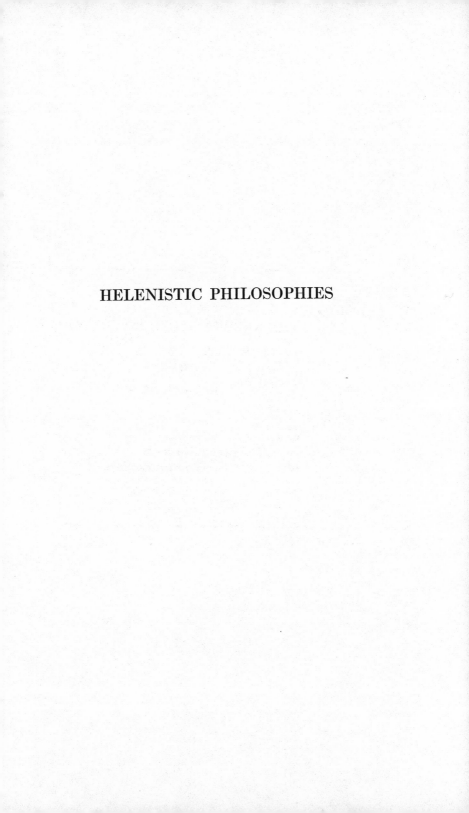

HELENISTIC PHILOSOPHIES

THE GREEK TRADITION

*From the death of Socrates
to the Council of Chalcedon*

399 B.C. TO A.D. 451

∽

HELLENISTIC PHILOSOPHIES

BY

PAUL ELMER MORE

Author of "Shelburne Essays"

GREENWOOD PRESS, PUBLISHERS

NEW YORK

CONTENTS

∞

CHAPTER I

ARISTIPPUS

OF the life of Aristippus, who founded the philosophy of pleasure which was to be developed and altered by Epicurus, not much is known. He was born in Cyrene, whence the name of his sect, but apparently abandoned his home at an early age. For a while, at least, he belonged to the circle that gathered about Socrates in Athens. In these years he seems to have been both learner and teacher, for, according to a story derived from Phanius, the Peripatetic, he was not only the first of Socrates' pupils who exacted money for his lessons, but on one occasion aroused the indignation of the master by sending him twenty drachmas from his earnings.

For some time he was in Syracuse at the court of the younger, perhaps also of the elder, Dionysius, where he exercised his wit at the expense of Plato. Once at a banquet, as the gossip runs, the tyrant bade his guests dance in purple robes; whereupon Plato refused, declaring,

> "I could not well a woman's garment wear."

But Aristippus complied, excusing himself with the apt quotation,

> "Even in Bacchus' wild alarm
> The modest woman suffers still no harm."

On another occasion, when Dionysius presented Plato with a book and Aristippus with gold, the wily Cyrenaic defended himself against the jeers of a friend with the observation: "I want money, Plato books." These anecdotes are from the inexhaustible storehouse of Diogenes Laertius; but Plutarch also tells us that the tyrant offered Plato money often and in large sums, and that Aristippus commented on Plato's refusal of the gifts with the remark that Dionysius was canny in his munificence, since he proffered little to those who needed much, and much to Plato who would take nothing.[1]

---

[1]*Dion* 19.—A good jest never dies. Dr. Johnson once undertook to browbeat a Cantabrigian by repeating the famous epigram:

> "Our royal master saw, with heedful eyes,
> The wants of his two universities:
> Troops he to Oxford sent, as knowing why
> That learned body wanted loyalty:
> But books to Cambridge gave, as well discerning
> That that right loyal body wanted learning."

To which the Cantabrigian made retort:

> "The king to Oxford sent his troop of horse,
> For Tories own no argument but force;
> With equal care to Cambridge books he sent,
> For Whigs allow no force but argument."

If the life of Aristippus is summed up in a few anecdotes, it is not much better with his philosophy. The books he wrote have been lost, and for the knowledge of his principles we have little more than a few sentences of Diogenes Laertius and of Sextus Empiricus, and even so it is impossible to distinguish clearly between what was taught by Aristippus himself and what was added by his successors. In general, the principles of the sect are thus summarized by Diogenes:

"Those who abode by the Aristippean rule of life and were called Cyrenaics held the following opinions: There are two affections which we feel (*pathê*), pain and pleasure, the former being a rough state of motion, the latter a smooth state of motion. Pleasure does not differ from pleasure [in quality, they mean], nor is one more a pleasure than another. Pleasure is approved by all living creatures, whereas pain is avoided. And the pleasure of the body, which they make their chief good, or end, is not that continuous and unperturbed state of repose arising from cessation of pain which Epicurus accepted as the end. They believe that the end is a different thing from happiness (*eudaimonia*); for the good we aim at is pleasure (*hêdonê*) in particular, but happiness is the sum of particular pleasures, in which are included those of the past and those of the future. The particular pleasure is

desirable for itself, whereas happiness is not desirable for itself but for the particular pleasures
that compose it. As a proof that pleasure is the
end, we have the fact that from childhood we are
attracted to it involuntarily, and that obtaining
it we seek nothing further, whereas there is nothing we so avoid as its opposite, pain. And pleasure, they assert, is a good even when it arises
from most unseemly causes; for even if the act
is disreputable, still the pleasure in itself is desirable and good. The removal of pain they do not
account pleasure, as does Epicurus; neither is
the absence of pleasure pain. For both pleasure
and pain consist in motion, or sensation, and
neither the absence of pain nor the absence of
pleasure is a motion, or sensation; in fact the
absence of pain is a state like that of one asleep.
. . . The absence of pleasure and the absence of
pain they called middle states. Moreover they
held pleasures of the body to be better than those
of the mind or soul, and distresses of the body to
be worse. . . . But however pleasure in itself
may be desirable, the causes of some pleasures
often result in the contrary state of distress, so
that the assemblage of pleasures which produces
happiness seems to them a matter of extreme
difficulty. The life of the wise man, they admit,
is not one of continuous pleasure, nor the life of
the fool one of continuous pain; it is a question
of predominance. . . . Nothing, they say, is
just or beautiful or ugly intrinsically and by nature, but by law and convention. Nevertheless a

sensible man will not do anything shocking, by
reason of the penalties imposed and for the sake
of popular opinion."

Sextus in his treatment of the school dwells
naturally more on the rational basis of their theory. The only criterion of knowledge we have is
in the sensations, or immediate affections (*pathê*) ; these alone are comprehensible and intrinsically true, whereas of the causes of these sensations we have no sure knowledge. We know
when we have the sensation of white or sweet,
and can affirm that we have at this moment such
or such a sensation, veraciously and with no fear
of contradiction; but of what lies behind or beyond this sensation we can say nothing certain.
We cannot even say that a particular object is
white or sweet, for in another person, or in ourselves at another moment, this same object may
produce quite a different sensation. Nor have
we any right to suppose that the particular sensation which we call white or sweet is the same
as that which another person calls by the same
name. We know only our own sensations, and
all that is common in such abstractions as white-
ness or sweetness is merely the word.[2]

Fitted together the expositions of Diogenes
and Sextus may be summed up in the three max-

[2]*Adv. Math.* VII, 191.

ims: Sensations alone are comprehensible, sensations and not their causes; The end of life is to live pleasurably; The particular pleasure is desirable for itself,whereas happiness is not desirable for itself but for the particular pleasures which compose it.

Of all philosophies this, I take it, is the easiest to understand; and, granted its hypothesis that the only certain facts in our experience are the immediate sensations of pleasure and pain as these come and go and come again, granted so much as that Plato's Ideal world, or its equivalent, is a vapour raised by hope and nothing more, the "dream of a shadow," it is of all dogmatic philosophies the most rigidly logical and the most thoroughly consistent and the most immediately persuasive. It is the wisdom of the world, preached in effect and practised long before Aristippus reduced it to a formulary. You shall find it in the poets of the old times, Mimnermus and Theognis and their kind, who sang in various notes to the refrain of *carpe diem*. Whether Aristippus really quoted much from them, we do not know; but it can be asserted of his hedonism that it was rooted in their voluptuary principles, and his admonitions, as Sextus said of other philosophers, might have been sealed by the authority of many a gnomic verse and stanza.[3] And it was equally a possession of the future to be followed by innumerable Cyrenaics who had never heard the name. As a manner of life it is of all time; as a reasoned theory it is affiliated manifestly with the principles of the more sceptical Sophists, particularly with the famous doctrine of Protagoras that man is the measure of all things, as this was taken in conjunction with the widely accepted aphorism of Heraclitus: All things pass and nothing abides.[4] How these two principles flowed together in a purely sensational and atomistic theory of knowledge, Plato has shown at length in the *Theaetetus*.

The puzzling question is rather to understand how two such divergent schools as the Academic and the Cyrenaic could have been created by men who professed allegiance to one and the same person. Plato's relation to his master is clear enough; but what business had this denier of the gods, this repudiator of the living reality of justice and all moral law, this hardened materialist, with the honest disciples of Socrates? Yet it is a

[3]*Adv. Math.* I, 271.
[4]The historical affiliation cannot be doubted. The logical relation of the various schools of sensationalism and scepticism to Heraclitus, Democritus, and Protagoras will be discussed in our last chapter.

fact, as we learn from the *Phaedo,* that he was close to the master, so close that his absence was noted from the little band who stayed with Socrates through the last day in gaol.

The explanation, one may say, is that in Socrates' mind the various elements of the Platonic philosophy lay side by side without having been merged together into a homogeneous system; hence it was possible for men of such utterly divergent tempers as Aristippus and Euclides and, as we shall see, Antisthenes to find in his words substance for their reflexion and confirmation of their aims. For his part, Aristippus simply laid hold of the hedonism which, if we accept the *Protagoras* of Plato as historical in this respect, formed an integral part of the Socratic doctrine, and developed this independently in a manner which Socrates certainly would have repudiated. Socrates apparently took happiness as the criterion of right conduct, and understood happiness rather naïvely as a balance of pleasures, without attempting to reconcile such a criterion with his affirmation of the everlasting realities of good and evil. He left it to his great disciple to effect such a reconciliation, or perhaps we should say modification, by drawing a distinction between pleasure in the ordinary sense and another feeling, which he called happiness (*eudaimonia*), akin to pleasure superficially but associated with an essentially different sphere of the soul's activity. Such was not the way of Aristippus. The apparent paradox of Socrates he escaped by accepting only the hedonism and rejecting everything that might conflict with it. And then, having attained this point of consistency, he further altered the Socratic point of view by defining pleasure in terms of the Protagorean sensationalism and the Heraclitean flux. So it was that the Socratic hedonism became the Cyrenaic pursuit of the passing pleasures of the body. It is true that Aristippus saw, as anyone must see who thinks at all, that some pleasures bring very disagreeable consequences, and must be forgone; yet it was still the momentary sensation he made his end, as the one thing sure and desirable.

So far one can see how Aristippus may be called a perverted, or at least an imperfect, Socratic, but on another side he was truer to the spirit, if not the spirituality, of the master. Probably, after all, what drew and held the inquisitive young men who congregated about this strange teacher and preacher of the streets was not so much any particular doctrine as it was the power

of his life, his imperturbable courage and cheer
in a world where these were terribly needed, a
sense of mastery that emanated from his glance
and his very gesture, the central calm in his heart
beyond the reach and understanding of idle curiosity yet strangely visible and fascinating to
those who approached him nearly,—the embodi-
ment, as it were, of everything summed up in
the Greek tradition by those hauntingly beautiful words *eleutheria* and *asphaleia,* liberty and
security. Here was liberty, the free man, the
man secure in himself against all the chances of
life, the man sufficient unto himself, *autarkês.*
Now it is evident that Aristippus was impressed
by the need of attaining something like this same
liberty and security of mind in his pursuit of
what the fleeting moment might yield; otherwise, he saw, there could be no joy in the pursuit
but only a tortured dependence on the fluctua-
tions of success and failure. It is, indeed, this
conception of liberty and security meeting together in self-sufficiency as a necessary factor of
the life of pleasure, that makes him a philosopher and something more, if not better, than the
idle voluptuary. To this end he would be always
master of himself, and, so far as possible, master of events by adapting himself voluntarily

and adroitly to the changing conditions of fortune and society—"every colour and condition
became Aristippus." And so it was that Horace
could say:

> *Nunc in Aristippi furtim praecepta relabor,*
> *Et mihi res non me rebus subiungere conor.*

The formal precepts by which Aristippus inculcated this theory are gone with his books, but
we have a sufficient number of anecdotes which
indicate how he put his philosophy into practice.
One day Diogenes the Cynic,[5] who was washing
some potherbs, ridiculed him as he passed by, and
said, "If you had learnt to satisfy yourself with
these you would not have been serving in the
courts of tyrants." To which Aristippus replied,
"And you, if you knew how to behave among
men, would not be washing potherbs." Being
asked once what advantage he had derived from
philosophy, he said, "That I am able to associate
confidently with any man." To the question of
Dionysius why philosophers haunted the doors
of the rich but the rich did not frequent those of
philosophers, he retorted, "Because philosophers
know what they need and the rich do not." Another time, at dinner, when the tyrant was try-

[5] It is important to distinguish between this Diogenes of Sinope,
the Cynic, and Diogenes of Laerte, the historian of philosophy,
who lived much later.

ing to drag him into philosophical talk against
his will, he defended himself by saying, "It is
absurd if you are learning from me to discourse,
yet are teaching me when I ought to discourse."
Dionysius was vexed at this, and showed his dis-
pleasure by sending the philosopher to the bottom of the table. Whereupon Aristippus: "You
wished to make this place more respectable." At
another time, when Dionysius asked him why
he had come to Sicily, his reply was: "When I
wanted wisdom I went to Socrates, but now,
wanting money, I have come to you"; or, as the
story is otherwise related, "I went to Socrates
for instruction (*paideia*), to Dionysius for di-
version (*paidia*)." Again, he was begging a
favour for a friend, and, being refused, fell at
the tyrant's feet; and when someone reproached
him for his conduct, his retort was: "I am not to
blame, but Dionysius who has his ears in his
feet." Whether this biting retort was made in
the presence of the tyrant himself, does not appear from the record; but certainly in the ruler's
absence he could take down the arrogance of a
misguided courtier in a manner worthy of the
cynic Diogenes, whose savage disregard of the
proprieties he seems indeed sometimes to have
forestalled. And he was equally quick to defend

his own indulgences. A certain sophist, visiting
him and seeing the women he had about him and
the lavishness of his table, was unwary enough
to express censure. Aristippus waited a moment, and invited the sophist to pass the day
with him, and then, when the invitation was accepted, observed: "You seem to have a quarrel
with the expense and not the luxury of my din-
ners." Another time his servant murmured at
the weight of a sack of money he was carrying
for him on the road, and Aristippus merely said,
"Pour out what is too much for you and carry
what you can."

Perhaps some apology is needed for stringing
together these tales out of the only history of
Greek philosophy that has come down to us. But
in fact they are not so irrelevant as they may
seem; they show probably as well as any of the
author's works would have done the kind of versatility which the wily philosopher of Cyrene,
like another Odysseus, acquired in his search for
pleasure through many cities and many species
of men. They might perhaps all be summed up
in his one famous saying when reproached for
living with Lais the courtesan: "I possess her, I
am not possessed by her, since the best thing is
not to forbear pleasures, but to grasp them with-

out suffering their mastery." *Habeo, non habeor:* that is the key by which the Cyrenaic would open the door to the liberty and security of philosophy, while acknowledging no good beyond the indulgence in whatever the swift-flowing current of time might lay at his feet. Hedonism was no new thing in Greece, or in the world; but the poets who were its professing votaries had been so weakly uncertain of their tenure, rather had been so positively certain that happiness was the flower of one brief moment of life, and, going, left behind only the winter of discontent.

"Gather my youth, O heart, before it fly!
  Soon other men shall be, no doubt; but I
  An earthen clod in the dark earth shall lie"—

was the admonition of Theognis; and Mimnermus had sung the same truth in more despondent language:

"What then is life, what pleasure, when afar
  Sinks golden Aphrodite's star?
Ah, death for me, when love in secret lifts
  No more the heart, and honeyed gifts
Charm not, and slumber fails, and all the flowers
  That fill the garden of young hours.
  .   .   .   .
So as the leaves put forth upon the boughs,
  In springtide, when the sun allows,
Like these a little time the bloom of youth
  Delights us, and we know no truth

Of good and evil from the gods. Yet still
 The Fates are near to work their will,—
One with the term of age and palsied breath,
 One with the blacker term of death."

Call no man happy until the end! Not only
are such pleasures ephemeral at the best, but
there is always the danger that they may escape
us entirely. A little change, a grain of dust blow-
ing into the eye, a slip of the foot, pestilence walking in the street, the betrayal or the misfortune
of friends, the tyranny of enemies,—and the
power of enjoyment is gone, while the capacity
of suffering remains. Man is terribly subject to
chance in these matters, his will has the feeblest
grasp upon them, and in the end chance throws
off its mask and shows itself as a remorseless fatality. It was against this treachery of accident
and despotism of fate that Aristippus sought a
brave defence by the shifts of an infinitely clever
versatility and by calling himself the master and
not the slave of pleasure. *Habeo, non habeor.*
In his practice there was no doubt a latent dualism, an unacknowledged trust in some resource
of the soul apart from and superior to the succession of sensations evoked by contact with the
world; but at the last we are as we believe we are,
and our destiny is in the creed we profess. If

physical sensation is pronounced to be all, if we have no secure place save in the feeling of the moment, what is left but a dull vacuity when pleasure is absent, unless pain rushes in to fill the void? The boasted liberation of our philosophy turns out under the stress of life to be something very like mockery: *Habeor, non habeo.*

The inevitable end of the Cyrenaic creed if held sincerely and unflinchingly—as however in the complexity of nature few men actually do hold it—is the kind of grim jesting that runs through so much of the Greek Anthology:

"All is laughter, and all is dust, and all is nothing; for out of unreason spring all things that are."

"You speak much, O man, but after a little you are laid in the ground. Be silent, and while still alive turn your thoughts upon death."[6]

It is an oft-repeated truism that extremes meet; and so we see the Cyrenaic, who has staked his hopes on the accidental favours of this world, subscribing the same lesson as the Platonist, who was ready to risk all on his belief in another

[6]Glycon:

Πάντα γέλως καὶ πάντα κόνις καὶ πάντα τὸ μηδέν ·
πάντα γὰρ ἐξ ἀλόγων ἐστὶ τὰ γιγνόμενα.

Palladas:

Πολλὰ λαλεῖς, ἄνθρωπε. χαμαὶ δὲ τιθῇ μετὰ μικρόν ·
σίγα, καὶ μελέτα ζῶν ἔτι τὸν θάνατον.

world,—life is a study of death. It is the same
precept, but with what a change! Cicero tells of
a certain Cyrenaic named Hegesias, who argued
so eloquently for death as a release from evils
that he was forbidden by King Ptolemaeus from
teaching in the schools a philosophy which persuaded many of his pupils to commit suicide.[7]

[7] *Tusc. Disp.* I, 34.

CHAPTER II

EPICURUS

I

Of Epicurus, whose name has become a synonym for the philosophy of pleasure, we know not a great deal, but rather more than of his predecessor from Cyrene. He was born of an Athenian father, a school teacher, in Samos in 341 B.C. His mother, according to the *chronique scandaleuse* which passed in ancient times for the history of philosophy, was engaged in the disreputable business of selling charms and practising magical rites for the propitiation of the gods; and the boy helped both his parents in their trades. One can surmise that from his mother's occupation Epicurus acquired an early hatred of superstition. At the age of eighteen he went to Athens, where he stayed but a short time, and then led a more or less wandering life until he returned to the city in 306 as a teacher of philosophy with several adherents. Here he bought a garden beyond the walls for 80 minae (about $1600), where he set up his school, or where, one might say more precisely, he lived with his friends and pupils, men and women, in what might be called a state of plain living and moderately high thinking. At the time of his settling Plato had been dead forty-one years and Aristippus somewhat longer; Polemo was the head of the Academy and Theophrastus of the Lyceum; Zeno, a slightly younger man, was living in Athens, and probably had already opened his school in the Painted Porch. Death came to him in 270, at the age of seventy or seventy-one.

Epicurus was a voluminous writer, leaving behind him some three hundred separate treatises. It is curious that the great advocate of ease and pleasure should have cared little for the comfort of his readers. Ancient critics complained of his disorderly composition, and the modern student finds his language one of the most difficult, not to say repellent, styles of all the Greek philosophers. His primary works are lost, as is the so-called larger epitome of them made by his own hand. There was also a smaller epitome, parts of which, apparently, are preserved by Diogenes Laertius. We have besides this a remarkable summary of his doctrine in forty aphorisms or Master Sayings. The poem of Lucretius is based probably on the larger epitome, and there are a great number of allusions to and quotations from his works in other Greek and Latin authors. Altogether we have a pretty full report of the main tenets of his philosophy; how far we understand them is another matter.

The difficulty that confronts us when we try to understand Epicurus is the extraordinary paradox of his logic. What, in a word, is to be said of a philosophy that begins with regarding pleasure as the only positive good and ends by emptying pleasure of all positive content? There is no possibility, I think, of really reconciling this blunt contradiction, which was sufficiently obvious to the enemies of Epicurus in antiquity, but it is possible, with the aid of Plutarch's shrewd analysis,[1] to follow him step by step from his premises to his conclusions, and so to discover the source of his entanglement.

Epicurus began with the materialistic and monistic theses which had allured Aristippus, and which, mingled in varying proportions from the teaching of Heraclitus and Protagoras and Democritus, had come to be the prevailing belief of the Greek people; they were, indeed, no

---

[1] *Non Posse Suaviter Vivi Secundum Epicurum.* I draw freely on the racy language of the old English translation.

more than the essence refined out of the voluble
lecturing and debating of the so-called sophists
against whom Socrates and Plato had waged a
relentless but unsuccessful warfare. This visible
palpable world of bodies is the only reality, and
the only thing which to man, in such a world, has
any certain value is his own immediate physical
sensations. Pleasure we feel and pain we feel, in
their various degrees and complications; and we
know that all men welcome pleasure and shrink
from pain by a necessity of nature. Pleasure, in
fact, is simply a name for the sensation which
we do welcome, and pain for the sensation from
which we do shrink. The example of infants and
animals is before us to nullify any attempt to
argue away this primary distinction.

These are the premises of Epicurus, as they
had been of Aristippus, and to these he will cling
through thick and thin, whatever their consequences may be and however they may entangle
him in self-contradictions. He seems even to have
gone out of his way at times to find the grossest
terms to express the doctrine, whether his motive was to shock the Philistines of morality or
to fortify himself and his friends in their positive belief. The avowed programme of the school
was "not to save the Greeks, but to indulge the

belly to the limit of safety with meat and drink";
and in a letter to a friend Epicurus says: "I invite you to continuous pleasures, not to virtues
that unsettle the mind with vain and empty hopes
of fruition." The programme is simple enough
in all conscience, and might satisfy the most cynical votary of the flesh, but, desiring like his predecessor to be a voluptuary, Epicurus was driven
despite himself to be a philosopher, even more a
philosopher than the Cyrenaic, whether his wisdom came from deeper reflection or greater ti-
midity. His experience might be described as the
opposite of that of Johnson's humble acquaintance who had been trying all his life to attain philosophy but failed because cheerfulness would
break in. Aristippus could make a boast of his
Habeo, non habeor, but, however he might twist
about, his dependence on the fleeting sensation
of the moment left him at last a prey to the hazards of circumstance. Clearly the hedonist who
was enough of a philosopher to aim at liberty
and security must embrace a wider view of life
than the Cyrenaic; and so the first step of Epicurus was to take happiness, conceived as a continuous state of pleasure, rather than particular
pleasures, for the goal. This is the initial, and
perhaps the most fundamental, difference be-

tween the strictly Epicurean and the Cyrenaic
brand of hedonism.

But how, taking individual pleasures still in
the grossly physical sense, was a man to assure
himself of their consummation in happiness? It
was well to make a god of the belly and, in the
Epicurean language, of any other passage of the
body that admitted pleasure and not pain, but,
as soon as he began to reflect, the philosopher
was confronted by the ugly fact that the en-
trances of pain are more numerous than those
of pleasure, and that the paroxysms of pain may
surpass in intensity any conceivable pleasure.
He saw that there was something ephemeral and
insecure in the very nature of pleasure, whereas
pain had terrible rights over the flesh, and could
dispute her domain with a vigour far beyond the
power of her antagonist. Evidently, in a world
so constituted, the aim of the philosopher will be
lowered from a bold search for sensations to the
humbler task of attaining some measure of security against forces he cannot control; and so,
I think, we shall interpret the curious phenomenon that the greatest of all hedonists was driven
to a purely defensive attitude towards life. On
the one hand he knew, as Plato had shown, that
the recovery from disease and the relief from an-

guish do bring a sense of active well-being, and hence it was possible for him to define pleasure in negative terms without seeming to contradict flagrantly his grosser views about the belly and other bodily organs. Again, since positive pleasure and pain by some law of nature are so intimately bound together that the cessation of one is associated with access of the other,[2] then, clearly, the only pleasure free of this unpleasant termination is that which is itself not positively induced but comes as the result of receding pain. For the content of happiness, therefore, the Epicurean will look to sensation of a negative sort: "The limit of pleasure is reached by the removal of all that gives pain," and "Pleasure in the flesh admits no increase, when once the pain of want is removed; it can only be variegated."[3]

But the philosopher cannot stop here. Such a state of release, though in itself it may not be subject to the laws of alternative pleasure and pain, is yet open to interruption from the hazards of life. And so Epicurus, in his pursuit of happiness, is carried a step further. Not on the present possession of pleasure, whether positive

[2]This association of pleasure and pain was familiar to Plato. He refers to it in *Phaedo* 60B, and deals with it at greater length in the *Philebus*.

[3]*Sayings* 3 and 18. In my quotations I sometimes adopt the language of the excellent versions in R. D. Hicks's *Stoic and Epicurean*.

or negative, will he depend for security of happiness, but on the power of memory. Here, at least, we appear to be free and safe, for memory is our own. Nothing can deprive us of that recollected joy, "which is the bliss of solitude"; even what was distressful at the time may often, by some alchemy of the mind, be transmuted into a happy reminiscence:

"Things which offend when present, and affright,
In memory, well painted, move delight."[4]

The true hedonism, then, will be a creation in the mind from material furnished it by the body. Plutarch describes the procedure of Epicurus thus, and exposes also its inadequacy:—

Seeing that the field of joy in our poor bodies cannot be smooth and equal, but harsh and broken and mingled with much that is contrary, he transfers the exercise of philosophy from the flesh, as from a lean and barren soil, to the mind, in the hopes of enjoying there, as it were, large pastures and fair meadows of delight. Not in the body but in the soul is the true garden of the Epicurean to be cultivated. It might seem as if by the waving of a magic wand we had been translated from a materialistic hedonism to a region like that in which Socrates and Plato looked for

4Cowley, *Upon His Majesty's Restoration.*

unearthly happiness. But in fact there is no such
magic for the Epicurean. The source of the pleasures which compose our happiness is still physical, and only physical; the office of the soul, so-
called, is merely to retain by an act of selective
memory the scattered impressions of sensuous
pleasure and to forestall these by an act of selective expectation. If you hear the Epicurean cry-
ing out and testifying that the soul has no power
of joy and tranquillity save in what it draws from
the flesh, and that this is its only good, what can
you say but that he uses the soul as a kind of vessel to receive the strainings from the body, as
men rack wine from an old and leaky jar into a
new one to take age, and so think they have done
some wonderful thing. And no doubt wine may
be kept and mellowed with time, but the soul
preserves no more than a feeble scent of what it
takes into memory; for pleasure, as soon as it
has given out one hiss in the body, forthwith ex-
pires, and that little of it which lags behind in
memory is but flat and like a queasy fume, as if
a man should undertake to feed himself today
on the stale recollection of what he ate and drank
yesterday. What the Epicureans have is but the
empty shadow and dream of a pleasure that has
taken wing and fled away, and that serves but

for fuel to foment their untamed desires, as in
sleep the unreal satisfaction of thirst and love
only stings to a sharper lust of waking intem-
perance.

Memory, though it promise a release from the
vicissitudes of fortune, is still too dependent on
the facts of life, too deeply implicated in the recurrence of passionate desires. There is no final-
ity of happiness here, and so the Epicurean is
driven on to further refinement. If pushed hard,
he will take refuge in imagining a possible pain-
lessness of the body and a possible stability of
untroubled ease. Life itself, in some rare instances, may afford the substance of this comfort, and memory then will be sufficient; but if
the substance eludes us, we have still that within
us which by the exercise of free will can lull the
mind into fancying it remembers what it never
possessed. Step by step the reflective hedonist
has been driven by the lessons of experience from
the pursuit of positive pleasure to acquiescence in
pleasure conceived as the removal of pain; from
present ease in the flesh to the subtilizing power
of memory in the mind, and, when memory is
starved, to the voluntary imagination that life
has gone well with him. The fabled ataraxy, or
imperturbable calm, of the Epicurean turns out

to be something very like a pale beatitude of illusory abstraction from the tyranny of facts, the wilful mirage of a soul which imagines itself, but is not really, set apart from the material universe of chance and change. *Habeo, non habeor,* was the challenge of Aristippus to the world; the master of the Garden will be content with the more modest half: *Non habeor.*

There is something to startle the mind in this defensive conclusion of a philosophy which opened its attack on life under such brave and flaunting colours. There is much to cause reflection when one considers how in the end hedonism is forced into an unnatural conjunction with the other monistic philosophy with which its principles are in such violent conflict. For this ataraxy of the avowed lover of ease and pleasure can scarcely be distinguished from the apathy which the Stoic devotees of pain and labour glorified as the goal of life. This is strange. It is stranger still, remembering this negative conclusion of Epicurean and Stoic, by which good becomes a mere deprivation of evil, to cast the mind forward to the metaphysics of another and later school of monism which led the Neoplatonist to reckon evil as a mere deprivation of good. Into such paradoxical combinations and antag-

onisms we are driven as soon as we try to shun
the simple truth that good is good and evil is
evil, each in its own right and judged by its immediate effect in the soul.

It may appear from the foregoing that the
hedonist, in his pursuit of the *summum bonum,*
argues from point to point in a straight line;
in practice he seems rather to follow no single
guide, but to fluctuate between two disparate
yet inseparable motives. At one time, in a world
where physical sensation is the only criterion of
truth and the basis of all reality, the liberty of
enjoyment is the lure that draws him on; at another time, in a world of chance and change or
of mechanical law which takes no great heed of
our wants, it seems as if security from misad-
venture must be the limit of man's desire. Other
philosophers, the Platonist in his vision of the
world of Ideas, the Christian in his submission
to the will of God, may see their way running
straight before them to the one sure goal of spiritual happiness, in which liberty and security
join hands. The path of the hedonist wavers from
side to side, aiming now at positive pleasure and
now at mere escape from pain; and this, I take
it, is one of the curious reprisals of truth, that
the dualist should have in view a single end,

whereas the monist should be distracted by a
double purpose. Whether one or the other of the
revolving objects shall stand out clearer before
the hedonist's gaze, will depend perhaps chiefly
upon his temperament. With an Aristippus the
pleasure of the moment is supreme, though he
too will have his eye open for the need of safety;
with an Epicurus, more timid by nature and
more reflective, the thought of security at the
last will almost, if never quite, obliterate the en-
ticement of pleasure. It was still as a good Epicurean that Horace could write:

Sperne voluptates, nocet empta dolore voluptas.

II

Certainly, when we pass from consideration
of the chief good to the philosophical theories
which Epicurus developed to explain and justify his choice of that good, the idea of security
becomes altogether predominant; it is the keynote equally of his ethics, his science, and his attitude towards religion.

The ethical ideal of the Garden is summed up
in the famous maxim, "Live concealed" (*lathe
biôsas*), or, as Horace exquisitely phrases it, the

fallentis semita vitae. In this way alone would the perfect ataraxy be attained.

Now the hidden way is not that which we admire today, much as in other respects our thoughts have kept the colour of hedonism and utilitarianism. On the one hand, the pleasures pursued by the modern voluptuary are likely to be that of the busy and aggressive sort which cannot easily be dissociated from the noise of crowds and the distraction of ceaseless motion, and in comparison with which the Garden of Epicurus would seem to offer but a wan image of life. On the other hand, the only useful career we commonly understand today is one equally involved in the restless business of doing, and our commendation is reserved for those who are engaged in promoting the welfare or regulating the morals of other men. To shrink from the hazard of public adventure or to prize the refinement of secrecy is branded as cowardly, while concern for the salvation of one's own soul is likely to be reprehended as selfish and immoral. Hence it happens that both the vices and the virtues of the present age have brought into disrepute the ancient ideal of withdrawal from the distractions of life. That is as it may be. But at least we ought to keep the mind clear in these matters, and not to lose the sense of distinctions. The hidden way of the Epicurean has at first sight a startling resemblance to the Platonic and the Christian flight from the world, and to a certain point the two ideals are rooted in the same soil; but to ignore their difference while seeing their similarity, or to unite them in the same praise or condemnation, would be the error of a very blind psychology. When Gregory of Nazianzus, in accordance with the direct methods of the day, had been captured bodily and ordained a priest against his will, he first fled from this act of "spiritual despotism" to the monastic retreat of his friend Basil in Pontus, and then, admitting the obligation thrust upon him, returned to his charge. And this was in part his apology to the people for his precipitate flight:

"Into my heart had come a certain longing for the beauty of the quietness of solitude. Of this, indeed, I had been a lover from the beginning, as I know not whether any other votary of letters had ever loved it; and this, amid great difficulties and trials, I had made my vow to God. Some taste of it I had already known, having stood, as it were, in its vestibule, so that my desire was the more enkindled by experience; and I could not tolerate the tyranny that was thrusting me back into the midst of noise and tumult, and dragging me by violence from the better life

as from a sacred asylum. For nothing appeared
to me so desirable for a man as this, that, closing
the eyes of the senses, and withdrawing from the
flesh and the world into his inner self, and having no contact with all that concerns humanity,
save as need compelled, conversing with himself
and with God,—that so he should live above the
plane of visible things, and bear within him the
signs of divinity, pure always and unmixed with
earthly vagrant impressions, presenting his soul
as a clean mirror to God and the heavenly
lights."[5]

Gregory's apology, delivered in the remote
church of Cappadocia, might seem almost to be
a sermon on the Epicurean text, "Live concealed," which no doubt he had heard discussed
from every point of view during his student
days at the university of Athens. Yet if the se-
ductive phrase of Epicurus, as we may suppose,
had sunk into his mind so as never to be absent
from his thoughts, it is no less true that the hidden life for which he pined was divided, as pole
is separated from pole, from that, in some ways
not ignoble, withdrawal of the Athenian hedonist into his garden.

For Epicurus the purpose of retirement was
primarily the desire to escape so far as possible
the incursions of society, with no thought of fit-

[5]*Oratio* II, 6, 7.

ting himself for citizenship in another world. To this end political life was to be utterly eschewed; for how, indeed, could the philosopher maintain his precious calm of soul, while suffering the anxieties of ambition or the envies of office? To the same end marriage and the cares of a family were to be avoided, though not so rigorously as political entanglements. In one respect Epicurus was better than his creed. It is notorious that his school made much of friendship, theoretically and practically; and their kindly comradeship, even their readiness to sacrifice ease and possessions for a friend, threw something like a glow of romance over their otherwise unlovely profession of egotism. No doubt Epicurus could find logical excuses for this human weakness in the mutual protection offered by such unions; but in fact some inextinguishable nobility of mind carried him here quite beyond the bounds of his boasted principles. His hedonism might leave a place open for friendship as the greatest felicity which wisdom procures for the whole of life,[6] but he was surely forgetting the claims of the flesh when he added that it was of more account to know with whom we were to eat and drink than what we were to

[6] Diog. Laert., *Epicurus* 148.

eat and drink.[7] And his rejection of the Pythagorean community of goods (which had been so
alluring to Plato), because it shows some lack
of confidence in the generosity of friendship, is
one of the finest and, in the French sense of the
word, most *spirituel* of ancient maxims.[8]

Such was the social ideal of Epicurus, and his
rules for private conduct were of a piece with
it—they were directed as completely, considering the place of friendship in his social scheme
even more completely, towards the attainment
of that outer and inner security on which the
continuous state of pleasure must depend. To
this end morality of a sort is necessary: "It is
not possible to live pleasantly without living
wisely and fairly and justly, nor to live wisely
and fairly and justly without living pleasantly."
The exordium is well, and might lead one to expect a code of morals not altogether unlike the
Platonic eudaemonism; but such an expectation
is soon dispelled. In the Epicurean scheme there
is no conception of wisdom as a good to be sought
for itself, or of justice as a possession which of
itself brings peace and happiness to the owner;
how, indeed, could such a conception find place
in a purely materialistic philosophy? Not virtue

[7]Seneca, *Ep.* xix, 10.
[8]Diog. Laert., *Epic.* 11.

for its own sake is desirable, nor is justice conceivable for its own immediate reward in the
soul; the law of safety is the supreme law of
conduct, and "any means is a natural good by
which a man may acquire a sense of security from
other men." The state of nature would be like
that which a Thrasymachus and a Callicles upheld at Athens, and a Hobbes was to expound in
England. So far as justice exists as an obligation, it is merely a kind of compulsory engage-
ment by which we agree not to deprive others of
their possessions and comfort in order that we
may enjoy from them the same immunity. And
if men live up to such a compact it is only because
of the penalties imposed upon disobedience. "Injustice is not an evil in itself," and he would be a
fool who did not covertly grasp for himself what
he could, while preaching abstention to his neighbours, were it possible to do this with impunity.
"No one who in secret violates any article of the
social compact of mutual forbearance can be con-
fident that he will escape detection, even though
hitherto he has escaped a thousand times; for to
the end of life he cannot be sure that he is safe."[9]

9Mr. Hicks undertakes to condone this code of morality as being
"just the position taken up by modern international law and just
the attitude adopted by Christian nations" (*Stoic and Epicurean*
177). He has a word of protest against the Stoics who presented
the code "in an unfavourable light, as does Epictetus when he

And as it is with justice between man and man, so it is with the more personal virtues of prudence and temperance and courage. "The virtues are not taken for themselves but for the pleasure they bring,"—prudence because it sees the folly of striving for the unattainable, temperance because it protects us against perilous indulgences, courage because it enables us to overcome pain and to escape from empty fears. At the best, virtue becomes such a barter of pleasure against pain and of pleasure against pleasure as seemed to Socrates, in gaol and awaiting death, to miss all the nobler chances of life. At its ordinary level virtue is the caution of a soul that sees no real distinction between good and evil, but shrinks back from the bold adventure of licence:

"If the acts that give pleasure to the profligate absolved him from fears, . . . if they showed him the limit of desires, we should have nothing to censure in such a man; for his life would be

says: 'Not even does Epicurus himself declare stealing to be bad, but he admits that detection is; and because it is impossible to have security against detection, for this reason he says, Do not steal.'" I cannot see that the Stoics (to whom might be added the Platonists and Christians and all the other moralists save the followers of Epicurus) presented the code in a more unfavourable light than did he who first promulgated it. Discredit the belief th.t injustice by its own nature, and apart from any conventional penalties, works mischief in the soul that harbours it, and the position of Epicurus as interpreted by his enemies is the only logical one to take—though Epicureans might on occasion be illogical.

filled with pleasures flowing in from every side, and would have no pain of body or mind—pain which is the evil thing."

III

But there was another disturbance of human life more serious than that which came from the entanglement of the individual in society—viz. the disturbance from the tyranny and terror begotten by false notions of the universe. Security from the encroachments of society Epicurus sought, as we have seen, in his ethics; to attain like security from the world at large he looked to some formula for the universal nature of things which should enable the mind to pursue its even course without anxiety. "For," as he says, "there would be no profit in establishing security from men so long as we suffered from forebodings of what goes on overhead and under the earth and anywhere in the infinity of space." Now the great enemy of ataraxy, as Epicurus saw it, was religion. It is superstition that has filled our human life with hideous fears of the world to come and with criminal passions in this world, and to free mankind from these he will lay his axe at the root of the evil.

As for the sense of terrors to come it is hard
for us, with our impatience to admit the force of
any mythology but our own, to comprehend how
large a part it played in the life of the ancients,
how it hung like a lowering cloud in the air of
Greece, which we are wont to picture to ourselves as perfectly serene and untroubled by
those spectral portents that haunted the Middle
Ages and our own age until a very recent date.
Yet a little reading and a slight acquaintance
with the human heart ought to warn us against
such an error.[10] Plato saw clearly the havoc made
in the imaginations of his countrymen by the
gruesome tales of Hades, and undertook to liberate men by moralizing the future life and by
placing the fate of the soul within the power of
each man, as he chose the upward path of virtue
or the downward path of vice and misery. But
such a deliverance required the belief in moral
laws which were not recognized in the hedonistic
monism of Epicurus; the only way of escape
open to him was to find what comfort he might
in the conclusions of his naturalistic creed. There
is no future life, no immaterial soul which will
live and continue to suffer when the visible body
is dissolved; therefore the dread of what may

[10]For the sort of terrors current in antiquity see, *e.g.*, Lucian's
Lover of Lies 22, 25.

happen after that final event is as idle as the
shuddering that inflicts our dreams. But what
of the horror that still is left of empty darkness,
of annihilation, the thought of sinking into an
abyss of nothingness? why, that too is causeless:
"Death is nought to us; for that which is dissolved [as the body and soul are dissolved into
their elements at death] feels not, and that which
feels not is nothing to us." This was an argument to which Epicurus recurred again and
again,[11] as if by repetition of a charm he might
benumb the heart into a dull acquiescence. And
one recalls the retort of Plutarch, that such a
thought does not remove the terror of death, but
rather adds to its sting by demonstrating its
cause; for it is just this anticipation of complete
insensibility in the future that fills men with a
present distress.[12]

The tyranny of the future is but an extension,

[11]So Cicero, *De Fin.* ii, 31.

[12]*Non Posse* 1104ᴇ.—It might seem that Epicurus could have
made out a better case for himself by regarding death as the
great surcease of pain and so as the fitting consummation of
pleasure as he conceived pleasure. He might have quoted the
beautiful line of Electra in Sophocles:

Τοὺς γὰρ θανόντας οὐχ ὁρῶ λυπουμένους—

"Therefore receive me in thy narrow home,
As nought to nothing, in that world below
To dwell with thee forever . . .
For this I see, the dead have rest from pain."

But the spirit of religious resignation, even in its negative aspect, cannot be wedded to Epicureanism.

so to speak, of the monstrous oppression under
which man's present life labours from his belief
in the gods and in Providence. And here at least
Epicurus was dealing with an undeniable evil.
Cruel persecutions, the smouldering fires of religious bigotry, malignity dressed in the garb of
spiritual love, the passion of egotism stalking
about as a divine inspiration, the grovelling dread
of supernatural portents, the paralysis of the
human will,—who can think of these and what
they have done through the long course of history, without shuddering? All this Lucretius,
translating Epicurus into the language of poetry, summed up in one fiery picture of the sacrifice of Iphigenia on the altar of Artemis, with
its last stroke of indignation, terrible and unfor-
gettable:

Tantum religio potuit suadere malorum.

Here again Epicurus had been anticipated.
Plato too was keenly alive to the sum of evils for
which religion must be held responsible, but for
release from this oppression he could find a way
quite barred to the materialist. It was his privilege to liberate religion from the dark overgrowth of superstition by purifying our notion
of the gods and by moralizing the work of Providence; whereas for the pure hedonist the only

escape was simply to deny the fact of any intervention from above in the life of mankind, and
this Epicurus did absolutely and unflinchingly.
It might have been expected that he would follow
the logical consequences of such a creed into pure
atheism; but here, for one reason or another, he
drew back. Though the thought of Providence
was utterly repugnant to him, and though he
swept away, with one grand gesture of disdain,
the whole fabric of signs and portents and proph-
ecy, he still in a fashion clung to the existence of
the gods. It is easy to accuse him, and antiquity
did not fail to accuse him, of insincerity, as if he
were an atheist but, for fear of popular resent-
ment, concealed his genuine views. Possibly he
may have been influenced to some extent by this
motive, but his theology is capable of another
and more generous explanation; he really had a
need of the gods in his philosophy, and of precisely the kind of gods whom he admits, as may
be seen from his arguments.

In the first place, granted the existence of
gods, granted that their state is one of untroubled
felicity, granted that felicity is dependent on that
withdrawal from cares and obligations which was
the ideal of Epicurean hedonism, then it follows
that the gods will pass their time in unconcern

for the business of this vastly laborious world of ours. "The motion of the heavenly bodies, their solstices, eclipses, risings and settings, and what goes with these, all such things we must believe happen without the present or future intervention of any being who at the same time enjoys perfect felicity with immortality."[13] Nor will the gods suffer themselves to be affected and swayed by the distracted affairs of mankind: "That which is blessed and immortal neither has any troublesome business itself nor brings such trouble upon another; it is exempt from movements of anger and favour, for all this implies weakness." There is no room in such a theology for a divine Providence of creation or preservation. The gods, if they exist, will not be "good" in the sense which Plato attached to this word, but simply happy in the enjoyment of complete indifference and security; their home will be set apart in a Paradise beyond the shock and conflict of opposing forces, where, as in a celestial counterpart of Epicurus' own garden, they will spend the long aeons in pleasant intercourse one with another. Such the gods must be, if we grant their existence,—

[13]*Epist. Prima* 76.

"The gods, who haunt
The lucid interspace of world and world,
Where never creeps a cloud, or moves a wind,
Nor ever falls the least white star of snow,
Nor ever lowest roll of thunder moans,
Nor sound of human sorrow mounts to mar
Their sacred everlasting calm! and such,
Not all so fine, nor so divine a calm,
Not such, nor all unlike it, man may gain
Letting his own life go."

And in these lines from Tennyson's *Lucretius* we see not only how Epicurus[14] adapted Homer's picture of Olympus for his home of the gods, but why he admitted the gods into a philosophy which might have been expected to abut on pure atheism. After all, the divine state was no more than a carrying out by the imagination of that which Epicurus aimed at in this troubled world, but never could quite achieve. The *makarios bios,* "the blessed life," "the life of felicity," is a phrase often on his lips, and he was not unwilling to accept from his pupils terms of homage which fell little short of deification; yet withal how imperfect was the security he could actually attain against the encroachments of society and

[14]Tennyson's lines are taken from the third book of the *De Rerum Natura,* where Lucretius borrows from the sixth book of the *Odyssey;* but Epicurus, though he was not fond of Homer or the other fabricators of myth, would not have repudiated this picture.

the pangs of disease, and that last agony of dissolution, however bravely he might argue that
agony away. He needed this ideal of the divine
tranquillity to strengthen his own heart and to
put courage into his band of worshippers. He,
also, must have his religion, his dream of imitat-
ing God, at whatever price he bought it.

IV

Having freed man from the terrors of superstition by removing the gods far off from the
actual world, it remained for Epicurus to substitute some theory of nature's course which
should at once fill the place of Providence and
offer a secure foundation for his ethics. To this
end, being no inventor, he was content for his
physics to take over bodily, with, however, one
important addition, the atomic system of Democritus. And from his *Letter to Herodotus* one
can see the process by which his mind settled upon
this particular hypothesis as suitable to his general philosophy. All that we know is given to us
by the momentary sensations of the body. Hence
the world is corporeal, and the dividing reason
will cut this corporeal substance into ever smaller
and smaller particles until it reaches the concep-

tion of ultimate atoms which correspond to the
atomism of our sensations. If you ask why he
stays the dividing reason at this point and does
not permit it to proceed *ad infinitum,* he will return the simple and sufficient answer that, if we
do not pause somewhere, all things will be analysed into nothingness. But empty space also is
necessary for his system, since without it the
atoms would be crowded together; there would
be no division, but a solid mass, and there would
be no possibility of that motion of matter which
is a fact of observation. Hence the universe for
Epicurus is composed of an infinite void wherein are moving an infinite number of solid atoms.
And here it is in place to observe that this conclusion reached by the unrestrained action of the
analytic reason is as thoroughly monistic as is
the conclusion reached by the unrestrained action of the synthetic reason. Plutarch was keen
enough to note this, and to lay it against the
school: "For when Epicurus says that 'the whole
is infinite and uncreated and incorruptible without increase or diminution,' he certainly speaks
of the universe as a unity. And when in the beginning of his treatise he declares that 'the nature
of things consists of bodies and the void,' he has
made an apparent division where there is really

only one nature; for of his two terms one really
does not exist at all, but is called by you the im-
palpable and the void and the bodiless. So that
for you the universe is a unity."[15] The point of
Plutarch's argument is that naturalism, in so far
as it excludes from its view anything positive
and radically different from matter, is equally
monistic, equally arbitrary, whether it divides
its material substratum into innumerable atoms,
after the fashion of Democritus and Epicurus,
or conceives a continuous substance in a state of
everlasting flux, after the mode of Heraclitus
and Zeno.

Upon this hypothesis of atoms moving in the
void Epicurus built up a purely mechanistic explanation of all the phenomena of the world and
of life. Omitting the details of his exposition, we
may say, briefly, that by the mutual shock and
repulsion of the atoms, which vary indefinitely
in shape and size, more or less durable aggregations of matter are formed and vortical motions
are started, out of which are produced the solar
and sidereal systems. Living organisms owe their
origin to the same cause, the soul, or principle of
life, being simply a compound of finer atoms, a
sort of fiery vapour, enmeshed in the corporeal

[15] *Adv. Coloten* 1114A.

structure of grosser atoms and dissipating when its vessel is dissolved. Even the gods are material and subject to decay.

So far Epicurus seems to have followed pretty closely in the steps of the naturalists who preceded him. But in one momentous point he struck out for himself. In the Democritean theory the atoms were supposed to be moving primarily all in one downward direction, and the collisions out of which the aggregations arose were supposed to occur by reason of the fact that the heavier atoms would overtake the lighter. Now Epicurus was sagacious enough to see that no universe like this of ours could arise on such a basis. A regular and uniform flux of atoms might create a conglomeration of absolute law and order, but it would be a world without variety or variation of form, or indeed without any forms whatsoever, properly speaking. To escape this conclusion he added a significant modification: the atoms should all be falling downwards by their own weight as in the Democritean system (though he failed to give any intelligible meaning to the word "downwards" in space of infinite extension), but besides this primary motion each individual atom swerves a little to one side or the other by some principle of arbitrary declination within itself. Lucretius states the matter thus:

"This point of the subject we desire you to
apprehend, that when atoms are borne straight
downwards through the void by their own weights,
at quite uncertain times and uncertain places they
push themselves a little from their course, only
just so much that you can call it a change of inclination. If they were not wont to swerve thus,
they would fall down all, like drops of rain,
through the deep void, and no clashing could
have been begotten, nor any collision produced,
among the first-beginnings; thus Nature never
would have produced anything."[16]

By this clever device Epicurus shuns the im-
passe of absolute determinism, and introduces
the possibility at once of order and variety—
order from the systematic motion of the atoms,
variety from the spontaneous motion of each individual atom. The masses, organic and inorganic,
of which the world is composed are thrown out
by nature without design and in infinite variety.
Those which happen to be constructed suitably
and are fitted to their environment endure and,
in the case of living creatures, propagate their
kind; while the rest are broken up and perish

[16]*De Rer. Nat.* ii, 216-224. The translation is from John Masson's *Lucretius, Epicurean and Poet.* How far Epicurus was
justified in assuming that Democritus held the atoms to be falling eternally downwards is a question we need not consider. See
Burnet's *Greek Philosophy* 1, 96.

amidst the unceasing clash and conflict. In the sphere of organic life, at least, Epicurus connected the law of survival with the conception of development in time, and the fifth book of Lucretius presents a magnificent and really astounding picture of man's progress from the primitive state of savagery to that of a complex civilization.[17] But for one omission, Epicurus would have anticipated in principle the theory of Darwinian evolution; if we may judge from Lucretius, he had no hint of the gradual transformation of one species into another, but each species, as it was thrown out by chance, so endured if it was fit, or perished if it was unfit. The omission is large, no doubt; yet in view of the apparent inability of modern biologists to come to any agreement upon the law of variation, perhaps it will not be held so damaging to the intelligence of our ancient philosopher as at first it might appear. And apart from this, the Epicurean doctrine agrees surprisingly with the modern attempt to explain the nature of things on a purely materialistic and mathematical basis. In both the ultimate source of phenomenal evolution is reduced to the mechanical law of chance

[17]M. Joyau (*Epicure* 118) thinks that the picture of progress in Lucretius should not be carried back to Epicurus; it is certainly, I think, implicit in the Epicurean physics.

and probability, and endurance is made to depend on the law of fitness. Both fail to explain how there can be a law of probability in the sequences of chance, and both equally shirk the difficulty of giving any meaning to the word "fit" in a world not governed by an intelligence which is superior to mechanical forces, and which acts selectively in accordance with a self-justifying principle of rightness, or order.

It is a question how far Epicurus' anticipation of the atomic theory in its present form and of evolution should be set down to mere philosophical guessing, and how far in general he can be regarded as a precursor of the modern scientific spirit. According to Froude Epicureanism was "the creed of the men of science" in the time of Caesar; Sir Frederick Pollock held it to be "a genuine attempt at a scientific explanation of the world"; for Professor Trezza it "summed up in itself the most scientific elements of Greek antiquity"; Renan praised Epicureanism as "the great scientific school of antiquity," and to Dr. Woltjer "the Epicureans, with respect to the laws and principles of science, came nearest of all the ancients to the science of our own time." On the other side Mr. Benn, from whom I borrow these quotations, regards such comments as "absolutely amazing";[18] he can find in Epicurus no spark of the true scientific spirit. Perhaps it would be fairer to put it this way, that Epicurus was a great anticipator of science, but, like the hero of Molière's play, *malgré lui*. In fact not the least paradox of his logic rich in surprises was his adoption of a scientific, or semi-scientific, mode of explaining the world for the avowed purpose of undermining the very foundation of what we understand by science. It was the last thing he had at heart that, having adopted a theory of creation which eliminated Providence from the world, he should suffer his physics to set up a law of mechanical determinism in its place. Between the personal tyranny of theology and the impersonal despotism of science, if he had to choose, he would prefer the former as the less absolute and inhuman:

"Destiny, which some introduce as sovereign over all things, he [the wise man] laughs to scorn, affirming that certain things happen of necessity, others by chance, others through our own agency. For he sees that necessity destroys responsibility and that chance or fortune is inconstant; whereas our own actions are free, and it is to them that praise and blame naturally attach. It were better, indeed, to accept the legends of

18*The Greek Philosophers*2 367.

the gods than to bow beneath that yoke of destiny which the natural philosophers have imposed.
The one holds out some faint hope that we may
escape by honouring the gods, while the necessity of the philosophers [of science] is deaf to
all supplications."[19]

It was strictly in harmony with this hostile
attitude towards the postulates of science that
Epicurus denied the possibility of formulating
a single and final explanation of any phenomenon of nature. Only in the general law of atoms
and the void, upon which his whole philosophy
rested, did he admit any exception to this rule;
in all other cases, dealing with particular phenomena, we are simply to accept whatever theory may suit the conditions of our life and confirm our tranquillity, remembering always that
the theory accepted does not exclude an infinity
of others equally possible. So far his interest in
investigation would go, and no further; for the
pure inquisitiveness of reason, here as everywhere, he expressed unmitigated contempt.[20]

From any point of view it appears that Epicurus shaped his system of physics, not in the
interest of science, but as an aid to his ethical

[19]*Epist. Tertia* 133 (Hicks's translation).—For a similar attitude of a modern Epicurean, Samuel Butler of Erewhon, towards
science and religion, see *Shelburne Essays* XI, 198.
[20]*Epist. Secunda* 87, 93, 97, 104.

purpose; he was seeking here, as in his theology (which indeed to the Hellenist is a branch of physics), for such a liberation from the inroads of the outer world as would enable him to attain the equanimity, the ataraxy, which seemed to him the only secure ground of pleasure. Hence his famous declination, or arbitrary swerving, of the atoms performed a double function: on the one hand it broke the rigidity of what otherwise would have congealed into a system of absolute determinism, and on the other hand it opened the door to a freedom of will which places the life of pleasure within a man's own choice. The nexus between atomic declination and human freedom is not clear.[21] They both, no doubt, imply spontaneity; but in the one case a spontaneity of pure chance, and in the other case a spontaneity of conscious purpose, and these two are more than different in kind, they are intrinsically incompatible from the Epicurean point of view. A dualist may solve this difficulty by

[21]See Masson, *Journal of Philology* XII, 1883, pp. 127-135.—In the second of his Boyle Lectures the great Bentley commented thus on the Epicurean attempt to deduce free will from a mechanical deviation of the atoms: " 'Tis as if one should say that a bowl equally poised, and thrown upon a plain and smooth bowling-green, will run necessarily and fatally in a direct motion; but if it be made with a bias, that may decline it a little from a straight line, it may acquire by that motion a liberty of will, and so run spontaneously to the jack." (Quoted in Jebb's *Life of Bentley*, p. 31.)

attributing mechanical chance to the material
world and conscious purpose to the realm of
spirit; but no such division was legitimately open
to a consistent monist. Apparently Epicurus
undertook to bully the logic of the situation by
a transparent device. His primary atoms are
described, as a true materialist should describe
them, in purely quantitative terms; they have
size and form, but no qualities, no sensation,
nothing inducive of sensation. Then, suddenly,
by the mere fact of aggregation, they have become
endowed with qualities and with sensation, and
in the finer atoms which constitute the soul mechanical chance has become converted into conscious free will. The transition is arbitrary, incomprehensible, subversive of the principles of
the Epicurean physics, as Plutarch was not slow
to point out;[22] but, then, logic is the last stronghold of tyranny, and Epicurus was ready to pur-
chase liberty at the price of any self-contradic-
tion.

V

This, indeed, is the staggering fact, that a philosophical theory, which in the name of reason begins with a repudiation of the dualistic

[22]*Adv. Coloten* 1111ʙ, 1118ᴇ.

paradox in the nature of things, should end in a
set of self-imposed and utterly unreasonable
paradoxes. Here is a philosopher who puts his
faith solely and unconditionally in the senses,
yet for the basis of his system goes beyond the
senses to an hypothesis of invisible atoms and
the void; who accepts all sensations as true, yet
holds part of the qualities given to us by sensation to be purely relative; who despises the forms
and rules of logic, yet argues on from syllogism
to syllogism; who recognizes only physical causes
and laws, and rejects all arbitrary and fanciful
effects, yet in his own doctrine of atomic deflec-
tion and human free will makes a law of unac-
countable spontaneity; who reduces all pleasure
and pain to corporeal feelings, yet looks to the
soul as the seat of the higher satisfaction; who
sees no motive but self-seeking egotism, yet in
practice followed the precepts of humanity, justice, disinterested friendship, even of self-sacri-
fice.[23]

All this is undeniable; but it is equally true
that the conclusions of Epicurus are no more
contradictory than are those of Stoicism and
Neoplatonism, or, indeed, of any monistic method. And, after all, it may be said that the physics

[23]Zeller, *Geschichte*[2] IV, 422.

and metaphysics of Epicurus are only the outer
fortifications thrown up, with whatever success,
to protect the inner citadel of his philosophy. In
taking pleasure as his starting point and end,
he chose what all men do naturally aim at and
desire—pleasure, or something corresponding
to it in the spirit. That is the simple fact to which
we must hold fast through all the shifts of reason; and those subtle logicians who have tried to
escape this law of nature by discriminating between pleasure itself as the end of action and the
object or act which results in pleasure have merely quibbled over a word. By grasping so firmly
this fundamental truth—though it be but half
the truth—of human life, Epicurus gave his name
to one of the broad and enduring philosophies of
life; and men of old and men of today call themselves Epicureans who have never read a line of
the master's writings. That, in fact, is characteristic of his influence. No founder of a sect was
ever more revered by his followers, and of all
the schools of Greece his was the only one which,
theoretically, underwent no change; although
in practice no men who call themselves by the
same name have so differed in their lives, as the
pleasure of their desires shifts from colour to
colour.

The great multitude, indeed, of those who have
called themselves, or whom we call, Epicureans
have been anything but scholars or sages or, in
any proper sense of the word, philosophers. This
is so true that it was common among the early
Christians, while making many concessions to
the other pagan sects, to deny utterly to Epicureanism the name of philosophy; among the
Jews the Greek name of the master of the Garden was used to denote a heretic or unbeliever
of any sort. "Be diligent," said Rabbi Lazar,
"to learn Thorah, wherewith thou mayest make
answer to Epicurus."[24] What the creed of pleasure too often means to the world Cicero has told
in his oration against Piso, the despoiler of Mace-
donia. In his disorderly youth this Piso met with
a Greek philosopher who undertook to expound
to him the doctrines of the Garden. But the teacher did not get far. "No doubt you have heard it
said that the Epicureans measure all things desirable to men by pleasure"—it was enough; like
a stallion neighing in excitement the youth leapt
at the words, delighted to find an authority for
lust where he had expected a sermon on virtue.
The Greek began to distinguish and divide and
explain; but "No," cried the young man, "stop

[24] *Sayings of the Jewish Fathers* 40, edited by Charles Taylor.

there, I subscribe, your Epicurus is a wonderful
fellow!" And the Professor, with his charming
Greek manners, was too polite to insist against
the will of a Roman senator.[25]

Pleasure is a power that needs no encomium
to inflame the desires and to fascinate the understanding, and a philosophy which throws such a
word about broadcast, however it may modify
and protest, cannot be absolved from a terrible
responsibility. It will be said that such a charge
may be fair enough against the Cyrenaics, who
were rather voluptuaries than philosophers, but
is a grave injustice when applied to the true
Epicurean brand of hedonism. And, no doubt,
there is some force in this excuse. As for Epicurus himself we have seen that the craving for
security prevailed so strongly with him over the
grasping at positive indulgence in the compound which he called by the name of ataraxy,
that the body in the end is almost refined out of
his philosophy. By whatever devices of logic and
ambiguities of definition, however he came by
the possession, one cannot but feel that in his
heart he did hold a treasure of wisdom. He was
tried by bereavement and in his later years by

[25]*In Pisonem* 28.—Lucian (*The Parasite* 11) shows that the pro-
fessional toady has laid hold of the *telos* of Epicureanism better
than Epicurus himself.

painful disease, yet through it all he seems to
have remained lord of himself and of that tranquillity of soul which he preached as the genuine
fountain of pleasure. To one of his friends, just
before his death, he sent a letter of which this
fragment is preserved:

"And now as I am passing this last and blessed
day of my life I write to you. Strangury has laid
hold of me, and wracking torments beyond which
suffering cannot go; but over against all this I
set my joy of soul in the memory of our thoughts
and words together in the past. Do you care for
the children of Metrodorus, in a manner worthy
of your devotion to me and to philosophy."

Strange termination, you will say, to a creed
which began by denying reality to everything
except the immediate sensations of the body; yet
there it is. Were it not for the flaunting paradox
of the phrase, one would declare that of all Epicureans he who gave them their name was the
least an Epicurean.

And the world has seen many other noble
souls who have found a measure of comfort and
strength and grace and something very like spiritual elevation in the more refined philosophy of
hedonism. Transplanted to Rome, such a creed
could inspire Lucretius with a passionate longing to liberate mankind from the slavery of im-

aginary fears, and with an agony of adoration,
one might say, for that Nature by whose will the
atoms were maintained in their everlasting majestic dance, and who offered to the souls of men
one fleeting glimpse of her tremendous face and
then dropped upon them the thick curtain of
annihilation, kindly in what she granted, kind-
lier in what she withheld. The same creed could
carry a sensitive lover of the earth's bounties like
Atticus unscathed through the brutalities of the
Civil Wars, a man of infinite resourcefulness in
the service of his friends by virtue of his complete abstention from the hazard of public affairs.

In England of the nineteenth century the tradition could still rouse a Pater to break the calm
of Victorian propriety for the valorous adventure of an artistic hedonism distilled out of the
more positive doctrines of Aristippus and the
stricter discipline of Epicurus. "Every moment
some form grows perfect in hand or face; some
tone on the hills or the sea is choicer than the
rest; some mood of passion or insight or intellectual excitement is irresistibly real and attractive to us—for that moment only. Not the fruit
of experience, but experience itself, is the end."
And so the pursuit of philosophy shall be no

cold consultation of books or dull hoarding of wisdom; for, with a "sense of the splendour of our experience and of its awful brevity, gathering all we are into one desperate effort to see and touch, we shall hardly have time to make theories about the things we see and touch."[26] Under a new name the old philosophy of the Garden could teach Mill, as a utilitarian, to look for private happiness in devotion to the well-being of others, and, as a hedonist, to grade the

[26]Ancient Epicureanism covers every form of hedonism except the artistic. I can find nothing in antiquity quite corresponding to the philosophy developed by Pater on the principles of Aristippus, or to the aesthetic of Croce, nothing corresponding to the theory of art for art's sake of modern times. As for Epicurus himself, he was so far from conceiving an artistic hedonism that he virtually rejected aesthetics altogether from his doctrine. He will admit a kind of pleasure in music, but will not take it seriously and forbids any discussion of it as an art. He excludes the study of rhetoric and commands his pupils to have nothing to do with τὴν ἐλευθέριον καλουμένην παιδείαν. For Homer he has only abuse. Sextus Empiricus was referring mainly to the Epicurean views when he said (*Adv. Math.* I, 298) that, so far as it lies with the poets, their art is not only useless to life but actually injurious; for poetry is a stronghold, or confirmation, of men's passions. (Aristippus was probably more liberal; see preceding chapter, p. 6). The breakdown of ancient hedonism is owing to the fact that it fails to give the desired security from the chances of life on which its happiness depends. Just this security the modern theory of aesthetic hedonism proposes to offer by seeking the source of pleasure in an art entirely dissevered from the business of life. But the result is an art denuded of solid content and a life without meaning. Epicurus was nearer to the truth than is Pater or Croce. For a profound criticism of the source of the modern theories in Hegel's aesthetic I may refer to the work of my friend Prosser Hall Frye, *Romance and Tragedy.*

kinds of pleasure by a scale of spiritual values
which theoretically he denied.

Epicurus can number among his followers a
sufficient line of artists and scientists, great sol-
diers and statesmen, sages and prophets; and if
a philosophy is to be rated by its finest fruit, hedonism may hold up its head among the schools.
But even so, taken at its highest, as a true philosophy and not as a mere incentive to the instinctive lusts of the flesh, Epicureanism still
suffers a grim defeat by any genuine pragmatic
test. At the best it was founded on a half-truth.
Its error is deep-rooted in the initial assumption
of a materialistic monism, and that fault it could
never entirely correct, though in practice it elud-
ed by an inconsistency the grosser consequences
of its origin. Certainly, the heart of man craves
happiness as its inalienable right; but the *hêdonê*
which Epicurus could offer as the reward of wisdom, the pleasure whose limit is determined by
the elimination, or even by the mental conquest,
of all physical pain, is a poor possession in comparison with the *eudaimonia* which Socrates and
Plato found in the soul that has raised its eyes
to the everlasting beauty of the Ideal world; or
beside that "joy in the Holy Ghost" which leaps
out of the language of St. Paul. No doubt the

human heart needs to be liberated from the vicissitudes of fortune and the visions of a disordered imagination and the terror of death; but the security of the Epicurean is a pale substitute for the fair and great hope of the Platonist, or for the assurance of the Christian: "Ye shall know the truth, and the truth shall make you free."[27]

It was the final charge of Plutarch against the philosophy of hedonism that a life of pleasure was impossible under the rule of Epicurus; and Professor Martha closes his penetrating and generous study of Lucretius with the judicial sentence, that "the true refutation of the doctrine which preaches pleasure is the sadness of its greatest interpreter." So much must be weighed against any theory of the world which ignorantly or wantonly shuts its eyes to the reality of

"Things more sublime than mortal happiness."[28]

[27]The Christian was not afraid of the Epicurean watchword. So Basil (Letter ccxlv): Μηδὲν προτιμότερον τῆς ἀληθείας καὶ τῆς οἰκείας ἑαυτῶν ἀσφαλείας τιθέμενοι. See *The Religion of Plato* 301.
[28]William Chamberlayne, *Pharonnida* III, ii, 52.

CHAPTER III

CYNICS AND STOICS

I

THE long line of Cynics and Stoics, in some respects the most important and significant of the Hellenistic sects, begins with Antisthenes, an Athenian, born about the year 440 B.C. At one time he was a pupil of Gorgias, and to the end his doctrine retained a strong sophistic bias; but later in his career he succumbed, like his antagonist Aristippus, to the Socratic spell. It is said that, living in Piraeus, he used to walk daily the forty furlongs up to the City to hear Socrates, and we know from Plato that he became intimate enough with the master to form one of the faithful group who stayed with him through the last day in gaol. At some date, probably after the death of Socrates, he set up his own school in the gymnasium Cynosarges. Hence, presumably, the name Cynic which attached to his followers, although popular etymology delighted to connect it with the word for dog (*kyôn*).

In one respect the father of the Cynics agreed with his fellow-pupil from Cyrene: they both, as imperfect Socratics, rejected all the spiritual side of Socrates' teaching. Both were materialists and sensationalists, in whom the master's deep concern with the human soul and with its eternal rights and responsibilities struck no answering chord. Antisthenes, apparently, was what Plato would call a semi-atheist: some kind of God he accepted as a power more or less identical with Nature; but it was a God remote from mankind, while the popular worship, to which Socrates conformed, with a shade, it may be, of ironical reservation, was to the Cynic a matter of jest and contempt. So also he repudiated vehemently the Ideal philosophy which Plato developed from the spiritual affirmations of Socrates. "O Plato," he is said to have exclaimed, "a horse I see, horseness I do not see." He was the first of the avowed nominalists, or conceptualists, for whom Ideas have no objective reality, but are only names or conceptions in the mind. And he was honest enough to carry this nominalism out to its logical conclusion. If our Ideas are pure conceptions of the mind, evocations only of our own thinking power, with no corresponding reality outside of the mind to which they should conform, and by which they should be controlled, then all Ideas are equally real and equally justifiable, and there is no distinction between true and false, no place for contradiction. "Whatever we say is true: for if we say, we say something; and if we say something, we say that which is; and if we say that which is, we say the truth." Here was room for a pretty feud, the memory of which remained as a source of amusement to the scandal-mongers of a late generation.[1] Antisthenes satirized Plato in a scurrilous book; and though Plato mentions his antagonist only once, and then merely to include him among those who were present at the death of Socrates, yet the later dialogues are much concerned with refuting this fundamental heresy, which makes a mockery of the philosophic quest of truth.

And if Antisthenes was at one with Aristippus in rejecting the whole spiritual half of the Socratic doctrine, we can see, I think, how he was still drawn to Socrates by the same traits which fascinated the young visitor from Cyrene. He too was looking for freedom and security, freedom from inner perturbations, and secur-

[1]See *e.g.,* Athenaeus v, 63; xi, 115.

ity from a world that seemed indifferent, if not hostile, to man's happiness; and in the *autarkeia* of Socrates he saw these qualities embodied in a manner that piqued his curiosity and dominated his will.

So far Antisthenes and Aristippus, as naturalistic monists, were in harmony, but at this point their paths diverged. To the Cyrenaic it appeared that liberty and security might be obtained, at little cost, by a prudent calculation in the pursuit of pleasure, through the hedonism, that is to say, which formed a part undoubtedly, but not the whole, of the Socratic teaching. To the Cynic, with his different temper and mind, such a creed appeared not exactly subordinate to a higher truth, as it did to Plato, but intrinsically dangerous and subversive of life. He saw that the boasted *Habeo, non habeor* of Aristippus was no more than the gilding on the chains of servitude. He felt too clearly the seductions and enervation of pleasure, the pitfalls it dug for unwary feet, and turned from it as from an implacable foe. To such an extreme he went in the expression of this antipathy that he used to say, "Rather let me be mad than feel pleasure";[2] by which he meant, apparently, not that he was

2Diog. Laert. VI, 3: Μανείην μᾶλλον ἢ ἡσθείην.

opposed to the mere gratification of the senses,
for in some respects he was ready enough to indulge the flesh,[3] but that he refused to distinguish between pleasure and pleasure in such a
way as to suffer his conduct to be governed by
the need of choice. Virtue (*aretê*), not the free
dalliance with pleasure, was the parent of self-
sufficiency; that should be the goal of his striving, and all things between virtue and vice should
be disregarded as indifferent, except as they
contributed to this or that end. If any one aspect
of the Socratic doctrine is to be isolated from
the rest, this at least is a more orthodox code
than the Cyrenaic or the Epicurean hedonism.

But for Antisthenes, who discarded the pursuit of pleasure as a snare, and to whom the Ideal
happiness of Plato could have no meaning, virtue was necessarily left without a positive motive or outcome, and took the form of a mere
hardening of one's resolve against any accom-
modation with the world. It could go no further
than that quality of steady endurance (*karteria*)
on which alone the indomitable valour of Socrates might seem to depend. Or if virtue assumed
a positive character at all, it would be by inten-
sifying passive endurance into a deliberate wel-

[3] *E.g. ibid.*: Χρὴ τοιαύταις πλησιάζειν γυναιξὶν αἳ χάριν εἴσονται.

come of the bracing hardships of life. That, I
think, is the significance of the Cynic identification of virtue with *ponos,* a word not easy to define. It means either "labour" or "pain," as the
case may be, or both together with shifting emphasis on one or the other element of the compound; as "labour" it signified for the Cynic
that philosophy was a matter of life and action,
not of words or syllogisms or learning; as "pain"
it would inculcate an indifference to pleasure
extending even to a preference for discomfort
and privation. The accepted morality of the
world would be nothing more than an imposition of words, an unauthorized convention (*no-
mos*), in opposition to which he would set up
the law of nature (*physis*), or the consideration
of things as they are on the lowest possible basis
of estimation; all that creates the comfort and
ease and grace of life, and at the same time
softens the possessor so as to leave him a prey
to the hazards of fortune, he would strip off as
superfluous. The philosopher should be absolutely self-sufficient in his apathy, or as nearly self-sufficient as the necessities of physical
existence permit—liberated from desires and
fears, superior to want, inured to hardship, contemptuous of opinion, licensed to do and to say

whatever occurred to him, a model for other men.

Only in one point did Antisthenes yield to the softer emotions. Somehow he found it possible to combine some sort of sympathy with his apathy, and to preach some sort of universal citizenship along with his exaggerated individualism; he was the first, unless Socrates preceded him, to call himself a cosmopolite. But of this strange paradox we shall have more to say when it appears in the Stoicism of Epictetus.

Such was the life and lesson of Antisthenes. As our gossiping historian puts it: "From Socrates he took the quality of endurance and apathy, and so founded the school of Cynicism; and that *ponos* is the chief good he proved by the instance of the great Heracles and of Cyrus, drawing one example from the Greeks and the other from the barbarians." Antisthenes is a shadowy and somewhat ambiguous figure; for the later generations his fame was quite swallowed up by that of Diogenes, or of the legendary saint of philosophy into whom the real Diogenes was soon converted.

II

The line of Cynics runs from Antisthenes through Diogenes of Sinope, Crates, Bion of Borysthenes,

Teles, and spreads out into a body of genuine ascetics and cunning impostors, who wore the folded cloak and imitated the surly manners of their leaders for the edification of society or the gratification of their own vanity and greed. Cynicism remained to the end a mode of life rather than a system of thought. Meanwhile the current was diverted in part to an allied, though in some respects very different school.

Zeno, probably a Phoenician by race, was born in the Cyprian town of Citium about the year 336 B.C. When still a young man he came to Athens, and there, stirred by the reading of Xenophon's *Memorabilia* and Plato's *Apology,* was drawn to the Socratic philosophy and placed himself under the tutelage of the cynic Crates, though he studied also with the masters of the Megarian and Academic sects. In time he founded his own school, delivering his lectures in the Stoa Poikilê, a colonnade near the Agora adorned with paintings, from which his followers came to be called Stoics, or men of the Porch. He died in 264, having taught publicly for some forty years, and having won the esteem of the Athenians for his integrity of character and frugality of life.

The affiliation of Zeno's doctrine may be gath-

ered by reading together two passages from antiquity; one from the historian of Laerte, who
says that Antisthenes laid the foundation of the
city by anticipating the apathy of Diogenes, the
continence of Crates, and the endurance of Zeno;
the other from a late Stoic who declares that by
the counsel of God Socrates took for his province
the examination of souls, and Diogenes the art
of rebuking in royal fashion, whereas Zeno made
philosophy didactic and dogmatic.[4] As Epicurus, following Aristippus, laid hold of the Socratic hedonism and developed this into a systematic philosophy, so Zeno took the Socratic
virtue of endurance and self-sufficiency from
the Cynics and out of these constructed an elaborate scheme of optimism. And, again, like Epicurus, he accepted the Xenocratic division of philosophy into physics, logic, and ethics, and undertook to lay a solid basis for his ethical structure in a harmonized theory of the nature of the
universe and in what seemed to him a sound criterion of knowledge.

In forming his physical system to this end it
is clear, I think, that Zeno had in view the Platonic cosmos and especially the mythological
scheme of the *Timaeus*. Like Plato, he felt the

---

[4]Diog. Laert. VI, 15; Epictetus, *Discourses* III, xxi, 19.

working of two forces in the composition of the world, which he also identified with a creating God and brute matter. This dualism, manifestly Platonic in conception, runs through the Stoics' creed and colours what may be called their philosophic emotions at every step; but it does so, one might say, despite themselves and in a manner quite inconsistent with their fury for rationalizing. For this would seem to be a distinctive note of the Stoic mind, that it was not content to abide by the paradoxical data of consciousness and to employ reason in the service of these data, but was convinced that reason can transcend the facts of experience and explain the nature of things by an hypothesis of its own. Any hope of a self-sufficient life, they thought, must be based on a theory of the world in which we live as itself self-sufficient, with no disturbing defect and no inherent inconsistencies, a reasoned and perfect unit. The process by which they satisfied these demands of rational optimism is fairly clear, and the results beautifully simple—if only they had any basis of truth.

In the first place reason looks for a continuous and comprehensible system of cause and effect, and in this demand it finds itself baffled at the outset by the relation between spirit, or the

immaterial, and matter. The problem is not peculiar to the Stoics, and the solution has been repeated whenever rationalism has usurped the
field of thought. Thus it goes. We are aware, as
it seems to us, of two factors in ourselves making a composite creature, mind and body, spirit
and matter. We know also that in some way
these two elements of our constitution act and
suffer together: we are sick, and the mind is affected; we think or feel, and the body is affected. There appears to be some kind of interaction
between the two elements, yet no investigation
of psychology or physiology has ever succeeded
in laying a finger on the nexus of cause and effect, and indeed any such bond is incomprehensible, even repellent, to reason, so long as we
conceive body and soul, the material and the immaterial, as belonging to two distinct orders of
being. Hence rationalism, in its search for a
closed system of cause and effect, has invariably
tended to escape this dualism by defining mind
and soul in terms of matter and body, or by defining matter and body in terms of mind and
soul. The former of these adaptations is the eas-
ier, for the very simple reason that body forces
itself peremptorily upon our senses, whereas
soul is elusive and can more readily, so to speak,

be argued out of sight; and this, consequently, has been the path commonly pursued. Certainly it was the course taken by Zeno, as may be shown by putting together several of the Stoic arguments:

"Nothing incorporeal feels with (*sympaschei,* 'has the same affection with,' 'is connected causally with') body, nor does body feel with the incorporeal, but body with body. Now the soul feels with the body in sickness or under the knife, and the body feels with the soul, turning red when the soul is ashamed and pale when the soul is afraid. Therefore the soul is body."

"There are those who think that nothing can cause motion which is itself motionless, but that everything that causes motion is itself in motion. And evidently this was the view of those ancient philosophers who held that the first principle, whether one or multiple, was corporeal; and among the moderns it is the view of the Stoics."

(In the following sentences the writer is criticising from the Peripatetic point of view) : "We ought not to begin from the ultimate principles of causation, that is to say, from concussion and thrust; nor should we surrender our contention with the Stoics who hold that an agent produces its effect by propinquity and contact. It is better to say that all causes are not by propinquity and contact."

"Death is a separation of soul from body. But nothing incorporeal is separated from body, as on the other hand there is no contact between the incorporeal and body. But the soul is in contact with body and is separated from body; therefore the soul is body."

By reasoning such as this Zeno reduced soul, or spirit, or the divine, or whatever one may choose to call the immaterial element, to a purely mechanical operation. His definitions, to be sure, left room for a troublesome distinction between energy and matter to be explained away before a thoroughly materialistic system could be established; but the Stoic was not a man to be frightened by any such bogey of the intellect, and he will evade this dualism of mechanics by defining energy and matter as nothing more than the active and passive aspects of one and the same thing. To be sure it is rather a puzzler for the monist to explain how a uniform substance can act on itself as agent and be acted upon by itself as patient, and perform both operations at the same time; but his vocabulary is not exhausted, however his reason may be disconcerted, and the *tonos* of Chrysippus and the later writers was devised, apparently, for just this purpose of finally identifying energy and matter. However, as no critic of antiquity seems

to have comprehended the precise function of
this famous and furiously debated term, we may
avow our own ignorance unabashed, and pass
on. Whether logically or illogically, Zeno had
reached a completely mechanistic conception of
the universe, in which energy is only another
name for matter.[5]

His next problem was to reduce the apparent
diversities of matter itself to one uniform substratum. Here he proceeded, so far as I can see,
by a sheer plunge of the reason rather than by
logical steps. Falling back upon the ancient hy-
lozoistic philosophies, which found the source of
nature in some one primordial stuff possessing
the characteristics of life, and more particularly
upon Heraclitus, he declared that the universal
substratum of things was fire, or an element like
fire in its fineness and fluidity. So stated, the
theory sounds crude enough to ears accustomed
to the modern conception of combustion; but if
for the moment we suppress our knowledge of
chemical processes and accept the terminology
of the Stoics, the physical substratum assumed
by Zeno is near enough to the nebular hypothesis of Kant to command our respect though it
may not warrant our assent. At any rate reason

[5]See Appendix A.

had done its work; the great leap had been taken from the dualism of experience to a metaphysic of absolute monism.

To account for the actual condition of the world in its manifold diversity, Zeno had recourse to the process of evolution. In the beginning is fire. This primary substance is potentially active and passive, and by some law of its being the passive principle in it thickens and coarsens, becomes separate from the active principle, and develops stage by stage into the four elements of the phenomenal world: fire, air, water, earth. Meanwhile the active principle remains unchanged, and penetrates the coarser elements as the forming, creating, governing energy of the cosmos. In the gleaming stars of the firmament it appears with uncontaminated splendour, and through the descending scale of creatures it manifests itself as reason in man, soul in animals, nature in plants, and *hexis* in inorganic objects. At the conclusion of time's period the process of evolution is inverted, and by gradual steps the world is absorbed back into the primordial element from which it sprang; fire again becomes all in all, until once more the law of diversification begins its work. The alternating expansion and contraction, evolution and involution, are, as it were, the diastole and systole of the world's great heart, the everlasting recurrence by which the same series of events endlessly repeat themselves: what is happening now, has happened before, and will happen again, as regularly and as fatefully and as mechanically as the swing of a pendulum.[6]

Such, briefly summarized, is the physical theory of Zeno, which was carried on by his followers with little change. Speaking as scientists and in the cooler moments of reason, they reduce the universe to a mere machine conceived in the most grossly materialistic terms. All things that really exist are bodies, and those phenomena which other men define in terms of immaterial energy are explained by the interpenetration of body in body or by the mixture of body with body. Nor, denying the existence of empty space within the confines of the world, are they repelled by the conclusion that such a theory of interpenetration implies the existence of two bodies in the same place at the same time.[7] So they account for the operation of fate and Providence and for that sympathy of part with part which binds the universe together into a perfect unity. All

[6]The same process of evolution and involution will be met with again in the spiritual monism of Plotinus.
[7]J. von Arnim, *Stoicorum Vet. Frag.* II, 475.

these things are the mechanical effects of a diffusion of the primordial element throughout the visible body of the world, as it were matter dissolved in matter, not by juxtaposition of particle to particle, but by coöccupation of the same space.

And it is characteristic of the Stoic mind that, just as their desire to define all activity in a purely mechanical formula forces them in the end to play fast and loose with the first law of mechanics, so their boldly formulated panhylism, if I may invent the word for the theory of material solutions, can suddenly and without warning, slip over into an equally bold pantheism. Almost, one might say, at the whim of the writer the immanent cause of the world may be described in grossly materialistic terms, or it may be dignified as God, Providence, logos, the universal soul, with all the spiritual connotation of such words as they are commonly used.[8] That is the sort of logical legerdemain to which the monist is inevitably brought at last by the stern necessity of facts; and so it happens that the same philosophy after many centuries has fathered the science of a Huxley and the romanticism of

[8]This is a residue of the Timaean mythology which clung to the Stoics as it were despite themselves. But it also goes back to the original discrepancy of the Heraclitean fire and logos as two ill-consorted principles of evolution. See Aall, *Geschichte der Logosidee* I, 18, 129.

a Wordsworth. For the pantheistic turn of Stoicism, which will colour all the thoughts of such
later writers as Epictetus and Marcus Aurelius
and Seneca, we can go back to the second master
of the school, Cleanthes, whose *Hymn to Zeus*
fortunately has been preserved. It contains, as
Mr. Adam has observed, "what is perhaps the
most famous expression in Greek literature of
the profoundly religious as well as philosophical doctrine of man's celestial origin and nature"
—the most famous, undoubtedly, in religion
owing to St. Paul, but, with certain phrases of
Plato echoing in my mind, I should be slow to
say the most profound in philosophy. The translation which follows is from Mr. Adam's *Vitality of Platonism:*

"O God most glorious, called by many a name,
Nature's great King, through endless years the same;
Omnipotence, who by thy just decree
Controllest all, hail, Zeus, for unto thee
Behoves thy creatures in all lands to call.
We are thy children,[9] we alone, of all

[9]'Εκ σοῦ γὰρ γενόμεσθα.—The reader needs no reminder of Paul's
words at Athens (Acts xvii, 28) : 'Εν αὐτῷ γὰρ ζῶμεν καὶ κινούμεθα καὶ
ἐσμεν· ὡς καί τινες τῶν καθ' ὑμᾶς ποιητῶν εἰρήκασι, Τοῦ γὰρ καὶ γένος ἐσμέν.
The last clause is taken from Aratus (*Phaenomena* 5), but Paul's
use of the plural "poets" may indicate that he had also in mind
the equivalent words of Cleanthes, as indeed by his time the sentiment was a commonplace of philosophy. Mr. Adam, comment-
ing on the clause, "in him we live and move and have our being,"
observes that a Stoic would rather have said, "God lives in us."

On earth's broad ways that wander to and fro,
Bearing thine image wheresoe'er we go.
Wherefore with songs of praise thy power I will forth
    shew.
Lo! yonder Heaven, that round the earth is wheeled,
Follows thy guidance, still to thee doth yield
Glad homage; thine unconquerable hand
Such flaming minister, the levin-brand,
Wieldeth, a sword two-edged, whose deathless might
Pulsates through all that Nature brings to light;
Vehicle of the universal Word, that flows
Through all, and in the light celestial glows
Of stars both great and small. O King of Kings
Through ceaseless ages, God, whose purpose brings
To birth, whate'er on land or in the sea
Is wrought, or in high heaven's immensity;
Save what the sinner works infatuate.
Nay, but thou knowest to make crooked straight:
Chaos to thee is order: in thine eyes
The unloved is lovely, who didst harmonize
Things evil with things good, that there should be
One Word through all things everlastingly.
One Word—whose voice alas! the wicked spurn;
Insatiate for the good their spirits yearn:
Yet seeing see not, neither hearing hear
God's universal law, which those revere,
By reason guided, happiness who win.
The rest, unreasoning, diverse shapes of sin
Self-prompted follow: for an idle name
Vainly they wrestle in the lists of fame:
Others inordinately riches woo,
Or dissolute, the joys of flesh pursue.

Now here, now there they wander, fruitless still,
For ever seeking good and finding ill.
Zeus the all-bountiful, whom darkness shrouds,
Whose lightning lightens in the thunder-clouds;
Thy children save from error's deadly sway:
Turn thou the darkness from their souls away:
Vouchsafe that unto knowledge they attain;
For thou by knowledge art made strong to reign
O'er all, and all things rulest righteously.
So by thee honoured, we will honour thee,
Praising thy works continually with songs,
As mortals should; nor higher meed belongs
E'en to the gods, than justly to adore
The universal law for evermore."

For the basis of his logic Zeno took the organon of Aristotle, but consistently with the
materialism of his physics, made sensation the
ultimate source of all thought and knowledge.
This department of the Stoic philosophy was for
many decades the subject of fierce attack from
the sceptics on the one side and from the idealists
on the other side. It is not within my province
to trace the long and tangled course of this history; only a word must be said in regard to the
phantasia kataléptikê as the Stoic criterion of
knowledge, since with it is involved the ethical
system which is our real concern.

Now the use of the phrase *phantasia katalép-*

tikê was more or less modified to meet the hostile criticism it evoked, but in the main and ultimately its meaning is clear enough. A *phantasia* is the impression made in the mind by some external object through the senses, and this impression was often understood in a gross manner as resembling the figure made upon wax by a seal. *Kataleptikê* ordinarily would signify grasping, or comprehending; but it may also, in accordance with the common ambiguity of active and passive in Greek, signify grasped, or comprehended; and there has been a good deal of dispute among modern critics as to whether a *phantasia* so defined implies an impression made when the sense clearly grasps and comprehends the object perceived, or when it is grasped by the object, or indeed as to which of the two grasps or is grasped.[10] In either case it was an impression so distinct and vivid and consistent and permanent as to carry its own conviction of certainty and to be its own criterion of truth. Through such impressions the objects of sense are, so to speak, exactly reproduced in the mind, and we

[10]Sextus Emp., *Adv. Math.* vii, 257, describes the kataleptic process vividly: Μόνον οὐχὶ τῶν τριχῶν, φασί, λαμβάνεται, κατασπᾶσα ἡμᾶς εἰς συγκατάθεσιν.

attain to a perfect comprehension, *katalêpsis*, of the nature of the world as it is.[11]

It is no wonder that the malicious critics of the Porch jumped at such a thesis and worried it as a cat plays with its victim. By such a criterion, they would ask, how do you distinguish between a wise man and a fool, when each swears with equal conviction to the vigour of his impression and the clarity of his opinion? It was apparently Arcesilas, founder of the Middle Academy, who started the mischief, and for a century and more there was a running battle between the Stoic supporters of *katalêpsis* and the sceptical maintainers of *akatalêpsia* ("non-comprehensibility"), which seems to have afforded vast entertainment to all concerned. One of the stories of this warfare is commonly passed over by the historians of philosophy as too frivolous for their graver Muse; but as it was quoted by the godly Eusebius in his *Preparation for the Gospel*, and as it really has some significance—at least for

[11]The part played by judgment as distinct from sensation in the final act of comprehension, the existence or not of phantasies derived from an immaterial source, are questions much agitated. I do not pretend to have any firm foothold on this quaking ground where Stoic psychology and epistemology meet. At bottom it should seem that the Stoics were trying to find some equivalent for Plato's definition of knowledge (*Theaetetus* 208ʙ) as ὀρθὴ δόξα μετὰ λόγου, but by their monism, which leaves no place for a distinction between δόξα (*i.e.* αἴσθησις) and λόγος, were driven about in a vicious circle. Fortunately my theme absolves me from entering upon this argument; Bonhöffer (*Epictet und die Stoa* 222ff. *et al.*) discusses it at sufficient length.

any one who is inclined to take lightly all theories of knowledge, ancient or modern,—it may find a place in these pages. It is related of a certain Lacydes, the successor of Arcesilas as head of the Academy, and so, nominally, a follower of Plato.

Now this Lacydes, we are told, was a stingy fellow who used to dole out the stores to his household with a tight fist. But though he acted as his own steward, he did not like to carry the keys about with him; and so he adopted this habit. Having locked the pantry, he would put the key in a desk, seal the desk with his signet, and then throw the signet through the keyhole into the pantry. When next he wished to enter the room, he would break the seal of the desk, get the key, and so on. Naturally the slaves soon got wind of this procedure, and took advantage of it. In his absence they would raid the pantry, and then lock the room just as their master had done. Lacydes to his surprise would find empty vessels where he had left them full, and could not understand how this happened unless his eyes deceived him. However he had heard that Arcesilas, of the Academy, was expounding the doctrine of incomprehensibility (*akatalêpsia*) against the Stoics, that is to say, was teaching that we can derive no certain knowledge from what we see and hear. So to school to Arcesilas our Lacydes went, and was convinced that the new doctrine of incomprehensibility explained the deception of his eyes. One day he invited a friend to his house, and began to lay bare the mysteries of scepticism, giving his experience with the pantry as a proof of the fact that our senses are no criterion of knowledge. "What," he argued, "could Zeno himself answer to my demonstration of incomprehensibility? With my own hands I lock up everything, seal the desk, and throw the signet into the room; and then when I come back, there are the signet and the key just where they should be, but the stores have all the appearance of not being as I left them. What's to be made of it? No thief could have got in, because the key is sealed up. It's just that we can't put any dependence on our senses." At this tale the friend, who was a merry wag, broke out into uproarious laughter, and explained to the victim what had happened. Lacydes thought it prudent to carry the signet about with him after that, and no longer used his storeroom as a demonstration of incomprehensibility; nevertheless, he continued his sceptical studies just the same. But the slaves were not to

be outdone. Whether from some wicked Stoic
or otherwise, they got their instruction, and made
their plans accordingly. They simply broke the
seal on the desk, took the key, pilfered the pantry, locked it up, put the key back in the desk,
which they then left unsealed or sealed with any
signet they could find. When Lacydes saw the
state of the desk and accused them of tampering
with the seal, they calmly assured him that his
senses deceived him and that everything was
exactly as he had left it. "For you know," they
would say, "one can't form any sound opinion
from what one sees; and as memory is a kind of
opinion, that too is quite untrustworthy. You
yourself were saying as much to a friend in our
hearing." Then Lacydes would argue, and the
slaves would counter-argue, until it sounded as
if all the denizens of the Academy and the Porch
were at one another's throats, and no one could
tell who was Academician and who was Stoic.
Lacydes kept this up until he got into a state of
utter distraction, and could only cry out in rage
to gods and neighbours. At last he settled the
difficulties by staying at home and keeping watch
on the door. To the slaves who tried to ply him
with the old doubting questions, he would say:
"My boys, that's the way we talk about these

things in the schools, but we live differently."[12]

Lacydes, at least as he comes to us in the tradition, is not much more than a buffoon, playing a farcical interlude on the stage of the Academy between the solemn parts of Arcesilas and Carneades. But out of the mouths of fools wisdom sometimes proceeds, and perhaps the soundest conclusion to all epistemological debates is the genial ejaculation that we talk one way in the schools and live another way. What else is to be made of any argument on the process of knowing when every step of the argument must be based on an assumption of this same process of knowing.

The ethical creed, for the sake of which Zeno built up his physics and logic, can best be studied in the teaching of Epictetus, who in the main returned to the original principles of the sect, though no doubt something of the Platonic tone introduced by certain schismatics still clung to his mind. It will be sufficient to note here two points. In the first place, the Cynical contempt for the conventions of decency remained as a kind of *amari aliquid* in the Stoic school, contrasting painfully with its finer vein of moralizing. There are sayings quoted from the early

[12]I have paraphrased the story as quoted by Eusebius (*Praep. Ev.* XIV, vii) from Numenius.

masters of the Porch expressing their, theoretical at least, indifference to the most abhorrent
of unnatural vices. And this, too, is a logical sequence of a monism which denies all ultimate
distinctions, as Plato showed in the *Gorgias*. In
the second place, it is clear that the whole rational system of Zeno was worked out for the purpose of achieving that inner and moral security
which was the desire also of Cyrenaic and Epicurean but was plainly incompatible with a philosophy of pleasure and atomistic chance. Only
in a world absolutely rational and continuous,
absolutely at one with itself, and only by a criterion of knowledge which enabled us to reproduce such a world exactly in our own reason,
could man, as the Stoic believed, be secure in the
rational government of his own life. This is the
significance of the famous maxim "to live consistently with nature," or "in accordance with
nature," which from the time of Cleanthes was
repeated as the catchword of Stoic ethics. But—
and this is the dire Nemesis that tortured their
logic—by the means adopted for attaining such
security they deprived themselves of the liberty
which was, and is, equally the aim of philosophy.
When reason has reduced the world to a fatalistic machine, any talk of freedom (and the Stoics

talked much of it) becomes a pitiful mockery.
If Cyrenaic and Epicurean saw in the world a
place of liberty without security, it may be said
that the Stoic universe is for the soul of man a
place of security without liberty. Yet both Epicurean and Stoic knew and felt deeply that our
security and liberty cannot be severed, but are
craved as one thing.

Meanwhile, to return to the historical development of Stoicism, it is sufficient for our purpose to mention the fact that after Cleanthes
the leadership of the school passed into the hands
of Chrysippus (*ca.* 280-205), who remains, when
all criticism has been made, one of the supreme
masters of dialectic. The task of Chrysippus was
to develop and organize the doctrines laid down
by Zeno into a vast metaphysical system. It was
said of him: "Had there been no Chrysippus,
there had been no Porch." Then came the panic
and the defection of the so-called Middle Porch.
From the virulent attacks to which the contradictions inherent in their principles laid the
Stoics bare, Panaetius (†111 B.C.) and Posidonius (†91) sought relief by trying to merge a
Platonic psychology with the rigid monism of
Zeno. No doubt the results of this "conflation,"
or "contamination," were interesting, and since

the publication of Schmekel's study of *Die Mitt-lere Stoa* (1892) Posidonius in particular has become for the historians of philosophy a figure of almost superstitious reverence, to whom they are prone to trace in one way or another the spiritualistic currents that prevailed in later Greek thought. But there is a good deal of pure conjecture in all this; and at bottom the changes introduced by Panaetius and Posidonius, so far from relieving the Stoic system of its inherent difficulties, only added a new source of mental confusion. The radical dualism of Plato and the absolute rationalism of Zeno can never be made to lie down comfortably together.

CHAPTER IV

EPICTETUS

I

Epictetus was a Phrygian-born slave of Nero's freedman Epaphroditus. He was lame, from birth or by disease, as the cause is variously reported. But Celsus, the anti-Christian, has a different story: "When his master was twisting his leg, Epictetus only smiled, and said calmly, 'You will break it.' And when it was broken, 'I told you so.' Did your God [Jesus] say anything like that under torture?"[1] Whatever may be the truth of this, Epictetus, at some time, gained his freedom, and set up a school of philosophy in Rome, continuing the Stoic lessons he had learned under Musonius Rufus. His language was Greek, which he spoke with vigour and precision, if not with elegance. In the year 94 (?) Domitian banished the philosophers, and Epictetus transferred his classes to Nicopolis in

[1]Origen, *Contra Celsum* vii, 53.

Epirus. He died in old age, having won respect
for himself as a man, and wide renown as a
teacher.

Epictetus wrote nothing. But one of his hear-
ers, the historian Arrian, took notes of his lectures, probably in shorthand, and published the
gist of these in several books of *Discourses,* out
of which he also compiled a brief compendium, or
Manual. Fortunately Arrian, as he declares in
his preface and as the text confirms, has reproduced pretty faithfully the direct, unadorned
speech of the lecturer, with the result that, though
we know so little of Epictetus' life, he is extra-
ordinarily vivid to us as a teacher; it is as if we
were actually in the class-room, and heard the
lame old man, as he calls himself, delivering his
rather disjointed, but direct and powerful appeals. We can almost see the pupils as they sit
taking notes, asking a question now and then or
putting in an objection. For the most part they
would seem to have belonged to the upper and
official classes, young men who came over to this
provincial town to find some guide which should
take the place of the older religious sanctions,
or to learn the way to strength and a quiet heart
in a world filled with fears and alarms, or merely to acquire such readiness of tongue and such

adroitness in argument as would enable them to
shine in a polished and disputatious society.
These last were apparently the more numerous;
at least their presence vexed the soul of the stern
disciplinarian, and over and over again he turns
aside to ridicule their vanity and to warn them
that they are wasting their time. He is not there
to impart cleverness in the exchange of paltry
phrases, but to train the will and prepare for the
rude contest of life. "The ship is sinking," he
cries out to those who wish to jump immediately
into the subtleties of logic, "the sea is breaking
over you, yet you would hoist the topsails!"[2]

Occasionally some traveller strolls into the
hall where this strange professor of philosophy
is holding forth, whose fame has reached him
through the noise of the Empire's business; and
sometimes the sightseer is greeted with such
words about himself as must have sent him out
with tingling ears. A notable scholar, who had
been detected in adultery, ventures in, and hears
a terrible diatribe on the baseness of such a sin.
What, one wonders, were the pupils doing while
the master was pouring denunciation on the
poor victim? How did the victim take it? Did he

[2]This is the tone and almost the words of Buddha in regard to
metaphysical dispute.

sit patiently, with a Stoic smile, through the storm?

Constantly also the master talks about himself, humbly, proudly, with wistful earnestness. Once he has been telling about a pardoned exile who had been in charge of the corn-supply in Rome, and who had protested to Epictetus, on his way back, that the rest of his life should be devoted to retirement and tranquillity—only to plunge, as Epictetus predicted, more deeply than ever into ambitious schemes on reaching Rome. And then Epictetus suddenly thinks of himself:

"Do I say that the creature man is not to be active? Heaven forbid! But what is it that fetters our faculty of action? Take myself first: when day comes, I remind myself a little as to what lesson I ought to read to my pupils. Then in a moment I find myself saying, 'But what do I really care what sort of lesson I give to this man or that? The first thing is for me to sleep.' And yet, how can the business of those worldlings be compared in importance with ours? If you attend to what they are doing you will see the difference. They do nothing all day long except vote, dispute, deliberate about a handful of corn or an acre of land, and petty profits of this sort. Is there any resemblance between receiving and reading a petition such as this: 'I beg

you to let me export a little corn,' and a petition
such as, 'I beg you to inquire from Chrysippus
how the universe is governed, and what position
the rational creature holds in it; inquire too who
you are and what is good for you, and what is
evil'? What have these petitions in common? Do
both demand the same attention? Is it equally
shameful to neglect one and to neglect the other?

"What is my conclusion? Are we elders alone
indolent and sleepy? Nay, the fault is much
rather with you young men. For, indeed, we old
folk, when we see young men playing, are only
too eager and ready to join their play. Much
more, if I saw them thoroughly awakened and
eager to share my studies, should I also be eager
myself to take my studies seriously."[3]

II

As for the system of philosophy expounded by
Epictetus, there was not much of originality
here, and, indeed, originality in the matter of his
teaching was the last thing he aimed at. In the
main his lectures, apparently, took the form of
reading and interpreting the Stoic doctrine of
Chrysippus, though this formal side of his in-

[3]Most of the quotations from Epictetus in this chapter are from
the excellent translation by P. E. Matheson (Clarendon Press,
1916). But in some cases I have altered the language freely, so
that Mr. Matheson should not be held responsible for any word
or phrase without reference to his work.

struction is for the most part passed over by
Arrian. Philosophy for Epictetus, as for the
other teachers of his day, was divided into three
heads: physics, ethics, and logic; and if he had
little to say about the first of these branches, its
subject matter, nevertheless, lay in his mind as
the background of all his reasoning. The materialism of the earlier school had been softened in
the course of time; there is scarcely a hint in
Epictetus of the primitive stuff of the world,
and he would willingly let us forget that the
soul is only a finer substance than those of which
our bodies are composed. The identification of
that fiery element with reason (*logos*) had become more complete, and his thoughts turned
rather to God and to God's providential government of the world than to any mechanical
law of nature. Yet if the materialism of the
school has been shoved into the background,
their monism, theoretically at least, has suffered no relaxation. The Providence of God is an
absolute fatality, and whatever is, by virtue of
its necessity, of its very being, is right.

Confronted by the great problem of evil as a
disturbing factor in the nature of things, Epictetus, in what may be called his objective theory
of ethics, contented himself with the familiar

paradox which the Stoics had learnt from Plato, while passing over Plato's alleviation of its irritating inadequacy.[4] For the composition of the universe as a whole it is necessary that there should be an infinite number of parts each incomplete in itself. What seems evil to any individual member of the corporate body is this inevitable incompleteness. The perfection and well-being of the whole are conditioned by the imperfection and limitation of the parts. To this explanation Epictetus followed his predecessors in adding another, which is nothing more than the same physical paradox expressed in the terms of ethics: our character—and the happiness springing from character—depends on the strength derived from resistance to opposition; the suffering which we call evil is merely the gymnastic exercise by which we acquire self-mastery, and as such is our good in disguise. So Heracles would never have been himself or realized his divinity but for his victory of endurance through the twelve labours. It is patent that such an explanation leaves the heart of the matter untouched, and affords no answer to the troublesome query *why* the perfection of the world as a whole should require the conscious

4See *The Religion of Plato* 145 ff., 235.

imperfection of the parts, or *why* our good must be wrung out of suffering. But we need not be too severe with Epictetus for juggling with a sophism which, time-worn and frayed as it is, still goes on doing duty after these thousands of years.

Indeed, Epictetus himself was aware of the insufficiency of such an answer, taken alone, to the insistent problem of philosophy. He was always and above all a moralist, and the voice of conscience was still an ugly fact which he had to meet. Thinking of the world wherein men live, he might say that whatever is is right, but thinking of man himself, speaking from the depths of his own consciousness, he was bound to consider the *prolêpseis,* as the Stoics called them, the primary presuppositions, or preconceptions, of good and evil, the conviction common to all men that some things are well with them and other things are not well with them. The task of the Stoic philosopher, then, was to find some term of reconciliation for the optimism of his monistic physics and the ethical dualism which as a true moralist he could not escape.

So much will be clear from the Stoic point of view: since the world itself is absolutely determined and absolutely right, the distinction of

good and evil lies not in the nature of things, but
is purely subjective; it is in ourselves, involved
somehow in our act of imagining such a distinction. It is we who have eaten of the tree of the
knowledge of good and evil, and for ourselves
corrupted what is incorruptible. "All things are
opinion,"[5] said Marcus Aurelius—which is not
equivalent to the Shakespearian maxim: "There
is nothing either good or bad but thinking makes
it so," but means rather: All things are good
although thinking may make them to appear ill.
That is the beginning, and that is the end, of
Stoicism, summed up in the one word *dogma*
("judgment," "opinion," "the way things seem
to us"), which runs through all the chapters of
Epictetus like the binding refrain of a chant.

What, then, more precisely are these dogmata? The reply to this question breaks into a
group of propositions which occur either alone
or in various combinations with almost dam-
nable iteration; they form what I may call the
Stoic Wheel, though the phrase itself was not
in use.

THE STOIC WHEEL

1. What are dogmata?
    Certain things are *ours,* belonging to us,
    in a sense we.

[5] xii, 8: Πάντα ὑπόληψις.

Other things are *not ours,* another's, foreign, alien, not we.

2. What are ours? what not ours?

Ours are things *in our power,* under our
control.

Not ours are things *not in our power,* not
under our control.

3. What are in our power? what not in our power?

In our power are things *voluntary,* matters of our will, choice.

Not in our power are things *involuntary.*

4. What are voluntary? what involuntary?

We can exercise our will in the *use of
impressions,* or phantasies.

We cannot exercise our will in the *impressions* themselves.[6]

But what is meant by this "use" of impressions which we have reached in our attempt to
define the nature of dogmata? Now an impression, phantasy, *phantasia,* in the simplest terms
is the change produced in the mind by an external object, the image that corresponds with what
we perceive and that remains after the immediate act of perception. The difference between
an impression and the use of an impression may
be illustrated thus. A man is on a vessel at sea,
and looking out receives an image, or picture, of

---

[6]Ours, ἴδια; not ours, ἀλλότρια; in our power, τὰ ἐφ' ἡμῖν; voluntary,
προαιρετικά; will, προαίρεσις; impressions, φαντασίαι; use of impressions, χρῆσις τῶν φαντασιῶν.

a boundless expanse of water; that is a phantasy. Then, perhaps, there comes upon him a feeling of awe or terror at the thought of his own littleness and helplessness amidst this vast, weltering, inhuman power; that is not a phantasy, but his own use of a phantasy. Again, a storm arises, and the picture is formed in his mind of rushing winds and beating waves; that is a phantasy. The story of men drowned at sea recurs to memory, and this too produces a phantasy. But suppose he allows these images to unman him with fear: that is not a phantasy, but the use of a phantasy; it is not the bare image of death that causes his distress, but the thought, or dogma, that death is a fearful event.[7]

Thus the use of impressions is our thought about them, our judgment of their character and consequences, in a word our dogmata; and so the circle is completed, the Wheel has come full around to its starting point. Then, again, from dogmata we may proceed as before. What is a dogma, we ask again; and the answer is the

[7]*Phantasia* means not only an immediate image created by some impression from without, but is used also for the chain of images that may follow in the mind. When a distinction is made between *phantasiai* and the use of *phantasiai*, the *phantasia* is an immediate image not under our control, while the "use" includes the successive images and judgments raised by the imagination and so under our control. In this sense the word for imagination is *anaplasis*. (see III, xxiv, 108 ff.)

same, the judgment that certain things are ours
and certain other things foreign to us, not ours.
But the last link of the chain is now in our definition as well as the first, and these things that
are ours we know to be the use of impressions as
distinguished from the impressions themselves
which are not ours (since their cause is outside
of us) ; and the use of impressions we know to
be just the dogmata we form about them. So of
the second step. The things that are ours are
those in our power, and the things that are foreign to us are those not in our power. But again
the definition has this new content: we know also
that the things in our power are the use of impressions, whereas the things not in our power
are the impressions themselves, and the use of
impressions we know to be just our dogmata. It
may seem that our so-called Wheel is merely a
vicious circle, since the reasoning, if reasoning
it be, amounts to no more than this: we have
dogmata that certain things are ours, and these
things which are ours are nothing but our dogmata; or, things themselves are not in our power, but it is in our power to form judgments concerning them, and the judgments we form are
that things are not in our power. Certainly that,
taken alone, if it is not what logicians term a

vicious circle, is at least a wheel revolving upon itself and carrying us nowhere. Somehow the fact of good and evil, as a matter of dogma, seems to have slipped in between impressions and the use of impressions, but as yet we have been brought no closer to knowing just what good is and just what evil is.

Now it is from difficulties of this kind, Epictetus says, that education and philosophy take their origin. Men are so constituted by nature that some things seem to them for their profit, other things for their harm. In this sense all men are born with preconceptions, or innate ideas, of good and evil. So far we are all alike; but the moment we apply these preconceptions to particular cases, the moment we say this man is good, or this act is right, or this condition is well, or the contrary, that moment there is disagreement and discord.[8] What else was the cause of the Trojan war but such a disagreement between Menelaus and Paris? And what brought about the long calamities of the Greek host but a similar conflict of opinion between Agamemnon and Achilles? Philosophy, then, will be the endeavour to find some rule by which we can give practical content to the abstract no-

[8]To this extent the whole Stoic philosophy is anticipated in the *Euthyphro* of Plato.

tions of good and evil, or, to use the technical
term of the Porch, it will be the Application
(*epharmogê*) of our general preconceptions of
right and wrong, advantage and disadvantage,
to particular cases. And education in philosophy
will be to the end that men may arrive at concord through such a rule. To this point all the
schools would be in agreement; but for the Stoic,
with his assumption that the world itself is right
and that evil is only in our dogmata, the application would be, if the metaphor is not too harsh,
by giving some forward motion to that Wheel
which seemed to be revolving about a fixed
centre.

In the working out of this application into a
complete code we meet with the one important
contribution made by Epictetus to the Stoic
philosophy. In general he was content to adhere
closely to the system developed by Zeno and
Cleanthes, and particularly by Chrysippus, of
whom he speaks in language of reverence like
that employed by Lucretius of Epicurus. But
in his division of ethics into three *topoi,* "departments," or "fields," at least in the detailed
use of that division, he appears to have struck
out for himself; and it is a notable achievement.
"There are three fields," he says, "in which a

man who is good and noble [*i.e.,* who is to apply
his preconceptions rightly to conduct] must be
trained. The first concerns desires and aversions; he must be trained not to fail of that
which he desires, nor to fall into that for which
he has an aversion. The second field is concerned
with impulses to act and not to act, and, in a
word, with what is fitting: that we should act in
order, with due consideration, and with proper
care. The object of the third field is that we may
not be deceived, and may not act at random;
and, generally, it is concerned with assent." In
a loose way these three fields correspond with
the normal tripartite division of philosophy, the
first with physics, the second with ethics in the
narrower sense of practical conduct, the third
with logic; but the correspondence, except perhaps in the case of the third pair, was never
drawn out explicitly by Epictetus, and should
not be pressed. All philosophy was virtually
ethics for him.

III

The First Field, or Department, of ethics is
concerned with our desires and aversions; and
if happiness is the end which all men seek, then
it should seem to follow simply enough that the

purpose of philosophy will be to instruct us how
to obtain what we desire and to avert what we
desire not. But we need no long experience of
the world to learn that it moves on at its own
sweet will, with scant regard to our desires. The
Cyrenaic and Epicurean had discovered this
truth to their great cost:

"The worldly Hope men set their Hearts upon
Turns Ashes—or it prospers; and anon,
    Like Snow upon the Desert's dusty Face,
    Lighting a little hour or two—was gone."

Not in that direction lies the path of philosophy, and he who would snatch at the fleeting
gifts of pleasure has staked his happiness on the
most fickle of all chances. The Stoic will turn
another way, and will alter himself to fit a world
which itself he finds he can so little alter. He
will make his desire sure, unhampered, unforced,
unhindered, and his aversion equally secure of
liability. And there is one way alone to accom-
plish this: by limiting his desires to those things
which are within his power and subject to his
will, to those things, in a word, which are his
own. Not his are the circumstances of existence;
not his are health and riches and prosperity, not
friends or wife or children or fatherland, not life
itself. These he can control but a little, if at all;
they are outside of him, coming and going by

their own right. They are indeed within him by the phantasies they produce in his mind, but over these phantasies also he has no arbitration; they are what they are. His domain extends no further than the voluntary use of these impressions, by forming of them what judgments he chooses. And in one way only can he judge of them so as always to have his desire: he must hold fast to the belief that whatever is is right and therefore for the interest of himself as a part of the whole, and that whatever is not cannot be desirable.

Such then is the first step in the application of general ideas to the particular needs of life. All men are born alike with preconceptions of good and evil; they disagree one with another because they apply these preconceptions to external objects and conditions. The Stoic will tell us that none of these things for which we contend is either good or evil, but in themselves all, without exception, are ultimately indifferent (*adiaphora*). The distinction of good and evil is not there, but lies within the scope of the human will; it is my good to conform my desires to things as they are, it is my evil to desire things to be other than God has ordered them or to set my will in opposition to the decrees of Provi-

dence. All the circumstances of life are indifferent, in the sense that in themselves they are neither good nor evil, but that we may create either
good or evil for ourselves by our attitude towards
them.[9]

It may appear that such a conclusion leaves
us still revolving in the same vicious circle of
dogmata: we have dogmata of good and evil,
and good and evil are our dogmata; but in fact
we have taken a long step forward. "What
then," Epictetus asks, "is the fruit of these dogmata?" And he answers: "The fairest and most
becoming fruit for those who are truly educat-
ing themselves—tranquillity, fearlessness, liberty"; to which may be joined the peculiar virtue
of Stoicism, apathy. Now the passions (*pathê*)
are those emotions that trouble the soul when it
fails to get what it desires or falls into that for
which it has aversion, and the apathetic man is
he who, by right dogmata, has raised himself

[9]It is not my fault if we have fallen already into a startling inconsistency. All things are right, and our dogmata cannot alter
this fact; yet in the same breath we are told that the circumstances of life are indifferent and become the source of good or
evil in accordance with our dogmata. This is the antinomy running all through Stoicism, as the world is regarded objectively
or subjectively: objectively regarded it is good, subjectively it
may be good or evil; but, and this is the crux, how in a monistic
system can there be any radical distinction between objective and
subjective?

above the possibility of just these emotions. He, too, is the tranquil man, since nothing can perturb him, and fearless, since nothing that he regards as misfortune can befall him, and free, because his dogmata are his own and are subject to no outer control. Stoic apathy, so understood, though it may be far from the Christian virtue implied in the same term,[10] must not be condemned as a state of sullen insensibility, a kind of death in life, unless tranquillity and fearlessness and liberty are held to be despicable possessions. Rather, Epictetus says, when perturbation and fear and servility, envy and jealousy and hatred, are gone, then, and then only, is the heart open to the true philosophic joy; then the soul has acquired that happiness for which all men are striving, while ignorantly impeding their own progress by dalliance with the false lures of pleasure. This is the ethical implication in the study of physics, that, knowing the constitution of the world, we should perceive the fatality which controls all things, and should obey the law with alacrity, as otherwise we must obey it sullenly.

The whole matter was summed up by Epictetus in the four so-called *procheira,* or maxims

[10]See *The Religion of Plato* 333 ff.

which the philosopher should have at hand under all the circumstances of life:

1. "Lead me, O Zeus, and thou, O Destiny,
   Where'er my lot is cast by your decree.
   I follow unafraid; nay, if my will
   Basely rebelleth, I shall follow still."

2. "Who rightly with necessity complies,
   In things divine we count him skilled and wise."

3. "Well, Crito, if this be the god's will, so be it."

4. "Anytus and Meletus have power to put me to death,
   but not to harm me."[11]

IV

So far our attention has been concentrated on what is our own, in our power, matters of the will, the use of phantasies; all the rest is neither good nor evil in respect to our inner life, but be-

[11]The first of these four *procheira*, from Cleanthes, is merely an expansion of the Stoic watchword "to live in accordance with nature." It was thus paraphrased by Seneca (*Ep.* cvii, 10):
> Duc, o parens celsique dominator poli,
> quocumque placuit; nulla parendi mora est.
> adsum impiger. fac nolle, comitabor gemens,
> malusque patiar, quod pati licuit bono.
> ducunt volentem fata, nolentem trahunt.

The second is from a lost play by Euripides. The third and fourth are condensed into epigrammatic form from passages in Plato, *Crito* 43 D and *Apology* 30 C. The fourth, which is more altered from the original than the third, seems to have been widely current. It is thus quoted by Plutarch (*apud* Stobaeus, *Eth.* vii, 32) and by Maximus Tyr., xii, 8A. Justin Martyr (*Apol.* I, ii, 4) uses it with noble effect in his appeal against the martyrdom of Christians.

longs to the sphere of indifference, and only by preserving this distinction in our dogmata is philosophic calm attainable. Nevertheless, it will be said, these indifferent things are about us, and in some way we must preserve the dogma that they are foreign to us yet must play a man's part in this life amongst them. How? The answer to this question is given in the Second Field of ethics.

In a passage already quoted, having distinguished the First Field, as concerned with desires and aversions, from the Second, which has to do with the impulses to act and not to act, Epictetus adds that this Second Department is "the sphere of what is fitting, of duties; for I must not be without feeling (apathetic) like a statue, but must maintain my natural and acquired relations, as a religious man, as son, brother, father, citizen." Elsewhere Epictetus states more clearly how and when in our philosophic training the transition should be made from the First Field to the Second. "Let us confine ourselves," he says to a pupil who was eager to advance too rapidly, "to the First Department, where we have almost sensible demonstration that we do not apply our preconceptions properly. Do you at this moment desire

things possible, and possible for you? Why,
then, do you feel yourself hindered and per-
turbed? Are you not now trying to avoid what
is inevitable? Otherwise, why do you fall into
trouble and misfortune? Why does a thing not
happen when you desire it, and happen when
you do not desire it, which is the strongest proof
of inner perturbation and misery?" Then, a little further on, speaking of the same pupil in the
third person, he continues: "Now, when he has
worked at this Department and made himself
master of it, let him come again and say to me,
'I wish to be free from passion and disquiet, but
also I wish, as one who has attained to piety and
philosophy and wise heedfulness, to know what
my specific duties are to the gods, to my brothers, my fatherland, to strangers.' Enter then on
the Second Department, I say; this, too, is
yours."

Now, if we examine these passages, we shall
see that the whole matter really hinges on the
definition of a few words—as indeed the Stoics
of all philosophers were the most given to defining and to drawing nice distinctions in the use
of terms. In the First Field the application of
our preconceptions is (1) to things that are our
own, (2) to desires and aversions in connection

with these, and (3) to absolute good and evil therein. In the Second Field the application is extended (1) to our relations (*scheseis*) with things foreign, (2) to our impulses to act and not to act (*hormai* and *aphormai*) in these relations, and (3) to the perception of our duty and of what is fitting (*kathêkon*) in such actions.[12] In the meaning of these three terms—relations, impulses to act, duties—is contained the law of conduct.

As for material conditions, such as health and riches, these may rightly be the objects of our activity in so far as they are preferred (*proêgmena*) above their contraries; to this extent the Stoic will compromise with the common instinct of mankind. But, while preferred, these things are still indifferent in the sense that, though we may work for them, we must not suffer our peace and happiness in any degree to depend ultimately on our success or failure. Nor should the pursuit of such things be permitted to interfere

[12]Mr. Matheson and other recent scholars avoid "duty" as a translation of *kathêkon,* since it "suggests a conflict which is not implied in the word." No doubt the connotation of "duty" has been changed by the Christian sense of a conflict between the will of God and the will of man; but on the other hand such words as "fitting" and "proper" miss the sense of obligation to a divine law, which is certainly strong in Epictetus' use of *kathêkon.* On the whole I regard "duty" as our nearest English equivalent.

with the religious and social obligations imposed on us by our nature.

All men, Epictetus says, and repeats with noble insistence, are the sons of one God and are thus related among themselves as children in one family; they are fellow-citizens of the one great City of God, which is the world; and so it is fitting, it is their duty we may say, to act towards God as towards a father and towards one another as towards brothers and fellow-citizens, and to check any impulse to act otherwise. Man is by nature a religious being, whose first duty is to worship the universal Father and Creator and Ruler; and he is a social being, whose second duty is so to play his part in the commonwealth that peace and concord and good will may be preserved. On these two commandments, the Stoic might have said, hang all the law and the prophets. They are summed up in the famous phrase "to live in accordance with nature."

But in this city of the world there are various things to do, many places to fill, many different associations to maintain. One man is set to rule, another to serve; one to trade, another to teach; one to marry, another to live without home or hearth. To each man there are the narrower relations to his particular city, to father, brother, wife, children, friends, strangers; and in each case he must act accordingly. The directions given are not very definite, you say; for the question is still left open how specifically we are to meet these obligations. And, in fact, Epictetus has few definite rules to offer. In the tenth chapter of the second book, after stating in general terms that the duty of a man is to act as a being distinguished from the lower animals by the possession of a rational will, and that the duty of a citizen is never to think of himself as solitary but always as a member of organized society, of a son to show obedience, of a brother to display a spirit of kindly concession—still not very specific rules, you will say—he adds: "Next, if you belong to a city council, remember that you are a councillor; if young, that you are young; if old, that you are old; if a father, that you are a father. *For each of these names, if properly considered, suggests the acts appropriate to it.*" The inference would be that there is no need to search over-curiously into the particular duties of life, for these have been discovered and sufficiently elaborated for us by the common experience of the race; they are embodied in the very words we use; and as in worship it is well to conform to tradition and the custom of the State, so in the various relations of man to man the voice of wisdom bids us to put away conceit (*oiêsis*) and humble one's self to the acceptance of what has been tried and found salutary.[13]

If there is originality in this branch of the Stoic ethics it is in the change from the Aristotelian method of defining virtues by some rule of measure in the activities themselves to this consideration of right conduct as determined by man's relations with other men. Here, as in other respects, Stoicism holds a curious halfway position between paganism and Christianity. One step was yet to be taken: the change from the abstract sense of relationship to the concrete emotion—love to God and to man as prescribed in the Golden Rule—which underlies and vivifies all these relations. Yet in another direction, as we shall see, the Stoic movement, so far as it remained true to its naturalistic origins, was un-

[13]This statement may seem to be contradicted by the fact that, in their passion for distinguishing and defining, some of the Stoics discussed particular problems of ethics in a manner which pointed the way to the scholastic science of casuistry. No doubt Stoicism is inconsistent here as elsewhere, but this is to be observed: the casuistical method was introduced by Panaetius and Posidonius —and so passed on to Cicero—as a defence against the attacks of Carneades, and is not inherent in Stoicism (cf. Schmekel, p. 368). An examination of the passages given by Bonhöffer (II, 201 ff.) will show that Epictetus, at least, uses σχέσεις as if their meaning and obligations were conveyed immediately in the ὀνό-ματα. For the appeal to συνήθεια, custom, convention, against Pyrrhonist and Academic, see *Discourses* I, xxvii, 15.

dermining the very basis of morality in the great
tradition of Platonism and Christianity.

V

In a way, the Stoic division of ethics into these
two Fields, or Departments, is no more than a
clear recognition of the double character of morality that runs all through the Greek Tradition. Plato first developed the idea, particularly
in his analysis of the virtues in *The Republic,*
where he assigns specific spheres of activity to
wisdom, bravery, and temperance, and identifies
justice with the compelling force behind all these
various activities. And this distinction, in one
form or another, was carried on by the later
schools.[14] But in the Stoic scheme the discrimination at first sight may seem harsh, even re-
pulsive, and at the same time obscure—harsh,
owing to the sharp assignment of good and evil

[14]I have discussed this distinction in *Platonism* 97-113. It seems
to have been first sharply defined by Aristo (see Arnim I, p.
85). A few further references to the continuation in the later
schools may be given; Aristotle, *Eth. Nic.* II, vi, 15, 17; VI, ix,
7; X, viii, 3 (with Stewart's notes) ; Philo Judaeus, *Leg. All.* I,
63 ff.; Clemens Alex., *Strom.* I, xx, 97; Chrysostom, *In Mat.* 96в,
189в; Socrates, *Ec. Hist.* IV, xxiii. Even the Epicureans draw a
like distinction between the ataraxy of a soul which possesses
itself, and the popular "justice" which implies conformity for
the sake of safety. Only the sceptics of the Pyrrhonic school reject the distinction absolutely.

exclusively to the First Field, whereas all the
objects of activity in the Second Field are denominated indifferent; obscure, because the law
of absolute morality does somehow extend down
into this region of indifference and because the
command to live in accord with nature is equally
operative in both Fields, "nature" being in one
sense the rational will that distinguishes man as
man and in another sense the sum total of man's
relations to the world. Yet, however paradoxical
the Stoics may be otherwise, they are really not
inconsistent here, as may be proved by the kind
of illustrations constantly recurring in Epictetus. Take the supreme test of character, death.
Now death, in the Stoic system, must be held a
matter of complete indifference, in itself neither
good nor bad, for the reason that it is something
over which we have no control, and which as a
consequence cannot be reckoned as ours. Nevertheless, the threat of death stirs in the mind an
impulse to act or not to act, and the action suitable to the conditions is our duty, our *kathêkon*.
There is responsibility here. Yet at the same
time our acts themselves are still in a manner indifferent in so far as they can be predetermined
by no fixed canon but must vary with circumstances; it may be fitting to face death unflinch-

ingly, or, under other circumstances, it may be
our duty to follow the impulse to avoid death.
So far we are in the Second Field, which has to
do with the experimental rules of practical ethics. We enter into the realm of absolute morality, passing to the First Field, when we consider,
not our specific conduct in regard to this death,
not the impulse to act or to refrain from action,
but the *telos,* or end, which lies behind and beyond all activity, and which concerns what the
Stoics call the desires and aversions of the soul.
However we act, whatever the event, our desire
and our aversion must be separated from the act
and the event, and this absolutely, for the reason that the thing itself, death or life, is indifferent.

Or take one of the common relations of life. I
am father, brother, son, husband, friend to such
a one, and he or she is related to me correspond-
ingly. In the very name of that bond I see the
obligations under which I am laid if I am to live
in harmony with my nature as a human being.
But at the same time that person, whether son
or brother, in himself is something foreign, not-
mine, in so far as I have no control over him and
am not responsible for his actions to me. Being
foreign, he is a thing indifferent, in so far as his

actions may make no difference in my conduct, or at least in my recognition of duty towards him. What if he is unkind, grasping, unfilial, must I therefore lose my humanity and fail in my obligations? Moreover, he is a thing foreign, not-mine, by the fact that I have no power to retain him; he is mortal and may die; he may go on a journey and so be lost to me. And in that sense also he is a thing indifferent, because the good and ill of my being must not depend on his presence, and my desires and aversions, in the citadel of the will, must be free of any relation. If he leaves me, as things mortal have a way of leaving, my desire shall not be attached to him, nor my peace broken, nor my liberty infringed, nor my submission to the divine will imperiled.

We touch here a mystery, and the frank, sometimes petulant, expression of an obscure truth has brought ill repute to the Stoics not always undeserved. So strong was their conviction of the ultimate independence of our will, our desire and aversion, upon any of these external relations, that they were wont to clothe their belief in words unnecessarily vehement. Suppose your friend dies, says Epictetus; shall you therefore sit and bewail? Shall you forget that he was born a mortal and subject to death? If the pot is

broken in which you boil your meat, do you not
send to the market and buy another? So be it in
your friendship.—Or, shall you stake your soul's
peace on the little son you love so dearly? What
harm if, when you kiss him, you murmur, "To-
morrow you will die"?—But I must go away,
you say, and my mother will grieve when she
does not see me. That is her affair, not yours.
Are you responsible because she will not learn
the lesson of philosophy? Your own sorrow you
may check absolutely, for it belongs to you; another's sorrow you shall endeavour to assuage
so far as may be lawful, not absolutely. Otherwise you will be fighting against God, and array-
ing yourself against His conduct of the universe.

These are not pretty sayings, let us admit;
but they should not be misunderstood. Epictetus did not mean to root out the natural affections which are so beautifully expressed by the
word *philostorgia*. One of his finest chapters is
that in which he rebukes a father who has run
away from a sick daughter because he could not
endure the sight of her suffering. "Suppose her
mother and her attendant also showed their love
like you by running away," Epictetus rejoins
indignantly; "was it right that the child should
be left desolate and helpless because of the great

affection of you its parents and of those about it?" No, this Phrygian slave, who was much alone in the world, and who did not shirk the harder doctrines of his school, was not in his heart callous to the softer ties of humanity, and there is a fund of tenderness under the rough language of his teaching. The critic who says that "Stoics made solitude in the heart and called it peace"[15] has turned a neat epigram, but he has not told the whole truth.

Yet, though it is a sad misreading of the text, to think of a typical Stoic like Epictetus as devoid of tenderness and natural affection, it is true that the deeper feeling of his mind is that of the Hindu epigrammatist:

> "These dear companionships are not for ever;
>   The wheel of being without end
>   Still whirls: if on the way some meet and sever,—
>   'Tis brother, mother, father, friend."

It is true that the relations of life are things ephemeral, foreign, and at the last uncontrollable, whereas inner peace, steadfastness of content, compliance to the will of God, are our own; not any power, not God Himself, can deprive us of the liberty of choosing what we will. And

[15]T. R. Glover, *The Conflict of Religions in the Early Roman Empire* 67.

when conflict arises, as sometimes it is forced
upon us, between what is ours to choose and our
attachment to what is not ours, when the bonds
of love are broken by accident or separation or
death, when the perversity of another renders
the mutual ties of life impossible, then the Stoic
will say that these things are indifferent and that
a man must withdraw into the citadel of his own
soul where his real treasure of good is to be defended. Where good and evil are, there finally is
our responsibility, and there happiness. And so,
putting this truth in compact language, the Stoic will declare: "It is better that thy son should
be evil than that thou shouldst be unhappy."[16]
Does that sound harsh, inhuman, paradoxical?
It may sound so, yet Christ could pronounce a
similar law in even sterner words. When one
said to him that his mother and brothers were
without, desiring to speak to him, thinking that
he was beside himself, what was his answer?
"Who is my mother? and who are my brethren?"
At another time, when the multitude was following him, he turned upon them, and cried: "If
any man come unto me, and hate not his father,
and mother, and wife, and children, and brethren, and sisters, yea, and his own life also, he

---

[16]*Manual* 12: Κρεῖττον δὲ τὸν παῖδα κακὸν εἶναι ἢ σὲ κακοδαίμονα

cannot be my disciple." Those are bitter sayings
that have caused many to wince and many to be
offended; but they cannot be evaded, nor is there
any contradiction, for one who knows the law
of religion, between them and the truly Christian sentences in the Epistle of St. John, "Who-
sover hateth his brother is a murderer," and "If
a man say, I love God, and hateth his brother,
he is a liar." I would not have it implied that I
see no difference between the Christian goal of
salvation and the Stoic pursuit of safety, or between the Christian love for one's neighbour and
the Stoic sense of duty in the relations of life;
there is in fact a profound difference. But, so
far as it goes, the Stoic distinction between the
First Field of ethics which teaches that absolute
good and evil lie in the right disposition of the
will and bids a man seek first his own happiness,
and the Second Field which embraces the obligations to other men,—so far as it goes this distinction is in the direction that was to be taken
by Christianity. As I said, we touch here a mystery.

Looking to the Orient, one is struck by a curious, almost a haunting, similarity of this Stoic
mystery with the practical wisdom of India as
summed up in the *Bhagavad Gîtâ*. No doubt the

difference here is as great as the resemblance, perhaps at the last analysis even greater. To the Hindu the world was not the purposed handiwork of God in any such way as it appeared to the Occidental philosopher; it was rather a mirage of illusion which offered no place for Providence or for submission to the divine will or for adjustment of the human will to the ordered progress of physical events. And on the other hand the eternal reality of the Atman is quite lacking to the Stoic distinction between what is mine and what is not mine. Nevertheless, in the application of these two orders of ideas East and West come together in a manner which must strike the imagination. In the East this application is expressed in the law of works and detachment:

"Whosoever abandoneth all desires, and goeth his way without craving,
Who saith not *This is mine! This is I!* he cometh unto peace.

"Therefore without attachment ever lay hand to thy peculiar work,
For he that doeth his work without attachment, he attaineth the Supreme.

"If all the doings of a man are devoid of the persuasion of desire,

If all his works are passed through the fires of knowledge, then will they who understand call him wise."[17]

Now it will be seen at a glance, I think, that
these couplets give as it were a summary of the
Stoic division of ethics into the First and Second Fields. The duties of a man to the world,
the obligations of his natural and acquired relations, are the Hindu works. And as these works
in the Hindu scheme are to be carried out without attachment to the subjects of obligation and
without ultimate concern for results, so precisely is it with the Stoic. Here, too, the duties
of our position must be fulfilled somehow without encroaching on our freedom from attachment (*prospatheia*), and the kindly affections
must be maintained without marring the soul's
private possession of apathy. Somehow the desire and aversion of the will must be removed
from our activities and their consequences to
the sphere of absolute good and evil. Only so,
Hindu and Stoic alike declare, is the path open
to peace and liberty and happiness, only so can
the law of the world be maintained. "It is difficult," Epictetus says, "to unite and combine

[17]For a fuller discussion of the Hindu creed I may refer to
Shelburne Essays VI, 43 ff. Mr. Edwyn Bevan has drawn attention to the parallel between Epictetus and the *Bhagavad* Gîtâ in
his *Stoics and Sceptics* 77 ff.

these two things—the care of one who devotes himself to the particular circumstances of life and the settled peace of one who disregards them—yet not impossible. Otherwise happiness would be impossible." Here, as elsewhere, what is dark and seemingly paradoxical in theory may be illuminated and simplified by its personification, so to speak, in a human character. Those who are familiar with the life of Marcus Aurelius have seen the union of Stoic aloofness with a tenderness towards all natural relations carried out in almost perfect harmony. Whether the Emperor's apathy did actually contain the elements of a positive happiness, is another question.

In the West, apart from the immediate teachings of Christ, the affiliation of this part of Stoicism is social rather than religious, and shows itself in the problem of the individual and the community, which troubled the eighteenth and nineteenth centuries and has not ceased to vex the drowsy ear of the present age. The antinomy goes back to Antisthenes, the first Cynic, who in some way not clear to us combined a harsh egotism with the doctrine of sympathy. From Antisthenes the antinomy passed to the Stoics, with whom it took the form of conflict between

self-interest, culminating in apathy, and a sense
of fellowship (*koinônia*) which, if not exactly
sympathy, resulted in practice very much like
it. On the one hand the Stoics insisted unwaver-
ingly that the highest good for a man must be
identical with his own advantage, while on the
other hand they were equally insistent on the fact
that men are bound together in one community
as the children of the same God and must concern themselves with their brothers' welfare.
Fellowship is the strong law of nature, and if,
like Epicurus, we deny the law, yet nature draws
us to her will, reluctant and groaning. The reconciliation between these contradictories was made
by Epictetus in a passage whose influence is still
felt, though its meaning may have been strangely perverted:

"This is not mere selfishness: for it is natural
to man, as to other creatures, to do everything
for his own sake; for even the sun does everything
for its own sake, and in a word so does Zeus himself. But when he (Zeus) would be called 'The
Rain-giver' and 'Fruit-giver' and 'Father of
men and Gods,' you see that he cannot win these
names or do these works unless he does some
good to the world at large: and in general Zeus
has so created the nature of the rational animal,
that he can attain nothing good for himself, un-

less he contributes some service to the community. So it turns out that to do everything for one's own sake is not unsocial. For what do you expect? Do you expect a man to hold aloof from himself and his own interest? No: we cannot ignore the one principle of action which governs all things—to be at unity with themselves."

Fellowship thus according to the Stoic creed is a part, an essential yet subordinate part, of self-interest. Ultimately a man's good, what he desires and must pursue, is that which he regards as advantageous to himself. But this good is placed in the realm of the will and the reason: man by nature is endowed with these faculties as his distinctive element, and his happiness as well as his duty is to live in accordance with his nature as a being so endowed. By nature also he is born one of a community of beings having the same endowment, and it is in accordance with his nature as a being so endowed to treat all men as fellows in the spirit, with generosity, helpful consideration, justice. But, it is important to add, as pleasure and the utility concerned with pleasure are not factors of his own real good, so they form no part, at least no essential part, of the bond of fellowship; and, secondly, though our obligation cannot be annulled by

the acts of another, our sympathy with another
ceases as soon as, and so far as, he in his turn
ceases to act as a reasonable and social being.

Now, whatever may be thought of this creed,
and however we may hold that it solves, or fails
to solve, the antithesis of the individual and the
community, certainly the modern attitude towards the question, though its origin goes back
to Stoicism, is radically different from that of
Epictetus.

The modern movement begins, or at least first
becomes important, with Shaftesbury,[18] whose
life and manner of thought, as he believed, were
regulated by a minute study of Epictetus, while
in fact he was introducing into philosophy a
spirit quite foreign to his teacher. To begin
with, from the Stoic principle of reason and will
Shaftesbury has removed the range of ethics
entirely to the emotions. In place of the ancient
command to acquire right dogmata, his precept
is: "Be persuaded that wisdom is more from the
heart than from the head; feel goodness, and

[18]For the earlier revival of Stoicism at the Renaissance see
F. Strowski, *Pascal et son temps,* chap. ii. But the peculiarly
modern tone, with its blend of Epicureanism, must be attributed
in the main to Shaftesbury, whose influence through the eighteenth century was immense. For his devotion to Epictetus, see
the *Philosophical Regimen* edited by Benjamin Rand.

you will see all things fair and good."[19] The key-word for Shaftesbury is not dogmata but the "affections." These he divides into natural (or public) and selfish (or private), and then sets them side by side as essentially hostile one to the other. "Whatsoever, therefore," he says, "is done which happens to be advantageous to the species, through an affection merely towards self-good, does not imply any more goodness in the creature than as the affection itself is good. Let him, in any particular, act ever so well; if, at the bottom, it be that selfish affection alone which moves him, he is in himself still vicious. Nor can any creature be considered otherwise, when the passion towards self-good, though ever so moderate, is his real motive in the doing that to which a natural affection for his kind ought by right to have inclined him." Now certainly, whatever we may think of this doctrine, it is a radical departure from the Stoic attempt, as seen in the quotation just given from Epictetus, to derive the natural duties (*kathêkonta*) from

[19]This and most of the following quotations are taken from Thomas Fowler's *Shaftesbury and Hutcheson.* Dr. Fowler gives an excellent summary of Shaftesbury's views; but it is hard to understand how, after showing the true weakness of Shaftesbury's ethical mixture (p. 92), he should add (p. 98): "It would not be too much to say that there is no modern writer whose views on morals approximate so closely to the classical way of thinking on these subjects as his."

one ultimate principle of self-interest. And the
practical consequences of this departure carry
us very far. Instead of a rigid law of subordination extending from right dogmata to a right
understanding of what is ours and thence to a
right disposition towards what is not ours, we
are to discover a rule of conduct in the balance
of public and private affections, or between the
feelings of sympathy and egotism.[20] If there is
any governing principle behind this mechanical
balance, it is not the Stoic reason or will but a
kind of instinctive taste or aesthetic sense, which
is affected by harmony or disharmony of character just as it is by proportion or disproportion
in a work of art. "And this, after all, the most
natural beauty in the world is honesty and moral
truth; for all beauty is truth," Shaftesbury says,
in a vein of dubious Platonism that was to be
echoed by Keats. Thus the Benevolent Theory
of Ethics merges insensibly into a pleasant and
easy kind of aesthetic hedonism as far removed
from the Porch as it is from the Academy. In
this facile blend of Stoicism and Epicureanism
there is no place for that strenuous discipline on
which Epictetus insisted, as one might say, in

[20]Shaftesbury may have got this notion of a balance between
egotism and sympathy from Panaetius through Cicero (see
Schmekel, *Die mittlere Stoa* 220, 369); he did not get it from
Epictetus.

season and out of season; instead we have the beginning of the new theory of natural goodness and moral *laissez-faire* which has been the dominant note in modern ethics and sociology from that day to this. To Epictetus wisdom and goodness were to be attained, if at all, by the labour of a lifetime; to Shaftesbury goodness appears so natural that it almost requires labour to be vicious: "Nor can anything besides art and strong endeavour, with long practice and meditation, overcome such a natural prevention or presupposition of the mind in favour of this moral distinction [between the amiability of virtue and the deformity of vice]."[21] As in Platonism, so it was in Stoicism, and so it will be in Christianity,—the first step towards an understanding of the doctrine must be in tearing away the masques which conceal their true features. To some it may appear also that the path of wisdom points in the same direction.

VI

The First Field of ethics, as we have seen, was concerned with the adjustment of the will to the great law of physics. The world is a vast flux, wherein all things are moving and changing by

[21]*Inquiry* I, iii, 1.

force of necessity and all things, taken together, are right, even as they are necessary. It is the business of the philosopher to recognize that he too is a part of this system, but not the whole of it, and that his good and evil, his happiness or misery, depend on the recognition of this fact; the world is not his to alter or control, but it is in his power to accept, or refuse to accept, things as they are.

The Second Field had to do with practical conduct, or with the division of philosophy called ethics in the narrower usage of the word. Having accepted the world as not ours, and so indifferent to us, we have still to know how to behave in relation to outer things.

The Third Field applies to life the division of philosophy called logic. The earlier Stoics, Chrysippus especially, had developed the organon of Aristotle in many directions, and had much to say about hypothetical arguments, variable premises, epichiremes, enthymemes, and the rest of the syllogistic machinery; all of which Epictetus took over as a part of the philosophic discipline, though evidently with some reluctance, and with outspoken irritation against those who came to him merely to acquire dexterity in debate. Yet Epictetus was well aware of the importance of this study at the proper time; and he saw that it had a double function. Negatively we need to have our wits sharpened by logical exercise in order that we may be ready to defend ourselves against the attacks of scepticism and may refute false and misleading arguments. But there is a positive use of logic also. Our conduct in the Second Field in the end must be determined by logical distinctions and by the application of syllogistic arguments to our relations; "for really, in every circumstance of life, our aim is to question how the good man may fitly deal with it and fitly behave." And the use of reason extends still higher into the First Field, for, after all, our attitude towards the sum of things that constitute the world will follow as a kind of syllogistic conclusion upon the premises we accept in regard to them. Reason in the end is that which makes all things articulate and complete, and life itself, unless it be that kind of unexamined and untested existence which to Socrates was no life at all, resembles nothing so much as a syllogism in practice. "In fact," Epictetus says, "we must behave in life as we do with hypothetical arguments"; and then he illustrates his meaning by this curious example:

" 'Let us assume it is night.'

" 'Granted.'

" 'What follows? Is it day?'

" 'No, for I have already assented to the assumption that it is night.'

" 'Let us assume then that you believe that it is night.'

" 'Granted.'

" 'Now believe that it really *is* night.'

" 'This does not follow from the hypothesis.'

" So too it is in life. 'Let us assume that you are unfortunate.'

" 'Granted.'

" 'Are you then unfortunate?'

" 'Yes.'

" 'What then, are you unhappy?'

" 'Yes.'

" 'Now believe that you are in the midst of real evils.'

" 'This does not follow from the hypothesis: and Another (God) forbids me.' "[22]

[22]*Discourses* I, xxv. Plato also (see *The Religion of Plato* 42) bases his philosophy on an hypothetical argument at once curiously like and unlike this of Epictetus. Plato's syllogism may be paraphrased as follows:

Let us assume that the just man, appearing to be unjust, is misunderstood by men and neglected by the gods.

Granted.

Then will he not suffer all the external consequences of injustice in this world with no hope of recompense in the next?

Yes.

What then, is he in the midst of real evils?

Yes.

Now, believe that he is unhappy.

This does not follow from the hypothesis; the nature of justice forbids me.

Plato will admit that a man may be in the midst of real evils, but

In such a way life presents itself to the Stoic as offering a series of hypothetical propositions, to each of which he must assent or refuse to assent. And so this Third Field, starting with the dry bones of formal logic, brings us at last to that mysterious word Assent (*synkatathesis*), in which it is not too much to say that the whole psychology of the Porch culminates. Here is the problem: What is this act of assent? or, more specifically, What is it that assents? What is that to which it assents? Evidently the answer to these questions will involve our conception of the Self and the world, of personality and the meaning of good and evil.

Now, at the first blush, the Stoic answer to the question, What is it that assents? would seem to present no difficulty. Over and over again it is said that good and evil are in the *proairesis,* that this alone is free, that this alone is ours, and so in a way *we*. That sounds simple and final. But is it? A difficulty arises when we undertake to transfer the term *proairesis* to English. We commonly translate it "will," and this, with proper reservations, is perhaps the

will not admit that he is therefore necessarily unhappy; Epictetus will admit that a man may be unhappy, but will not admit that he is therefore in the midst of real evils. That is the gulf between Platonism and Stoicism.

nearest equivalent we have. But, taken absolutely, our "will" is a synonym for the Latin *voluntas,* rather than for *proairesis;* by etymology and usage the Greek word signifies rather a mental process than a dynamic faculty, rather the *act* of choosing, the *act* of giving and withholding assent, than that which chooses and assents. What determines the act? What lies behind the *proairesis?*

And here, again, the step would seem to be easy. We are brought at once to the familiar catchword of Stoicism, the *hêgemonikon,* or Governing Principle as it is commonly translated, whose very meaning indicates the determining power of the will and the agent in the act of choosing. But, again, there are difficulties. Repeatedly the command is given to preserve the Governing Principle in accordance with nature, since therein lies our good. What is it then that preserves and determines this faculty? "As in walking," Epictetus says characteristically, "you take care not to tread on a nail or twist your foot, so take care not to harm your Governing Principle." What is this "you" that governs the governor, that guides the will, that assents or dissents? It is reason, the Stoic might reply. God Himself, or that subtle spirit out of which all the world evolves, is intelligence, knowledge, pure reason, and man has within him a portion of God; his soul is, as it were, a fragment of the divine reason. That is the essence of the Governing Principle, right reason. The answer is clear enough, one thinks; but again difficulties surge up. Reason is given us, it is said, for the purpose of using and controlling our impressions; but in the same breath we are informed that it is itself a system framed out of impressions of one kind or another (I, xx, 5). It is untrammeled contemplation; yet when erroneous dogmata affect it concerning things good and evil, there is a necessity upon us to act unreasonably. What is this that determines the reason, that governs the governor, that guides the will, that assents or dissents? It is rather like the house that Jack built, or, in the more dignified language of the schools, a *recessus ad infinitum*.

Some light is thrown on this vexatious problem in a chapter of the *Discourses* with the unpromising title, "That we ought not to be angry with men: and concerning what things are small and what are great among men." Here Epictetus asks the question categorically, "What is the cause of our assenting to anything?" and proceeds to give this answer:

" The appearance that it is. To that which appears not to be it is impossible to assent. Why? Because such is the nature of the mind—to agree to what is true, to disagree with what is false, to suspend judgment on things unknowable (*adêla*).

" 'What is the proof of this?'

" Feel (*pathe,* be persuaded, assent to the proposition) now, if you can, that it is night.

" 'It is impossible.'

" Put away the feeling (*apopathe,* be dissuaded, dissent to the proposition) that it is day.

" 'It is impossible.'

" Either feel or put away the feeling that the stars are even in number.

" 'It is impossible.'

" When a man assents, then, to what is false, know that he had no wish to assent to the false: 'for no soul is robbed of the truth with its own consent,' as Plato says, but the false seemed to him true."

Now this necessity of our nature to assent to what appears a fact, a truth, extends, as the argument goes on to show, from the sphere of perception to the sphere of action. Whatever object appears to a man good, that perforce he desires; whatever action appears to him for his interest, that perforce he has an impulse to carry out: "for the measure to man of all doing is appearance (*phainomenon*)." To this at last come even the great events of history which have thrown the world into commotion. It was appearance that caused Paris to run away with the wife of Menelaus, appearance that drew Helen to follow him; and if it had appeared to Menelaus a gain instead of a loss to be relieved of such a woman, there would have been no *Iliad* or *Odyssey*—on so little a thing depended effects so vast. Hence whatever happens, whatever we see a man doing, we can only say: "So it seemed to him, such was his dogma."[23]

In our search for the source of assent and responsibility we have come a circle back to the dogmata with which the whole discussion of ethics began. But these dogmata, as we now see them, are purely passive, with no element of freedom in them, no place for that apathy which was the aim of philosophy, no promise of security from the fatal pressure of the world. The will as a free faculty of choosing and the Gov-

[23]*Manual 42*: Ἐπιφθέγγου γὰρ ἐφ᾽ ἑκάστῳ ὅτι ἔδοξεν αὐτῷ. The closing phrase here is equivalent to δόγμα αὐτοῦ. Dogma, in fact, means etymologically not so much an active judgment as a passive appearance, a *phainomenon*. The Stoic ethics end in the same confusion between active and passive as that from which their physics began.

erning Principle have simply vanished away.
Is there then no responsibility in the choice of
good and evil, no morality, no distinction between mine and not-mine, myself and not-my-
self, nothing but a dull mechanic exercise of impressions?

Now, whatever else we may think or demon-
strate, we cannot get away from the immediate
belief in a distinction between mine and not-
mine, myself and that which is not myself. No
possible argument can relax our hold on this
primary dogma of consciousness; everything
may proceed from that dogma, nothing can obliterate it, and therefore the Stoics were justified in applying this distinction to the theory of
moral responsibility.

It is a fact that, considering the lives of other
men, looking at that which is not we, we seem
to discover only passive determination, and no
choice or responsibility at all. Good men and
evil alike are the playthings of circumstance,
their character is the product of heredity and
environment, their emotions and actions are controlled by laws they did not make, and so their
consequent happiness or misery is only their al-
lotment in the vast network of fate, or chance.
That is what the Stoic had in mind when he de-

clared that "the measure to man of all doing is appearance," and then, as putting a curb upon the attempt to pry into the moral responsibility of others, added, "It is not possible for a man to follow what appears to you, but only what appears to him. . . . Therefore, whatever happens, say to yourself, 'So it seemed to him.' " No precept is more frequent in Epictetus than this, that the motives and deeds of other men are not ours to judge, that we should not permit these things to influence our own sense of obligation to the world, that we should never find fault, never give way to anger or hatred or reproach. Only in this way can our peace of mind and the even current of our life be maintained, and only so can we preserve our conscience free of blame. "This is education, to learn what is ours, and what is not ours."

Turning now to our own immediate experience, we see something like that which we observed in the conduct of other men, yet with something added. Here too we are carried on through a consideration of the will and the Governing Principle to dogmata. "To every one the cause of his doing anything is his dogmata," it is said categorically; and our dogmata are simply that which appears to us, "for the measure

to man of all doing is appearance." And again:
"When we are impeded, or disturbed, or dis-
tressed, let us never lay the blame on others, but
on ourselves, that is, on our dogmata. To accuse
others for one's own misfortunes shows a want
of education; to accuse one's self is the beginning of education; to accuse neither others nor
one's self shows that one's education is complete." That would seem to obliterate the distinction between impressions and the use of impressions so far as any responsibility for them is
concerned, and to leave man a helpless victim of
the world. Nevertheless the Stoic was above all,
and despite, if necessary, his reason, conscious
of his own moral responsibility. One step yet
remained for him. He might, in accordance
with his fatalism, admit that impressions and, if
pushed to the wall, his use of impressions, his
dogmata, and his positive will, were imposed upon him without his choice, but one thing was still
his own: though he could not create impressions
or dogmata, and though, in the end, he must act
as the prevalent dogma bids, he could still for a
time hold his dogmata in check. This is the faculty which he called *epochê,* "suspension of assent." How this suspension operated may be
gathered from a few statements of Epictetus:

"Where does your work lie? In desire and aversion, that you may not suffer failure in desire nor force in aversion; in impulse to act and not to act, that you may not err therein; in assent and suspension of assent."

"First of all, do not be hurried away by the suddenness of the shock, but say: 'Wait for me a little, impression; let me see what you are, and what is at stake; let me test you.' And, further, do not permit it to go on picturing the next scene. If you do, it straightway carries you off whither it will."

"Third comes the field of assents, concerned with things plausible and attractive. For, as Socrates bade men 'not live a life without examination,' so you ought not to admit an impression without examination, but say, 'Wait, let me see who you are and whence you come,' just as the nightwatch say, 'Show me your token.'"

"When you imagine some pleasure, beware, as in the case of other impressions, that it does not carry you away. Wait awhile and give yourself pause. Then remember two things: the time you will enjoy the pleasure, and the after time of repentance and self-reproach. . . . And if it seems to you opportune to realize the pleasure, take heed that you be not mastered by its winning sweetness."

"Wherefore make it your first endeavour not to be carried away by an impression; for if once you gain time and delay you will be more master of yourself."[24]

The process is fairly clear. Upon the mind, already crowded with memories of the past, a new impression is made by some object or event. Our response in desire or aversion, in positive or negative impulse, will depend upon our use of this new impression; our use of it is coincident with our judgment of it; our judgment is an act of assent or dissent, and our assent, *when given,* is determined by the way the object or event appears to us. All the consequences flow from the impression itself and from the memory of former impressions; the mind creates nothing, and knowledge comes to us by passive adaptations. We are carried about in a circle of fatality, and there is no freedom except in that one clause, *when given.* The consequences to ourselves may be of one sort if assent and judgment follow immediately upon the impression; they may be of an entirely different sort if we suspend assent for a time, and so allow our judgment to be modified by the stored-up body of experience.[25]

[24]*Discourses* I, iv, 11; II, xviii, 24; III, xii, 14; *Manual* 34, 20. Cf. Plutarch, *Adv. Coloten* 1122 c.

[25]The term "suspense" (*epoché*) is common to both Sceptics and Stoics, but it has a different meaning in the two schools. The Sceptic applies his suspense of judgment to all final conclusions

In the last analysis that which is mine, the
me, as distinguished from all that is not mine,
the not-me, is driven back by negation after negation to a power of suspension, which is sometimes called the Inner Check. We have a philosophy superficially resembling Platonism, but
with a fundamental difference. For Epictetus
the soul, considered positively, is not a dual compound of reason and the passions as Plato conceived it, but is one and indivisible, a portion of
the pure reason of God. If passions break in to
perturb the quiet current of our life, it is because
the soul as a unit turns in a wrong direction and
ceases to function in accordance with its nature.
If you ask why and how such a perversion occurs, the answer apparently will be that the natural operation of a reasonable soul is to act as a
stay upon the flux of impressions that continually invade it from the world, and that, in its
evil case, it fails so to operate. Evil in the soul
would thus be not so much a positive change in
the nature of that which is essentially good, as a
kind of relaxation of energy, an atony or temporary sluggishness, to which it succumbs. Its

concerning the nature of things; appearances he simply accepts
at their face value as appearances. The Stoic exercises a suspension of assent to appearances in order to maintain the final
judgment that all is really good.

passions are then a true passivity rather than an active principle of evil.[26] But to the further question why the soul suffers this relaxation, and assents when it should not, there is no answer. Neither was any answer given by Plato; but in the case of the Stoics the very possibility of the question is an arraignment of the ultimate monism of their physics.

And an equally troublesome question springs up from the other side: Why is there any need of that staying power of the will or reason? What is it in the nature of things that lies in wait for us, so to speak, and takes advantage of the soul's indolence? To explain this the Stoics have a beautiful and, to me at least, haunting phrase, first apparently introduced by Cleanthes, certainly used by Chrysippus, and not forgotten by Epictetus—"the seductiveness in things," "the plausibility of circumstances," "the persuasion of appearances," as the words are variously translated.[27] We are, as it were, ravished by the

[26]This is the *rhathymia* of which I have written at length in *The Religion of Plato* 253 ff. In Stoicism the actual word used is *atonia*. The notion is connected with their principle of *tonos*, energy, the active principle as contrasted with the passive, which diminishes in force as the evolutionary process extends further and further from the primeval source. Taking into account the mechanical terms in which *tonos* is defined, one might say that the Stoic conception of passion and will is a materialistic counterpart of the Neoplatonic conception.

[27] Ἡ πιθανότης τῶν πραγμάτων.

persuasive beauty of the world and by its lure of
pleasures, and so the refraining will succumbs
to precipitate judgments, assenting indolently
where it should exercise suspension, admitting
that as good and desirable which a slower judgment would recognize as really foreign to the
soul. The error of judgment, or false dogma,
would resolve itself at last into a darkening confusion of the soul and the world, or, in the more
technical language of the school, into forgetful-
ness of the difference between what is mine and
not mine. I am inclined to accept this account of
error and evil as perhaps the finest in the history
of philosophy. It is at bottom a paraphrase of
the theory implicit in the Platonic ethics, and a
foreshadowing of the theory which will be held
by some of the wisest of the Christian theologians. It raises no logical difficulty there where
it belongs, though it may still leave the ultimate
problem of metaphysics unsolved and insoluble. But no Stoic will tell you why or how, in a
world identical with God and perfectly organized, the plausibility of things should have this
power to seduce the will, turning reason into
passion and producing evil out of goodness. Nor
will he tell you why the morality of our specific
acts may depend on a suspension of assent, while

the root of all morality depends on our unhesi-
tating assent to the universe as it is and to life
as a whole. On the other hand, no genuine Stoic,
however he may feel towards other men as though
they were passive instruments of their dogmata,
will admit that he is not himself finally responsible for his assent to error and for his own mis-
takes and unhappiness.

VII

The fact is that Stoicism, by a fault inherent in
its method, was perhaps of all philosophies the
most paradoxical. Seduced by the fascinations
of the combining reason, it started with an absolutely monistic and deterministic theory of
the world, and then, in abhorrence at the immoral consequences of such a theory, accepted
the non-rational and dualistic intuitions of good
and evil. The inevitable result is a succession of
flaunting paradoxes which radiate from these
two contradictions: the world is totally good, yet
human experience is full of evil; and, all things
are fatally determined, yet man's will is free.
Evil, the Stoics assert in one breath is not real
but only apparent, the necessary imperfection
of the parts contributing to the perfection of the

whole; yet almost in the same breath they are painting man's life on earth in colours of the blackest pessimism. The inconsistency is most striking in Marcus Aurelius, who does not shrink from the strongest, even the most revolting, terms to describe the miseries of the body and of society; but Epictetus is not free of the same pessimism. Instruction in his school was directed to nerving the pupils against a world bristling with hostile forces: "Life is a soldier's service; one man must keep guard, another go out as a scout, another take the field." Yet these same pupils are rebuked if, sent out as spies to reconnoitre the land, they do not report, as did the Cynic Diogenes, that "no enemy is near, all things are full of peace." One is reminded of Jeremiah's scornful words, "Peace, peace, when there is no peace." And then, if a man suffers defeat in this battle, is it that he has been borne down innocently by superior force, or shall he be held responsible? No one is deprived of the truth willingly, no one errs willingly, Epictetus will insist in various language, and insist all the while with equal fervour that every man is free and need only exercise his will to be good. It is no solution of these entanglements to maintain that all things are good and only thinking makes them evil.

Whence the evil thought? Whence the terrible
earnestness in a conflict with unreal shadows?

> "To question to and fro
> And to debate the evil of the world,
> As though we bore no portion of that ill,
> As though with subtle phrases we could spin
> A woof to screen us from life's undelight.
> . . . How vain are words,
> When that which is opposed to them is more."

These embarrassments were not overlooked
by the ancient critics of the Porch—as indeed
how should they be? At the very beginning the
Stoic had to meet the arguments of the Epicurean who could at least see the difficult position of a philosophy which commanded men to
live according to nature, yet took no account of
pleasure and pain or even went so far as almost
to glory in pain. Surely pleasure is a natural
good, a thing desired by all men, and pain a
natural evil. The Platonist, who also made little
of pleasure and pain, could answer that he did
so because pleasure was in fact insignificant in
comparison with the happiness to be found in a
realm of the spirit quite apart from nature; but
the Stoic left no such retreat open against his
adversaries. Then came the leaders of the so-
called Middle Academy, Arcesilas and Car-

neades, who for a hundred and fifty years plied
the Stoic stronghold with every weapon of scepticism. It was easy for these trained logicians,
especially Carneades, to show the untenability
of a monistic optimism by simply pointing to the
innumerable instances of actual evil; it was easy
to set forth the inconsistency of clinging to the
belief in Providence and conscious design in a
universe of absolute determinism; and more vir-
ulently, as we have seen, they drove the Stoic
from point to point in his criterion of knowledge.
This warfare between the Academy and the
Porch was not forgotten, and long afterwards
Plutarch summed up the results in a crushing
essay *De Stoicorum Repugnantiis*. But for the
heart of the matter we may turn to the Christian
critics, to Justin Martyr, for instance, who struck
home in this notable passage:

"Everywhere right-minded lawgivers and
thinkers show this [the inherent sense of responsibility in man for good and evil] by their commands that such things we shall do and from
such things we shall refrain. And the Stoic
philosophers also in their ethical theory show a
strong respect for these same truths, so that it is
clear there must be some fault in their naturalistic doctrine of first principles. For let them say
that human actions are due to fate, or let them

say that God is nothing but transitory matter always taking new forms and dissolving back into itself again, the Stoics are caught on this dilemma: either they will be found to acknowledge only corruptible things and to teach that God Himself as extended through the whole and parts of the universe is involved in the sum of evil, or else they must declare that there is no such thing as good and evil."[28]

It is curious and illuminating to hear William James in our day applying the same dilemma, in still more vigorous terms, to a modern equivalent of the Stoic paradox:

"My trouble, you see, lies with monism. Determinism=monism; and a monism like this world can't be an object of pure optimistic contemplation. By pessimism I simply mean *ultimate* non-optimism. The Ideal is only a part of this world. Make the world a Pluralism, and you forthwith have an object to worship. Make it a Unit, on the other hand, and worship and abhorrence are equally one-sided and equally legitimate reactions. *Indifferentism* is the true condition of such a world, and turn the matter how you will, I don't see how any philosophy of the Absolute can ever escape from that capricious alternation of mysticism and satanism in the treatment of its great Idol, which history has always shown. . . . Either close your eyes and adopt

28*Apology* II, vi, 7.

an optimism or a pessimism equally daft; or exclude moral categories altogether from a place
in the world's definition, which leaves the world
unheimlich, reptilian, and foreign to man; or
else, sticking to it that the moral judgment *is*
applicable, give up the hope of applying it to
the *whole.*"[29]

The logic of the Porch in fact was terribly
vulnerable, and as a result of the attacks delivered from the sceptics of the Academy the leaders of the school tried to fortify their position
by various outworks, so to speak, built of thefts
from Aristotle and even more flagrantly from
Plato. The result was the so-called Middle Porch
of Panaetius and Posidonius, answering to the
Middle Academy.

But however Stoicism by these modifications
may have averted an immediate danger, it did
not render itself really immune; it enlarged the
sentimental scope of its doctrine and humanized
its ethics, but it did so only by utterly confound-
ing a logic already sufficiently confused. Both
Panaetius and Posidonius clung to the physical
monism and determinism of Zeno, and then, in-

[29]*Letters* I, 238, 257. See also p. 245. Unfortunately James,
doughty foe as he was of every form of absolutism of the One,
by his theory of pluralism came very close to the opposite absolutism of the many. Hence, with all his brilliancy and insight,
his failure to bring true spiritual relief from the prison house of
metaphysics.

stead of holding that human nature also was one
and purely rational, and facing full front the
embarrassments of such a psychology, they undertook to slip Plato's dualistic conception of
the soul into an utterly incompatible metaphysic.
I am not writing a history of Greek philosophy
and have no need to go into the details of this
impossible mixture; it is sufficient to say that
Epictetus was evidently shocked by the mess—
the word is not too strong—into which Stoicism
had been thrown, and, in the main, reverted to
the earlier and authentic doctrine as it was developed by Chrysippus.

One admires the honesty of the reformer's
purpose, one is deeply impressed by the solidity
and rigour with which he carries out the ancient
tenets and applies them to life; but the old inconsistency still lurks like a serpent at the heart
of the system, scotched but not killed. It is one
of the irreparable misfortunes of philosophy
that some great thinker did not arise who, with
clearer vision and more radical hand, should
have thrown over the Stoic rationalism for the
Platonic dualism, and then, on that sounder
foundation, should have adopted and adapted
the large achievements of the Stoic teachers in
the field of ethics. Such a conversion was per-

fectly practicable, and the result might have
been a body of thought unshakable at the base
and majestic in its superstructure.[30] The Stoic
creed of dogmata would not be denied, but en-
riched with new significance. It would still be
true that all our philosophy and all conduct depend on right or wrong judgments—yet with a
difference. We should not say that no actual
wrong exists in this absolutely determined world,
and that things only seem wrong by a false judgment, and so in a way are evil to us, with the
stubborn question still unanswered why we so
judge when we are parts of such a world. Rather, we should say that both good and evil are really here in the sum of things, but that for us the
world may become a place of good or evil in accordance with our judgments. For when we
judge truly, and our opinion of right and wrong
coincides with the eternal laws, then the world
does indeed become good to us in so far as the
evil in it cannot invade the citadel of our being,
and we understand what Socrates meant when
he declared that no harm can befall a good man
either in this life or the next. The true office of
philosophy is to overcome evil, not to deny it.

[30]This in a measure was actually done by Plutarch (*e.g.,* the last
sections of *De Tranquilitate Animi*) and other syncretists, but
never, as it seems to me, with full comprehension of the problem.

Then the Stoic Wheel, as I have called it,
with its distinction between mine and not-mine
and the other pairs that follow, would not be
left to revolve *in vacuo,* so to speak, but would
correspond to a final distinction in the nature of
things. And a like transformation would take
place in applying the Wheel to the three Fields.
Good and evil would depend on the character of
our desires and aversions, but a new and positive
content would be given to this direction of the
soul.[31] The *idia,* things that are ours, to which
desire should be directed, would now be identified with the Platonic Ideas where the interest
of the true self lies, and our aversion would be
turned towards the positive forces of evil in the
flux of phenomena. The bleak negation of the
Stoic would acquire a positive aspect in the true
life of the spirit. And so with the impulse to act
or not to act: how much of the inconsequence
observed in the obligations of life would be removed, if we kept the sense of responsibility for
our part in a great drama of creation with its
eternal and ever-present issues; how the unreality felt in the duties prescribed by human
relations would be overcome, if the institutions
of society were regarded as necessary, though

[31]Cf. Plato *The Republic* 518ε.

faulty, copies of a divine order; how the cold-
ness that chills the theoretical brotherhood of
mankind would be warmed up, if the Stoic conception of the sage as a being completely superior to mortal frailty and emotion, impervious to
pain or sorrow, not even subject to temptation,
with no intermediary between his bleak, unattainable perfection and the total folly of ordinary men, were softened to the Socratic ideal of
the philosopher as one still striving for wisdom,
still contending with his passions, differing only
in degree of attainment from his unwiser com-
rade. For here again we are struck by the ano-
maly that a philosophy which begins with the
assumption of an impossible monism ends practically in a harsh and unreal dualism.[32] On the
other side, how much the profound intuition of
Plato might have gained in precise usefulness
through the subtle analysis of the Stoic ethics.
And then, in the Third Field, where the ethical
law is summed up in the word "assent," all that
the Stoics had added to philosophy might have
been retained, while the maddening query "assent to what?" would have lost its sting. Right-

[32]The wearisome question of the Stoic sage, or perfect man, and
the possibility or impossibility of such a creature, is not discussed dialectically by Epictetus. What he made of the sage as a
personality of history we shall see in our study of Diogenes.

ness of assent would still be defined as a consequence of that vigour of the soul which imposes
a stay upon the impressions surging through it
from the world, but the "seductiveness in things"
which makes such a suspension of judgment
necessary, and the passions of the soul itself,
would now have a substantial meaning.

And, lastly, the Stoic faith in the fatherhood
of God and the Stoic piety, how they would have
gained in fervour and security, if the foundation
on which such emotions ought to rest had not
been undermined. Even as it is, at whatever cost
of inconsistency, the religion of the Porch in
some respects marks a genuine advance upon
that of the Academy in the direction of Christianity. God, whatever He should have been logically, was in fact to Epictetus no such cold abstraction as He was becoming in the metaphysical school of the day, nor was He hard to know
and impossible to express quite as He had seemed
to Plato, nor was He a fancy to be grasped by
the imagination only. One cannot read Epictetus without feeling that in his realization of the
divine nearness he was almost a Christian; and
this is so true of a contemporary Stoic, Seneca,
that Tertullian and Jerome actually regarded
him as a disciple of St. Paul and the Council of

Trent cited him as it did the Fathers of the
Church. "In thyself thou bearest Him," says
Epictetus, "and art unaware that thou art defil-
ing Him with unclean thoughts and foul actions.
If an image of God were present, thou wouldst
not dare to behave so; but now God Himself
is present within thee, seeing all things, hearing all things, yet thou art not ashamed of thy
thoughts and deeds, O slow to understand thy
own nature and estranged from God!" Thus the
central act of religion for Epictetus, as for all
those from Plato to Chrysostom who did not utterly depart from the Tradition, was the endeavour to make one's self so far as possible like
to God:

"The philosophers say that the first thing one
must learn is this: 'that God exists and provides
for the universe, and that no man can act or even
conceive a thought or reflection without God
knowing. Next is to learn the true nature of the
gods. For whatever their nature is found to be,
he who will please and obey them must needs
try, so far as he can, to make himself like them.'
If the divine nature is faithful, he must be faithful too; if free, he must be free too; if beneficent,
he too must be beneficent; if high-minded, he
must be high-minded: he must, in fact, as one
who makes God his ideal, follow this out in every
act and word."

There is nothing original in this conception
of "becoming like," but in the spirit of devotion
that went with it one catches a note that had
never before been sounded so clearly in pagan
worship. One day the lonely exile in Nicopolis,
after pointing out the manifold bountiful works
of Providence, seems to have forgotten the school-
room and the pupils who so many of them came
to him for ignoble purposes, and breaks into a
chant of benediction to the great and good Father, greatest and best because He has given to
man the faculty to comprehend His beneficence.
Surely, all men ought at every moment to remember the divine goodness with thanksgiving:

"More than that: since most of you are walking in darkness, should there not be some one to
discharge this duty and to sing praises to God
for all? And what else can a lame old man like
me do but chant the praise of God? If indeed I
were a nightingale, I should sing as a nightingale; if a swan, as a swan: but as I am a rational
creature I must praise God. This is my task; I
do it, and I will not abandon this duty so long
as it is given me: and I invite you all to join in
this same song."

I know of nothing quite like that in the philosophers—not in Plato, not in Plotinus. It is
a note that will be caught up by the priests of a

new religion, and will find one of its sweetest
echoes in George Herbert:

"Of all the creatures both in sea and land
   Onely to Man thou hast made known thy wayes,
And put the penne alone into his hand,
   And made him Secretarie of thy praise.

"Beasts fain would sing; birds dittie to their notes;
   Trees would be tuning on their native lute
To thy renown; but all their hands and throats
   Are brought to Man, while they are lame and mute.

"Man is the world's high Priest. He doth present
   The sacrifice for all; while they below
Unto the service mutter an assent,
   Such as springs use that fall and windes that blow.

"He that to praise and laud thee doth refrain
   Doth not refrain unto himself alone,
But robs a thousand who would praise thee fain,
   And doth commit a world of sinne in one.

"Wherefore, most sacred Spirit, I here present
   For me and all my fellows praise to thee.
And just it is that I should pay the rent,
   Because the benefit accrues to me."

We repeat the devotional passages of Epictetus and Seneca and the other Stoics which echo
the magnificent hymn of Cleanthes, and we are
stirred deeply—and rightly, indeed, for of in-

sincerity or hypocrisy there is no suspicion in
these men—and then into our sympathetic emotion creeps the benumbing recollection that this
Being of their worship is only a subtle form of
matter pervading the grosser visible elements;
that this Providence which we are asked to cele-
brate in chants of praise is only another name
for a mechanical law of expansion and contraction, absolutely predetermined in its everlasting
recurrences; and that this worshipping soul, this
boasted spark of reason which distinguishes man,
is nothing more than a glimmering flame of the
universal fire caught for a moment in an ephemeral cage of flesh, with no assurance of separate
duration, no independence of personality,—is
nothing more at best than a bundle of dogmata
with no spiritual entity behind them. How different, one reflects, might have been the whole
course of the world's inner life, how much of the
estrangement between philosophy and religion
might have been avoided, if Panaetius and more
particularly Posidonius, in their reform of Zeno's psychology, had shaken off the tyranny of
metaphysics, and, going a step further, had accepted the fundamental dualism of Plato instead
of merely borrowing shreds and tatters of its
spiritual implications. Certainly the leaders of

the Porch, if ever any religious guides, made the great refusal.

And the result of that refusal is the note of sadness on which this philosophy ends—a sadness nobler in character, yet infinitely more pathetic, I sometimes think, than the final joylessness of the rival school of the Garden. All through the *Discourses* of Epictetus at intervals occurs the ominous phrase, "The door is open," "Open is the door." The practice of philosophy, he used to say, is summed up in the two words "bear" and "forbear" (*anechou, apechou*); and then, if the hand of the world became too heavy and temptation pressed too close, there was left to every man the one way of escape from failure and disgrace. I would not infer that this removal of the "canon 'gainst self-slaughter" implies anything weak or contemptible in the creed or lives of these men; there is no trace in Epictetus or in any other genuine Stoic of the "sickly inclination"[33] which led Donne to argue the legitimacy of suicide for a Christian. Voluntary exit from the battle field was permitted only when victory was impossible and defeat certain, and the signs were such that the sage could know surely the summons of the Captain to retire. The

[33]*Biathanatos* 17.

mere shirking of pain and danger was scorned by the Stoic as loyally as by the Christian, and the record of the deaths of Thraseas and Arria and the other political martyrs in Tacitus is the most stirring memory from the dark days of the Empire; yet there, after all, meeting us at every turn, is the bitter phrase, "The door is open,"— a strange admission to be wrung from the heart of men who taught that all things are for the best and that there is no real evil in this world.

But the sadness is not so much in the concession of the open door as in the thought of the emptiness that lies beyond: "When God fails to provide for you, then He is giving the signal of retreat, He has opened the door, and says to you, 'Come.'—Where?—To nothing fearful, but thither whence you were born, to things friendly and akin to you, to the elements"—and that is all. These are honest words, no doubt, instinct with that stubborn courage and that forced, almost sullen, tranquillity which to the popular mind—whether justly or not—sum up the meaning of the boasted Stoic apathy. Inevitably one compares this utmost comfort offered by Epictetus with the Christian triumph in martyrdom: "To the baser of mankind witness to the Lord by blood seems to be mere death and

that the most violent, for they know not that this
gate of death is the beginning of true life."[34] Like
the Epicurean, so the Stoic, notwithstanding his
much brave talk about a fatherland beyond the
grave and about his kinship to God, was deliber-
ately shutting his eyes on "things more sublime
than mortal happiness." Perhaps the most beautiful term in the Stoic vocabulary is the *eurhoia*
by which they expressed the even current of the
sage's life, moving on like a majestic river. It is
a noble ideal and no doubt often in large measure attained; yet for the Stoic the river of life
was hidden from the sun, and deep in his heart
he who sailed thereon must have felt himself as
a waif borne on a stream of endless and meaningless mutations. The words with which Mat-
thew Arnold closes his essay on Marcus Aurelius apply more exactly to the wistful Emperor
in his palace than to the exiled freedman of our
study, but they ought not to be forgotten in any
estimation of what Stoicism gave and failed to
give: "We see him wise, just, self-governed,
tender, thankful, blameless; yet, with all this,
agitated, stretching out his arms for something
beyond,—*tendentemque manus ripae ulterioris
amore.*"

[34]Clemens Alex., *Strom.* IV, vii, 44.

As for Epictetus, the old lame schoolmaster of Nicopolis, he is one of the supreme doctors of ethical experience, there is no doubt of it; yet he who would read him wisely, I sometimes think, must come to the *Discourses* as a Platonist and not as a Stoic, and must write between the lines and insert into the definitions a truth of which Epictetus himself had been robbed by the false usurpations of the *intellectus sibi permissus.*

CHAPTER V

PLOTINUS

The sects of Epicurus and Zeno go back through their predecessors to immediate association with Socrates, and are rivals of the Academy, if not openly anti-Platonic. The philosophy we are now to study was held by its founder, and is sometimes held today, to be rather a genuine restoration after many years of the teaching of Plato: it is called in the schools Neoplatonism. Yet to me, if anything is clear, it is that the dominating note of Plotinus belongs to a current of thought which is more a perversion than a development of what was learnt in the Academy.[1] And in view of the extraordinary revival of interest in the mystics shown today, and in Plotinus as the father of them all, it should seem to be a matter of some importance to get a clear notion of what Neoplatonism really was, and to consider how

[1] Dean Inge's otherwise illuminating and profound study of *The Philosophy of Plotinus* is in my judgment vitiated by the failure to observe the radical differences between Platonism and Neoplatonism.

far it is a source of true religion and of the purer
life of the spirit.

I

Fortunately we have for Plotinus, what we have
for no other of the ancient philosophers, a good
contemporary biography, composed by his pupil and literary executor, Porphyry. He was
born in Egypt about A.D. 205. In his twenty-
eighth year[2] he became interested in philosophy,
and frequented the most highly reputed professors in Alexandria; but with little satisfaction to
himself until he was directed to Ammonius Saccas, with whom he studied for eleven years. The
question was raised in antiquity, and recently
has been reopened, how closely Plotinus followed the teaching of Ammonius, and how far
he felt the direct influence of a certain Numenius of Apamea. It is probable that Ammonius
himself owed a good deal to Numenius, and that
in this way ideas of the Apamean philosopher
reached Plotinus. But there is reason to believe
that for the most part Plotinus was a faithful,
though by no means servile, disciple of Ammonius, who should therefore be recognized as the

[2]This is the year given by Porphyry, but, as will be seen, it allows little or no time for Plotinus' study with the preliminary
professors.

true founder of Neoplatonism. Porphyry tells us that Herennius, Origen (the pagan), and Plotinus agreed to keep the doctrine of their master secret, and that Plotinus held to this compact until his fellow students broke it. And there is another argument. Origen (the Christian) was also in his youth a pupil of Ammonius, and Origen's theology so strikingly resembles the metaphysics of Plotinus in many details that their common source is a natural inference. As for the education of Plotinus in other respects, it is singular in that it entirely missed the rhetorical training then regnant in the schools. His handwriting was slovenly, his spelling and grammar faulty, his pronunciation illiterate, his style so crabbed that the best scholar of his day found it unintelligible and the modern Grecian reads it with agony.

At the age of thirty-nine Plotinus joined the Emperor Gordian in his eastern expedition, being eager to acquaint himself at first hand with the practice of philosophy among the Persians and Indians. When Gordian lost his life in Mesopotamia, the inquisitive student escaped with some difficulty to Antioch, and from thence to Rome, where, at the age of forty, he opened a class in philosophy. After some eighteen years

Porphyry joined him, and continued in the school for six years. Then came changes. Porphyry went away to Sicily, and other pupils left him; friends had died; the Emperor who had protected him was murdered; he was afflicted with a distressing disease, and so, in solitude and suffering, he retired to Campania, where he died in the second year of the Emperor Claudius, at the age of sixty-six. He had summoned a friend and pupil, the physician Eustochius, to his bedside; but the friend was slow in coming, and the last words of Plotinus were these: "You see I am still waiting for you"; and then: "I strive to render up the Divine in myself to the Divine in the All."

So far as we can judge of the man, he had lived in harmony with his dying words; his life, in the full sense of the phrase used by Plato and so many other philosophers of Greece, was a continual study and practice of death. Such, we are told, was his shame of existence in the flesh that he would not speak of his family or the place of his birth. When urged by a favourite pupil to allow his portrait to be taken, he declined, with this excuse: "Is it not enough to carry for a time this image which nature has put about us? And must I consent also to leave behind me an image

of an image as a precious spectacle for poster-
ity?" Four separate times, according to Porphyry, he was caught up beyond all thinking
and all thought into ecstatic union with God;
and indeed always for him the goal and the vision lay near at hand. Through the metaphysical jargon that abounds in his works we can see
that his power over men was owing to a direct
experience of the Divine; and when he spoke
there came a light upon his countenance and a
new beauty upon his features as a testimony of
the truth.

Like other masterful mystics Plotinus appeared as a prophet of things forgotten, a dis-
coverer of things unknown, a guide in the spiritual way, preacher of a new Evangel. The empire in those troubled days of Gallienus was almost at its lowest ebb; faction and treason were
rife in the Capital; the barbarians were pressing
in from all sides; pestilence and poverty swept
through the lands; some terrible and final catas-
trophe seemed to be immanent over society. In
such a world and such an age, it is not strange
that the call of peace, the annunciation of a security that no present calamities could shake,
the promise of liberty for the soul, should have
appealed to many as a true voice from heaven.

Men of power and learning flocked to the school
of this teacher out of Egypt. One of these, the
Senator Rogatianus, went so far as to surrender
his property, emancipate his slaves, renounce
his political honours, and practise a life of religious abstinence. The house of Plotinus was
filled with boys and girls who had been entrust-
ed to his care by their dying parents. The emperor and his wife so venerated him that they
planned to restore an old ruined city, once according to tradition the home of (Pythagorean)
philosophers, and in this seat, rechristened Pla-
tonopolis, to establish Plotinus and his friends
under a constitution modeled upon Plato's
Laws. The scheme fell through, from jealousies
and intrigues at court as Porphyry believed.

Plotinus was readier with tongue than with
pen, and it was only under pressure from his
pupils that he consented to put his philosophy
into writing. During the period at Rome before
he was joined by Porphyry he composed twenty-
one treatises; then in the six years of Porphyry's
time he wrote twenty-four more, and, finally, in
the two closing years of isolation he added nine.
These fifty-four books Porphyry edited, and arranged in groups of nine, making the six so-
called *Enneads*.

The *Enneads,* composed and edited in such a manner, offer anything but easy reading. Besides the difficulty of Plotinus' language, there is a baffling obscurity in the connexion of some of his ideas, not to say in the ideas themselves. Of recent years it has become the fashion to explain certain fundamental inconsistencies by the fact that his books belong to three periods, governed by different influences.[3] There is something in this, no doubt; but it does not go far enough, and I fail to grasp any radical change from the Platonic books of the first period to the super-Platonic books, as one may call them, of the second period written under the influence of Porphyry. Something more than chronology is involved. There are, as I see it, two modes of thought running through the *Enneads* from beginning to end, essentially incompatible one with the other yet intimately merged together. One of these is a simple but profound philosophy, expressing a genuine psychological experience and closely related to Platonism; the other is a metaphysic, of Aristotelian and Stoic stamp, which not only suffers the kind of self-destruction that always attends the logic of unchecked rationalism, but works confusion in the philos-

3Such is the thesis of Fritz Heinemann's remarkable work, *Plotin.*

ophy of which it is a parasite. In our study of
Plotinus, therefore, we shall deal separately, so
far as this can be done, with his philosophy and
with his metaphysics, remembering however that
such a discrimination is our own and was not
made by him.

II

One cannot read much in Plotinus, at least I
cannot, without feeling that his philosophy begins, and in a manner ends, in a strong, almost
a morbid, sense of the inadequacies of our mortal state. His mood is one of dismay at the sub-
servience of the soul to its own mean and impure
desires, and at the unceasing change and instability of its mundane interests, with death hovering over all. Life, under these terms, seems to
him no more than "an expense of spirit in a waste
of shame." Such a feeling, indeed, lies close to
the origin of all philosophy, as of most poetry;
but with Plotinus this very discomfort forced
upon his mind an overwhelming conviction that
there is that within us which stands apart from
a world of confusion and disgrace. Whence the
desire to escape, unless there is something that
feels the desire and is aware of its own immutable purity?

"Plato, thou reasonest well.
It must be so; else whence this pleasing hope,
This longing after immortality?"

In these troubled nether regions the soul is
like the sea-god Glaucus, whom Plato describes
in *The Republic,* disfigured by clinging shells
and all kinds of overgrowth. If we would be free,
we must strip the soul clean of these excres-
cences, and, looking to its philosophy, discern
its true nature, its higher contacts, and its kinship with the divine. Of necessity evils parade
about the earth, Plotinus says, quoting now from
the *Theaetetus;* and our only way of escape is in
the acquisition of those celestial qualities whereby we are made like unto God. And so the philosophic life, that experience which springs from
obedience to deep-lying instincts of our nature,
will be a constant striving of the soul to know
itself and its God. Growth in wisdom will be
symbolized as an ascent from this world to another, a turning away from what is "here" to
what is "there." For the fatherland, where the
Father dwells, is not here, but yonder. This ascent of the soul will be by three paths, the aesthetic, the ethical, and the intellectual, by one or
all, according as the start, to use a distinction
known to Plato, is from the perception of the

I, i, 12

I, ii, 1

I, vi, 8

beautiful or the good or the true. And in each of
these paths there are three stages.

It is a little puzzling at first to find so ascetic
a writer as Plotinus, one so scornful of the graces
of language, touched by a passion for beauty
such as few other seers have felt. But so it is; and
the great sixth book of the first *Ennead,* together
with the eighth and ninth of the fifth *Ennead,*
fairly quivers with the aesthetic emotion of the
Phaedrus and the *Symposium,* while in some respects they enlarge and correct Plato's theory
where it is narrowed by ethics. Beauty, as we
first learn to feel it, is addressed to the eye and
the ear. But even here what attracts the philosophic observer is not merely the external sym-
metry of parts, since simple things can be lovely
as well as compound things; the appeal is rather
by that within the object which is akin to the observing soul. Beauty shines forth there where
the Idea has entered and made itself master of
what otherwise is ugly with disorder and inco-
herence and lawless multiplicity; that is how the
material object is transfigured—by communi-
cating in the Logos that flows from the Divine.[4]

[4]To this day there is no satisfactory English translation of the
Enneads. Thomas Taylor's version embraces only selections and,
though praiseworthy in some respects, rather blunts the sharp
outlines of the original. K. S. Guthrie has published a complete
translation, for which one must applaud his courage; but, one

But there are purer and loftier beauties than those of the eye and the ear, ravishing powers which are hidden from the many. For as it is not for those who have been born blind to speak of the graceful forms of the material world wrapt for them in darkness, so there is a beauty of conduct and learning and all that order of which it behoves those to hold silence who have never cared for such things; nor may they tell of the splendours of virtue who have never known the face of justice and temperance, beautiful beyond the lights of evening and of dawn. Such vision is reserved for those who see with the eye of the soul; and seeing they will rejoice, and a desire will fall upon them, which is not pain, deeper than all that colour and moulded shape can ever stir.

And still above rides Beauty—the solitary-dwelling Existence, the Good, the unique source, the secret hope of every heart. And he that shall know this vision—with what passion of love shall he not be seized, with what wondering delight, what longing to be molten into one with it!

regrets to add, it so teems with inaccuracies as to be utterly untrustworthy. Stephen Mackenna has completed a careful and scholarly version of the three first *Enneads*. He is free and sometimes unduly quaint, but his work, when finished, will be a notable addition to our philosophical literature. In my paraphrases and quotations of Plotinus I have drawn largely on this version, so far as it extends.

Surely, if he that has not yet seen this Being must hunger for it as for all his welfare, he that knows will be stricken by a salutary terror, flooded with unspeakable gladness.

But what must one do? How shall one prepare one's self for the arduous path? As there are purifications and the laying aside of garments for those who approach the holy mysteries, so it is with those who would ascend to the sanctuary of Beauty. He that has strength, let him arise, and withdraw into himself, leaving without all that the eyes know, turning away from the delight of fair bodies that once enthralled him. These he will no longer pursue, for he knows them to be copies, vestiges, shadows, and his desire is now towards the reality. And so, as if lightened of a heavy burden, he shall mount with swift and easy steps. But it is otherwise with those who cling to the pleasures of the flesh. For if any one follows what is like a beautiful shape playing over water—is there not a myth telling in symbol of such a dupe, how he sank into the depths of the current and was swept away into nothingness? It is thus with him who pursues the charm of material forms, forgetful that they are images fleeting over the abyss; he sinks down, not in body but in soul, to

depths of infinite darkness and sadness, sight-
less himself to have commerce only with blind
shadows.

The aesthetic ascent proceeds from the perception of visible objects of beauty to the invisible but gracious acts of the soul, and from these
to the uttermost fountain of all that is fair and
lovely. It is almost pure Platonism, with however two important exceptions. Plato nowhere
gives a hint of that mystical vision wherein at
last the seer and the seen merge together in one
indistinguishable act of objectless contemplation. Of this dubious development we shall have
more to say elsewhere. In another direction Plotinus made a valuable correction to the doctrine
of Ideas, and may be said, without quibbling, to
have been more Platonic than Plato. Art, it is
well known, except under the most stringent
discipline was always a matter more or less suspect to Plato, and his banishment of the poets
from his ideal commonwealth was a theme that
racked the invention of his apologetic admirers.
This is not the place to discuss at length what
has generally seemed an aberration in the most
Homeric of all philosophers, as he was called.
The point here to be observed is that in the tenth
book of *The Republic* he excused his suspicion

of art by describing the artist as merely an imi-
tator of imitations, and therefore as twice removed from Ideas and the realm of immediate
truth with which the philosopher is concerned.
Why, one asks, did not Plato, taught by his own
technique, understand that the great artist has
his eye fastened not on nature or manufactured
objects as on an opaque veil, but is really looking through these to the Ideas behind the curtain? Why did he not see that the artist is no
slave of nature, but at once her lover and, as it
were, her corrector and finisher, and more truly
a maker than he who fashions works of utility
with his hands? This is the question asked and
answered by Plotinus; and by so doing he justified Platonism as the artist's philosophy *par
excellence*.[5]

[5]*Enneads* V, viii, 1; ix, 2, 11.—Dean Inge, II, 215, observes:
"Here he [Plotinus] agrees with Philostratus, who in an epoch-
making passage [*Vit. Apoll.* vi, 19] says that great works of art
are produced not by imitation (the Aristotelian μίμησις) but by
imagination (φαντασία), 'a wiser creator than imagination [*sic*,
imitation], for imitation copies what it has seen, imagination
what it has not seen.' The true artist fixes his eyes on the archetypal Logoi, and tries to draw inspiration from the spiritual
power which created the forms of bodily beauty. . . . This is a
real advance upon Plato and Aristotle."—It may be said that
this theory of art was not entirely ignored by Plato, as *e.g.*,
Sophist 267c; but such a passage cannot weigh against the common trend of his criticism. James Adam, in his note on *Republic*
598 A, enters the defence that "Plato's own conception of a transcendent self-existing Beauty has proved an inexhaustible fountain of inspiration to some of the greatest artists, notably, for
instance, in connexion with the Platonic Academy at Florence

It will have been observed that in the middle
stage of the aesthetic ascent comeliness and virtue clasp hands, and that in the last stage they
are quite merged together in the Beautiful and
the Good, which are one. And so the transition
is easy to the second of the three ways, the ethical. We attain likeness to God, Plotinus says,
quoting Plato, by becoming just and holy and
wise. But, he adds, such a precept seems to imply that our human virtues are also qualities of
the divine Being; and how can that be? Is God
wise by reasoning as we reason, or brave because

I, ii, 1

in the days of Michel Angelo." And this is abundantly true. But
on the whole E. J. Urwick, in the eleventh chapter of his *Message of Plato,* has said the truer thing: *"Not so,* Plato would
reply; this is art's great illusion. The ecstasy of the art-inspired
soul is *not* the ecstasy of God-knowledge. It is only an emotional
shadow of the true ecstasy—fleeting, impermanent, unreal. Dangerous, too, as are all extreme emotional states. For if you think
these are real, you will never reach the true vision of God. . . .
And the penalty of all emotional states will overtake you. As certainly as emotion is unstable, so certainly will reaction follow on
realization. You will rise to the heights only to fall again to
deeper depths. . . . Make it [art], if you will, the basis of all
your early religious education: make it, as you must, the ground-
work of the good environment in which the learning soul should
live. Treat it in this way, as the servant of the spiritual life, and
its dangers are gone. But if it is protested, as it is today, and as
it was beginning to be among the Greeks in Plato's time, that
art cannot reach its highest development in *any* subordination
whatever, but must be free—a cult in itself, an end in itself—
then, like everything else which makes such a claim, it must be
'bowed out' of the good life." Mr. Urwick's book has been sharply criticised, and justly. I too would repudiate certain aspects
of his Oriental mysticism as applied to Plato; but I think, nevertheless, that he has done a work of vital importance as a correc-
tive of the Platonism prevalent in Germany and England today.

he has aught to fear, or temperate because He
has passions to restrain, or just because He has
aught to withhold? No, if virtue abides in the
divine world, it is not such as we practise in these
trammels of the flesh and amid these counter-
claims of individual souls; or rather, let us say,
virtue is here, while its source and law are there,
and by participation we become like to that
which is not like to us. The moral assimilation
to God, therefore, means not a mere growth in
kind, a change in degree, so to speak, but demands an alteration in nature and a conversion
of the soul.

As the soul is evil by interfusing with the body,   I, ii, 3
and sharing the body's moods and thinking the
body's thoughts, so its first step in goodness will
be by usurping the command in this partnership,
and by imposing measure and order upon instincts which of themselves are disorderly and
measureless. Hence the civic virtues, as Plato   I, ii, 2
calls them, the limit and bound set upon our desires, the removal of false judgments, the respect for equality. And this is the beginning of
the flight from the world and of the great purgation. The soul will rise to the second stage of
goodness by thinking its own thoughts, which is
wisdom, and by feeling nought for the body's

sake, which is temperance, and by fearing not
its separation from the body, which is fortitude,
and by holding its lower members in subjection
to reason, which is righteousness or justice. By
I, ii, 5   this purgation of virtue the passions are dispelled—anger, fear, and the like, with grief and
all its kin. The soul is disengaged and set free;
it lives then not virtuously, but in contact with
the principle of virtue; it is not measured, but is
itself the law of measure; it is not subject to reason, but is itself reason.

That is the second stage of the ethical ascent,
attaining which the soul has become like to God,
dwelling in undivided contemplation, which is
possession, of all beauty of the Ideal virtues. But
still beyond, in the philosophy of Plotinus, lies
that highest reach wherein likeness to God is
I, vii, 1   transformed into identity with the Good. To that
utter point are directed all aspirations, all loves,
every act; and therefore, when the soul has
mounted to this apex of its course, it no longer
aspires, no longer loves, no longer acts, having
no longer an end outside of itself; nor is there
any division within itself of desire and desired,
of seer and seen. It abides in its own peace; it is
not good, but Goodness.

There are several methods of explaining the

intellectual ascent, but the easiest of these perhaps, and that which shows most clearly the relation of this experience to the moral and aesthetic, will begin with the activity of the soul as
it contemplates the external world of sight and
sound. Out of a confused mass of impressions
and sensations that follow one another in time,
the soul, as a thinking mind, discovers a seeming
order in disorder. Gradually the plan and purpose of things stand out more sharply, the mind
is stirred to admiration at the beauty and rightness and wisdom of the whole, and begins to reflect more deeply on the significance of what it
sees, and on its own place amid the kaleidoscop-
ic phenomena of nature. It becomes more and
more aware of some power within nature that
moves and governs in conformity with its, the
soul's, own modes of thinking. The centre of interest shifts from contemplation of the world to
the act of contemplation itself. And so by degrees the reality of life will seem to be not a soul
reflecting on phenomena outside of itself in an
impenetrable sphere of time and space, but the
inner activity of a pure intelligence, or *Nous*,[6]

[6]*Nous* is the Hellenistic term for reason in this higher order of
mental activity. *Noumena* are the Ideas of the Nous, the objects
of its inner reflection as distinguished from phenomena as objects of contemplation outside of itself. *Noêta* are the same as
noumena, but rather more objectively considered, more distinct,
that is, from the act of reflection. It is very hard to avoid the
use of these technical terms.

communing with its own Ideas, or *noumena,* of
which the signs of intelligence displayed in the
world are an accidental outflow. But these noumena are in the Nous, of the Nous itself; "upward" and "inward" are synonymous terms to
the Neoplatonist; and the intellectual ascent
may thus be described as a passage from the soul
engaged in discursive reasoning to the soul engaged in intuition of its own multiple powers.

But there is a step beyond this, when the mind
begins to consider that these noumena are not
impressions forced upon it by some external
necessity, as the phenomena were, or seemed to
be, but are its own free activity, and that, by
withdrawing this activity, it can plunge, as it
were, into itself, passing thus from the one-many
to the One. Here all disquiet ceases. Here all
division, all multiplicity, come to an end; the
soul is no longer an intelligence communing with
its Ideas, it is not even an intelligence reflecting
upon itself (for such reflection still implies par-
tition and duality), but simply Itself, the Absolute One which is not thinking or thought, but
the goal of all thinking and thought.

The end of knowledge is not unlike a self-
denying ordinance, where truth and goodness
and beauty have dissolved together by losing

their distinctions,[7] and by this loss have transcended whatever we can name or think of as existence. The three ways by which the goal is reached might be likened to three mountain paths that start from different points at the base, and as they ascend draw ever nearer and nearer together. As the paths approach, the climbers thereon catch glimpses of one another in the open places, and hail one another with cries of greeting and encouragement; until, at the last, they meet on the summit in the wide light and the free air, with nothing about them, nothing above them, save a vast emptiness. There is nothing more to say but the *Neti, neti,* "It is not so, not so," of the Hindus. Plotinus himself, we are told, had suffered the ecstasy four separate times; and after the passages on beauty, in which his language glows with a fire caught from Plato, he is most impressive when, forgetting the difference of the ways, he strives to convey some intimation of the final vision wherein, seeing all, one sees nothing. In his arrangement of the *Enneads* Porphyry has appropriately placed last the book which may be called the Apocalypse of our western Bible of mysticism. This is the conclusion:

[7] At times, however, Plotinus repudiates such an identification, and insists that the Good is above the Beautiful.

"What, then, is the One and what Its nature?
We cannot be surprised to find It difficult to tell
of, since even Existence and the Ideas resist our
penetration though all our knowing is based upon the Ideas. The further the human Soul, or
Mind, ventures towards the Formless (to what
is either above or below Form and Idea), the
more is it troubled; it becomes itself, as it were,
undefined, unshaped, in face of the shifting variety before it, and so it is utterly unable to take
hold; it slips away; it feels that it can grasp
nothing. It is at pain in these alien places, and
often is glad to give up all its purpose and to fall
back upon the solid ground of the sense-grasped
world and there take rest. . . .

"Our greatest difficulty is that consciousness
of the One comes not by knowledge, not even by
such an intuitive Intellection as possesses us of
the lower members of the Intellectual Order,
but by an actual Presence superior to any knowing. The Soul, when it deals with matters of
knowledge, suffers a certain decline from its
Unity, for knowing is still an act of reasoning,
and reasoning is a multiple act, an act which leads
the Soul down to the sphere of number and multiplicity. The Soul, therefore, must rise above
knowledge, above all its wandering from its
Unity; it must hold itself aloof from all knowing and from all the knowable and from the
very contemplation of Beauty and Good, for all
Beauty and Good are later than this, springing

from This as the daily light springs from the sun. . . .

"The Supreme is not absent from any one— and yet is absent from all; present everywhere It is absent except only to those that are prepared to receive It, those that have wrought themselves to harmony with It, that have seized It and hold It by virtue of their own Likeness to It and by the power in themselves akin to the power which rays from It. These and these only, whose Soul is again as it was when it came from out of the Divine, are free of what Vision of the Supreme Its mighty nature allows. . . .

"It indeed does not aspire after us, in order that It may be conversant with us; but we aspire after It, in order that we may revolve about It. We indeed perpetually revolve about It, but we do not always behold It. As a band of singers, however, though it moves about the coryphaeus, may be diverted to the survey of something foreign to the choir [and thus become disobedient], but when it converts itself to him, sings well, and truly subsists about him;—thus also we perpetually revolve about the Principle of all things, even when we are perfectly loosened from It, and have no longer a knowledge of It. Nor do we always look to It; but when we behold It, then we obtain the end of our wishes, and rest [from our search after felicity]. Then also we are no longer discordant but form a truly divine dance about It. . . .

"The Soul restored to Likeness goes to its Like and holds of the Supreme all that Soul can hold, . . . that which is before all things that are, over and apart from all the universe of Existence. This is not to say that in this plunging into the Divine the Soul reaches nothingness: it is when it is evil that it sinks towards nothingness: by this way, this that leads to the Good, it finds itself; when it is the Divine it is truly itself, no longer a thing among things. It abandons Being to become a Beyond-Being when its converse is in the Supreme. He who knows himself to have become such, knows himself now an image of the Supreme; and when the phantasm has returned to the Original, the journey is achieved. Suppose him to fall again from the Vision, he will call up the virtue within him and, seeing himself all glorious again, he will take his upward flight once more, through virtue to the Divine Mind, through the Wisdom There to the Supreme. And this is the life of the Gods, and of Godlike men, a life without love of the world, a flight of the Alone to the Alone."[8]

III

Such is the ascent, and such the consummation of blessedness. It will have been observed that

[8]The fourth paragraph of this passage is taken from the translation of Thomas Taylor, the rest from the appendix to Mr. Mackenna's first volume.

this report of the upward way contains two related but not identical elements. In the first
place, and essentially, it gives the actual psychological experience of the man Plotinus, who
dwelt in Rome at a certain time, and who, amid
the distractions and fears of a dissolving world,
sought for himself and for others a plan of security and liberty. That, in a manner, is not
Neoplatonism alone, but the burden of all philosophy; for the world is always distracted, always filled with alarms and threatenings, and
always the cry is to find a refuge from its perturbations; the goal of wisdom is always an ataraxy in one form or another. With Plotinus the
search led inwards, into himself; and through
all his writings, mixed with much that is ex-
traneous and with some things that perplex the
mind, there runs the note of wonder and joy of
one who has discovered the majesty and everlasting value of his own soul. The ascent to the
height, the journey to the centre, is no more
than a figurative expression of this discovery,
which indeed is philosophy. Let a man, he says IV, vii, 10
to those who doubt, look to his soul stripped of
all that clings to her, rather, let him consider
himself and that which veritably concerns him,
and surely he shall see within himself a cosmos

all of mind and all of light, illuminated, as it were, from a central flame of Goodness which is the unexhausted fountain of outpouring truth and joy. His desire will be set no longer upon the visible and dying things of earth, but upon eternal, unbodied realities. Then shall he understand the words of Empedocles: "Hail and farewell, henceforth I am for you a deathless god." The way of purification is to the knowledge of our better selves, and our true science is within. For the soul does not run abroad when she would have vision of temperance and righteousness, but sits at home, and so, in self-contemplation and in recollection of what she has been, beholds those virtues as fair statues of gold, standing there, wiped clean of every stain.

That is the personal experience at the heart of the Plotinian philosophy. And with it goes the belief that a man's soul is not isolated in a world with which it has no bonds of sympathy, that philosophy is not private only but cosmic. The ascent is not made in a vast emptiness of unreality, but our inner change means at each step the consciousness of a new environment and of a new law, or, if you choose, a different aspect of the one all-embracing law. The first awakening IV, ix, 5 brings with it the hint of a world-soul, of which our individual soul is a member, and which is related to the visible universe as our soul is associated with the body, though without the disabilities of fragmentary existence. By that knowledge we feel our withdrawal into ourselves to be no selfish or sullen isolation, but a richer communion with the innumerable souls of others who, like us, are members of one sentient life. We rise higher into a larger sphere of the senses, wherein we see without distraction and hear without perturbation, being at once in the world but not broken by its multiplicity.[9] And then, as we withdraw from the senses, we are rapt into a noetic sphere, where the intuitive faculty of the soul, identified now with the cosmic Nous, enjoys the contemplation of those eternal Ideas of which the visible world is, as it were, an image hovering like a mirage over the abyss of chaos. Last of all, the ecstatic trance, in which the distinction between the mind and its Ideas, the self and self-knowledge, passes away, is not, so Plotinus would have us believe, a mere swooning and eclipse of the soul while the world goes booming on, but a flight of the Alone to the Alone. Sense and spiritual contemplation and

[9]This conception of a soul in the universe runs through Platonic, Stoic, and Neoplatonic philosophy. See *Philebus* 30 A; Arnim, *Fragm.* II, 1015; Plotinus IV, iii, 7; *The Religion of Plato* 116.

mystic union are psychological states corresponding to cosmic climes, and growth in self-
knowledge may be described also as a journey
of the soul through the universe to its far-off
home. Only this should be noted, that the actual
attainment of the noetic state, when once the soul
has been released from the bondage of rebirth,
brings a cessation of what we regard as personal
existence. The heaven of the Nous has no place
for memory of the soul's past lives, and Being
there is not an immortality that denotes conscious continuity; it is rather a blissful forget-
fulness. And the last stage of identification with
the One is a complete loss of identity.

But why does the soul attain to its native goal
so seldom, if indeed it attain at all, and why does
it sink away? Why, if that ecstatic union, as it
feels, signifies its true being, has it ever de-
scended to these earthly cares and distractions?
These were questions that Plotinus drew from
his own experience, and answered as best he
could.

IV, viii, 1   Often, he says, when I awake out of the slumber of this life, and from an alien world enter
into myself, I am amazed at the beauty of what
I behold. Then I begin to live, and am conscious
of a divine energy, and know that in that higher

sphere I am truly myself as I am at one with
God. But after a little the peace is broken, the
vision fades, and once more I am bound to the
senses and a slave to circumstance. Why this descent, this submission to the will of the flesh?
Thinking of these things I recall what Heraclitus taught long ago: the inevitableness of
change, the way up and the way down, the relaxation that comes with change, the labour and
weariness of abiding in one state. I remember
the belief of Empedocles and Pythagoras and
many others, that our fall hitherward was a penalty for sin, and our life in the body an incarcer-
ation of the soul. And then I think of the writings of Plato, which contain many beautiful sayings about the soul, but in this matter seem to
express two diverse views. For at one time he
too speaks of our existence here as of an im-
prisonment, and describes this world as a dark
cavern where the soul lies in chains, awaiting its
release and the journey upwards to the free air
and the blessed light of the sun. Yet elsewhere,
in the *Timaeus,* this same Plato has fair speech
of the world, and declares that God in His benevolence sent the souls hither in order that the
cosmos might be perfected as a divine creature

and a happy duplication of the Ideal pattern whereon His own eyes are set.

How is this discrepancy to be reconciled?

IV, viii, 2   Plotinus thinks we see a contradiction because we forget that there are two modes of governing and of exercising care. One is the royal way, when the ruler issues commands and calls forth order and beauty by the very power of his word, but himself needs not to stretch out his hand to the task. Another way is that of the servant, who is merged in his work and soiled by base associations. Now the world-soul takes the royal way, and, while shaping and moderating the chaos of matter, holds itself apart with clean hands and unperturbed gaze, and never leaves the company of the high gods. But these individual souls of ours, though they also by right share in the blessed life of Ideas, succumb weakly to the task imposed upon them, and, falling from communion with the world-soul, become immersed in a multitude of material cares and chained to these bodies as squalid and complaining captives.

For the reason of this falling away Plotinus has two theories, which may at first seem incompatible, but are really not so. While the indi-

IV, viii, 4   vidual souls are joined with the world-soul they

exercise lordship over the kingdom of matter
without passion or taint. But, according to one
theory, they become weary of this communion,
and their eyes grow tired with the steady vision
of Ideas which this passionless lordship demands.
They long for that ease in alteration of which
Heraclitus spoke, and so break loose from their
source, and in the weakness of their individual
existence sink down to the solid staying-ground
of these bodies. Elsewhere the cause of the sep-   v, i, 1
aration and the fall is laid, not to weariness, but
to a spirit of pride and a lust of the souls to be
themselves and their own masters. In either case
it is clear that Plotinus is merely translating into
a mythological event what he knew to be the
last discoverable source of evil in the soul,—that
slackness which succumbs to the fatigue of holding fast to higher things and turns to the ease and
comfort of change, the vanity that flatters us into believing we have no other end than to be ourselves and to follow our inclinations. Slackness
and vanity, these together are the dark remote
origin of our guilt; they are the cause of the fall,
and then of the misbehaviour of the soul amid the
trials which it has brought upon itself, whereby
it is plunged ever deeper into the abyss of evil.
Happy the soul that takes the penalties of life

for discipline, and, learning wisdom and grace
by suffering, turns again to the long ascent.[10]

IV

So far, by a process of separation, which, as I
have said, does some violence to the literary
method of Plotinus, we have been considering
his pure philosophy and mythology, that is to
say, his analysis of an actual and, up to a certain
point, normal experience, followed by the inevitable and, if properly understood, legitimate
hypostatizing of the stages of this experience as
cosmic realities. The conversion of the soul from
interest in the dead realm of phenomena to the
living world of Ideas is a simple daily occurrence
of which all men have a more or less vivid sense.
So, too, the feeling that the evil for which we are
responsible arises from an indolent and egotistic
yielding to the pressure of circumstance and the
drifting tides of temperament. To this extent
Neoplatonism is a fair development of the Platonic philosophy; nor, to say the least, can I
see any harm in permitting the imagination to

[10]For the Platonic conception of slackness and vanity see *The
Religion of Plato* 253. The κάματος which Plotinus borrows from
Heraclitus corresponds with the ῥᾳθυμία of Athanasius and other
Christian theologians; the τόλμα and the βουληθῆναι ἑαυτῶν εἶναι
with the Christian ἀπόνοια.

transform these psychological facts into a cosmic mythology. Whether Plotinus was justified in his peculiar interpretation of the doctrine of Ideas, and how far the mystical trance, which he superimposed upon Platonism, can be embodied in a sound philosophy, are questions of another colour, to which our answer may be deferred until our estimation of the value of the Plotinian system as a whole.

Our business at this point is with the metaphysical scheme in the *Enneads,* which introduces a mental procedure quite different in kind from what we have been considering. Reason now, instead of limiting its function to analysing and clarifying the psychological data at its service, will undertake to build up a theory of the cause and genesis of the total sum of things, the *rerum natura,* in harmony with its own demands for a logical absolute; and if the facts of our consciousness prove rebellious to these demands, so much the worse for the facts. Stoic and Epicurean had done this by means of a monistic naturalism, why should not the Idealist do the same in his own manner for his own edification?

Felix qui potuit rerum cognoscere causas,
Atque metus omnis et inexorabile fatum
Subiecit pedibus strepitumque Acherontis avari.

Whether warranted or not, the transition from philosophy to metaphysics is comprehensible enough. Reason, as Plotinus says, is the faculty that goes on dividing until it reaches the perfectly simple which is no longer susceptible of analysis; its unchecked course leads straight on to the dark and baffling abyss where all distinctions cease. Now just such a resting place is offered by the presumption of mysticism. The ecstatic trance will be accepted as a positive experience, and then will be wrenched from its psychological setting and conceived as an abstract Unity. This Unity will be hypostatized as the ultimate reality and hence as the cause of all things, while the multiple world of phenomena will be conceived as an effect flowing out by some mechanical process from the universal source of being.

To Plotinus it is evident that this transcendental monism, this metaphysic of the spirit, seemed to come straight out of Plato's Dialogues; and many, perhaps most, critics of the present day write as if Neoplatonism were an inevitable and proper development of the Platonic philosophy. That, emphatically, is not the thesis I would maintain. Neoplatonism, as I see it, derives its central dogma not from Plato at

all, but from a method of reasoning which was
introduced by Aristotle, and which, combining
with certain Oriental currents of theology and
merging into Neo-Pythagoreanism, carried philosophy in a direction quite contrary to the true
implications of Platonism. The question, as it
involves matters of the first importance, may
warrant a digression of some length before we
take up the Plotinian scheme analytically.

V

Plato's treatment of the problem of creation,
as the reader of the *Timaeus* need scarcely be
reminded, was not rationalistic or metaphysical,
but mythological. In the simplest terms, his theory means that we are conscious of two forces
at work in ourselves and in the world, a divine
cause and a lower cause. The realm of phenomena, in which our mortal life passes, is a composite of these two forces; or, in the language of
the religious imagination, God, with His eye set
on the everlasting and immutable Ideas, imposes form and order on an aboriginal chaos,
so far as the necessity therein permits. He himself creates the universe as a whole, a living
creature, the god to be; while to the lesser gods

He assigns the task of fashioning and governing the individual creatures in the world of genesis, or becoming.

Now the relation of Plato's mythological scheme to the Aristotelian metaphysics and to the subsequent course of religious philosophy may be seen by a glance at the diagram on the opposite page.

In the first place it is to be noted that for the dualism of Plato, corresponding to our innate and insurmountable sense of the divine and the "necessary" in our realm of experience, Aristotle has substituted a dualism justified, if it can be justified at all, on the demands of pure reason. Because no rational account could be given, as Plato himself admitted, of the relation between Ideas as divine entities and the forms of the phenomenal world, Aristotle denies the existence of any such Ideas, and ascribes the final reality of being to the intimate and inseparable union of form (or idea) and matter in individual objects. To existence in this sense God has no relation as cause or governor; the world in its substance is eternal and totally independent of divine interference. God, so far as He is cause, is regarded as the source of motion, not of being, and even as such He stands utterly remote from conscious

	Plato	*Aristotle*	*Numenius*	*Plotinus*
The divine term	The Creator, Ideas	The Unmoved Mover	One, the Good, Being, Nous The Creator The Creature	One, the Good Being, Nous Soul
	→		→	→
The phenomenal world	The Creature, the God-To-Be Genesis	Individual objects of form and matter	Genesis	Genesis
	←		←	→
The lower term	The Receptacle, Necessity		Matter, Necessity	Matter, Deprivation, Not-Being

and voluntary contact with the world. Here enters the wedge that was to split the dualistic view of the world in such a manner as to drive thought finally into an absolute monism. The process of reasoning by which Aristotle reaches this conception of the first cause displays strikingly and once for all the fallacy inherent in the metaphysical method.

The argument[11] starts from a supposed law of mechanics: every object in motion, according to Aristotle, presupposes a motor, which, as it is itself in motion, presupposes another motor. (That is a theory which seems to follow from our daily observation of the material world, and which conforms to Newton's three laws of motion to this extent that every change of motion requires an external motor.) But, Aristotle continues, we must pause somewhere; reason cannot abide the thought of a series of mobiles and motors regressing to infinity, it must have a beginning. (There is nothing in our knowledge of physical facts to justify this demand of reason. So far as our experience goes, the series is without beginning or end, or, rather, our physical

[11]The following statement of Aristotle's metaphysical argument is taken from Clodius Piat's masterly exposition in his volume of *Les grands philosophes* p. 110 ff. The comments and criticisms are of course my own.

experience has nothing to do with beginnings or ends. Aristotle's argument is of a purely metaphysical character having no connexion with mechanics.) There must, then, be a final motor, which, as such, is not moved by anything anterior to itself. It cannot be moved from without, because it is the first motor, or from within, because all motion requires an external motor; it is essentially and absolutely unmoved, and therefore motionless, being the complete actualization of all potential motion (whatever that may mean). It is the Unmoved Mover. How then does it move the world? Certainly not by means of a mechanical impulse, for this, by the law of mechanics, would imply a movement in itself by reaction. It will act upon the world as a final cause, as the end towards which all moving things aspire, as they are set in motion by an innate love of the Absolute which itself reciprocates nothing. And this final cause of all motion, itself unmoved, is God.

Here several observations are in order. In the first place, this consummation of Aristotle's reasoning offers no likeness to anything in human experience, whether spiritual or natural. Plato had defined soul as the self-moved mover, and so as the cause of all moving, logically antecedent to mechanical motion which demands an external motor. His language is not precise, as Aristotle pointed out,[12] since mechanical motion is spatial, whereas psychic activity is non-spatial. His theory thus leaves unexplained the really unexplainable connection, or *modus operandi,* between mind and matter; but it answers to this simple fact of our experience, that the soul, as free agent, possesses a spontaneous activity, whereas in the mechanical world, so far as we know it, there is no freedom or spontaneity, but only the action and reaction between inert bodies in motion. And thus the definition of God as the original self-moved mover, a spirit transcendent yet somehow operating by his divine will within the sphere of mechanical forces, may leave His nature a mystery, but a mystery akin to the relation of mind and body which meets us in every act of our diurnal life. By going a step further and defining God as the Unmoved Mover, Aristotle has passed from philosophy to metaphysics; that is to say, driven on by the insatiate impulse of reason to express itself in absolutes, he has defined the ultimate spiritual reality in terms which have no relation to anything we know from our own spiritual life, and,

[12]*De Anima* i, 3.

baldly stated, have no meaning at all. But at the same time—and this explains the pertinacious attraction of the error—he pretends to reach his conclusion by a straight argument from the universally acknowledged facts of our physical experience, not observing that his conclusion in an Unmoved Mover is not a derivation from, but a flat contradiction of, his premise that every object in motion presupposes a motor which is itself in motion. This pretension to lend the authority of physical fact, or scientific observation, to a theorem which is essentially contradictory to all our physical experience lies perdu in the very method of rationalism, and indeed in all so-called science which glides surreptitiously into metaphysical generalizations. The sceptics, as we shall see, laid hold of this inconsistency with deadly effect.

In a sense Aristotle's absolute might be described as a blending of Plato's God with the Idea of the True and the Good, while it heartlessly eliminates what is valuable in both. As the cause of all life and motion, it is God, but not the Creator, since it has no connexion with the being of individual objects or persons; nor is it the author of Providence, since it has no conscious concern with the unrolling of mundane

events. As the goal of all thinking, it is the Idea
of the True; but it is a truth evacuated of any
content, being the pure energy of self-contemplation, without difference or sequence or purpose or specific thought. As the end of all desiring, it is the Idea of the Good; but it is a good
devoid of meaning or value, since a gulf yawns
between it and the principle of form and order
which enters into the composition of individual
beings. Plato might seem to have had Aristotle's
absolute in mind when he exclaimed: "In the
name of God, what is this! Are we going to believe out of hand that the highest Being has in
fact no motion or life or soul or intelligence,—a
thing that neither lives nor thinks, but remains
forever fixed in solemn, holy, unconscious vacuity?"[13]

These may be reckoned harsh words to apply
to "the master of them that know"; and indeed,
if our design embraced a history of Greek philosophy in its various ramifications, we should
have a very different account to render of Aristotle's scope and significance. But even in the
secular branch of philosophy, I do not see how
the conclusion can be avoided that his introduc-
tion of metaphysics has been the source of end-

[13]*Sophist* 248 E.

less logomachies which bear no relation to the
facts of human experience. Certainly, in the religious sphere which is our special province, his
conception of God must be rejected finally as
an unwarranted assumption of the unchecked
reason, logically self-destructive, intellectually
confusing, ethically mischievous.

How far the later theologians, pagan and
Christian, were directly and consciously influenced by Aristotle, is a question not easy to answer. On the one hand the references to his works
are surprisingly rare throughout this whole period; Plotinus, for instance, seldom alludes to
him, whereas the reminiscences of Plato in the
Enneads are innumerable. Yet Neoplatonism is
undoubtedly more Aristotelian than Platonic
at the core, and Loofs can maintain that all the
positive theological dogmas of Dionysius the
Areopagite (whose mysticism is essentially Neoplatonic) go back ultimately to the Aristotelian
conception of God.[14] Among the Christian writers a distinction must be made. For the orthodox theologians of the first centuries Aristotle
scarcely existed; and this general neglect is ex-

---

[14]*Dogmengeschichte*[4] 320. It is at least questionable, however,
whether Loofs is correct in saying that Aristotle's God is the
erste Ursache und letztes Ziel alles Seienden. For a different
view, which I have adopted *supra,* see Boehm, *Die Gottesidee bei
Aristoteles.*

plained simply enough by Gregory Nazianzen's contemptuous reference to his "petty view of Providence, his technical method, and his mortal theories of the soul."[15] On the contrary it is characteristic of the major heresies that they all, openly or implicitly, turned for their philosophical basis from Plato to Aristotle, and we may surmise that the heretical treatises, if preserved, would display abundant allusions to the Peripatetic logic and metaphysics. Though Neoplatonism had already begun its work in the theology of St. Augustine, the direct entrance of Aristotle into the accepted theology of the Church occurred at a definite moment after the Council of Chalcedon, at the close of our period, when Leontius of Byzantium undertook to explain and support rationalistically the bare dogmatic statement of the creed as to the single personality and dual nature of Christ. By suffering itself to be seduced in this direction, scholasticism adopted the metaphysical method of the heretics as opposed to the Platonic method of the great orthodox Grecians, and it is a venturesome, but warrantable, thesis that the theology of the Church Councils, since the year 451,

15*Theol. Or.* I, 10: 'Αριστοτέλους τὴν μικρολόγον πρόνοιαν, καὶ τὸ ἔντεχνον, καὶ τοὺς θνητοὺς περὶ ψυχῆς λόγους, καὶ τὸ ἀνθρωπικὸν τῶν δογμάτων.

has been vitiated to a certain extent by the un-
orthodox, and at bottom anti-religious, logic of
Aristotelianism. If the Greek theology of the
third and fourth centuries is orthodox, then
heresy can be plucked with both hands out of
Thomas Aquinas.[16]

On the whole, then, in the absence of docu-
ments which would enable us to trace fully the
history of the subject, it may be said that, apart
from its double rôle in Christian theology, the
influence of Aristotelian transcendentalism
merged at an early date with various streams of
thought, Neo-Pythagorean, Oriental, and what
not, which however commonly regarded themselves as Platonic rather than Peripatetic, and
which reached their flower in the metaphysical
system of Plotinus.[17] Generally speaking, the
effect of this transcendentalism has been two-

[16]This is not the place to enter into the details of Christian theology. Those who are curious to see the relations between Aristotle and heresy may be referred to Whittaker, *Apollonius of
Tyana* 71; Tixeront, *Hist. des Dogmes* II, 22, 28, 40, 100; Robert-
son, *Regnum Dei* 153. For Leontius of Byzantium see H. M.
Relton, *A Study in Christology*. An illustration of the devastat-
ing effect of the Aristotelian metaphysic on medieval theology is
the doctrine of Transubstantiation.

[17]The Neoplatonists and their syncretic predecessors made a
conscious effort to reconcile Plato and Aristotle, and to this end
appealed to the supposed esoteric doctrine of Plato, hints of
which are found in the spurious Epistles. Numenius, for instance, wrote a treatise on the ἄγραφα δόγματα of Plato which he
entitled Περὶ τῶν παρὰ Πλάτωνι ἀπορρήτων. On this subject see the
excellent pages (82 ff.) of Chaignet's *Platon.*

fold: in irreligious minds it has tended to relegate God to a polite limbo of the Unknowable, resulting in agnosticism or more outspoken materialism; with the religiously inclined it has fostered a mysticism which holds itself from the sheer abyss of inanity by creating a variety of intermediaries between its remotest divinity and the world.

Aristotle himself, sought to bridge over the gap between his Unmoved Mover and the variously moving world by the insertion of a celestial sphere forever revolving about itself in an unvaried motion. But the tendency towards a mysticism mitigated by intermediaries comes clearly to the front in Philo the Jew, whose deity is a strange mixture—an unholy *mésalliance* I should like to say—of the Hebrew Jehovah and the Aristotelian Absolute. Between this God and the world, from which He is completely severed by His transcendental nature, Philo then inserts the Logos, a compound of the Platonic Ideas and the Stoic *logoi,* conceived as the animated, but not fully personified, mind of deity. And all this in Philo's eyes appeared to be pure Plato and pure Moses; Aristotle he scarcely recognizes.

More extraordinary was the course taken by

the Gnostics. They might differ in everything else, but in one thing they all agreed: in making a distinction between the true God, who dwells aloof from any contact with change and appearance and mortal life in a dark abyss of silence, and a lower deity, who is the Demiurge, or Creator, of the world and the more or less responsible author of suffering and evil.

In line with the Gnostics stands the rather enigmatical figure of Numenius of Apamea (see the diagram on p. 207), who flourished in the reign of Marcus Aurelius, and of whose works some fragments are preserved. He was professedly an eclectic, or syncretist, whose philosophical brew should contain the wisdom of the Brahmins, Hebrews, Magi, and Egyptians, dissolved in a medium itself compounded of Platonism and Pythagoreanism. Out of this concoction certain images emerge. The divine cause, which by Plato had been left as Demiurge and Ideas in parallel state, is split up into a trinity of subordinated causes. The first God, the One identified with Being and Nous and the Idea of the Good, is too remote to have any contact with the sphere of change and appearance. Below him stands a second God, who is not Goodness but good, the Demiurge of Plato's *Timaeus,* the

divine conceived as working in the sphere of
genesis. And there is still a third, who seems to
be a misunderstanding of the Timaean description of the universe as a living creature, "the
god to be." All this to Numenius was pure Platonism, or pure Mosaism, as you choose; for
"what," he says, thinking no doubt of Philo's
blend, "is Plato but Moses in Attic speech?"
As a Platonist he still maintains a strict dualism between the divine cause and the *hylê* (matter) underlying the phenomenal world, regards
evil as a spirit of ignorance and disorder in the
material substratum, and writes a history of the
Academy to show how the later leaders of the
school betrayed its founder.

VI

We can now see where the mystical monism
which closed the psychological experience of
Plotinus joined this metaphysical current from
Aristotle to Numenius. The highest member of
the divine cause for Numenius was the One, but
it could be described also as Being and Nous,
and thus was not utterly devoid of shadowy
qualities and activities. For Plotinus the One,
as the abyss into which contemplation plunges

in a kind of suicidal vertigo, must be lifted into the dark vacuity above both mind and being, which are relegated to a second place in a new triad. His First Principle will be, in the complete sense of the words, absolute and abstract— unqualified, undefinable, non-existent as super-essential. It may possibly be called the Good; but it is not good as Plato applied that term to the Demiurge, since it has no feeling for anything within itself or outside of itself, but is the unrelated source of all relations. It is the spiritual affirmation of Socrates transformed into a relentless negation.[18] The dualism of Plato, which still in Numenius contrived to hold a precarious place, has been eliminated to the utmost. There is no longer, properly speaking, a Creator in the scheme, nor a distinct act of creation, but the sphere of genesis overflows from the lowest member of the divine triad and expands infinitely into the emptiness of hylê.

The Neoplatonic problem, then, a very pretty problem, will be to explain *why* and *how* this concrete world of experience has been evolved from a metaphysical abstraction. For the *why*

---

[18]Even the One and the Good are, so to speak, courtesy titles and imply a positive addition to what is purely negative. The name "One," it is said (V, v, 6), perhaps means no more than the denial of multiplicity; and (V, v, 10) the "Good" is what the Nous remembers of It after the vision has passed.

Plotinus is rather vague; as indeed the mere possibility of such a question implies a flaw in his monism. Perhaps the nearest approach to a clear answer can be found in the principle of vision, contemplation, *theôria*. In one of the chapters of his great book *On Nature and Contemplation and the One* the question is put to Nature herself why she brings forth works, and she replies: "It would have been better not to ask but to learn in silence, even as I am silent and make no habit of speech. And learn what? That all becoming is my vision, seen in my silence; for I, myself sprung from vision, am vision-loving, and by this faculty bring forth vision." The visible world is thus the realization of a desire of vision in the heart of Nature. But this creative longing to see and behold does not begin, nor does it end, with the evocation of material phenomena; it extends up and down, throughout, everywhere, having no bound. All doing is for the sake of contemplation, and being itself is merely a by-work of visioning. But in perfect unity there can be no vision, no place for a seeing and a seen; if the One will contemplate it must lose its oneness. Hence, the Supreme, beginning as One, becomes pregnant from the love of vision; and there is multiplicity. Yet it

III, viii, 4

were well if this had never happened, for the
whence is better than the *whither;* and if the
question *why* is still urged, the only response
will be that command of Nature to keep silence,
or that dark word Necessity, *Anankê,* which for
Plato had signified the limiting obstacle to the   V, iv, 1
divine purpose, and is transformed by Plotinus
into a kind of fatalism impending upon the
whole system of the universe, a law of compulsion within the heart of the divine itself.[19]

In regard to the *how* of this expansion Plotinus is more explicit, and perhaps also more unintelligible, according to the rule that the more
explicitly one solves an insoluble problem the
less intelligibly. All sorts of verbal ambiguities
are involved: the double sense of *hen* as "one   V, v, 4

[19]It is in his poet's sense of vision that Plotinus remains most
faithful to the spirit of Platonism. And it is easy to see how
vision and necessity are transferred by him to his metaphysical
system. Thus (V, v, 12) he says that each thing is to be grasped
by the organ suited to it, one thing by the eyes, another by the
ears, while to the Nous there is vision of another kind. Those
who demand reality through the bodily senses alone have forgotten that which they have desired and striven after from the
beginning. "For all things reach after It and strive for It by a
necessity of their nature (φύσεως ἀνάγκῃ), having as it were a pro-
phetic sense that without the vision they cannot be." Thus, if the
being of all things depends upon the necessity of vision, and if all
things are an emanation from a First Principle, then the necessity of vision will readily be made the cause of emanation. This
whole chapter (V, v, 12) is a marvellous, and marvellously impossible, blend of the Platonic *theôria* in the *Phaedrus* and *Symposium* and *Republic* with the Aristotelian *theôria* of the *Ethics*
and *Metaphysics.*

which is composed of parts" and "one which is

v, iv, 1 without parts"; the double sense of *archê* as "what is first" and "what rules, exercises power," and I know not how many other amphibologies. In the main, however, Plotinus depends on

v, i, 6, 7 the Aristotelian distinction between power in a state of potentiality and power energizing, or in a state of actuality.[20] The First Principle, he says, is perfect, and, as the Sovereign Power, must surpass in efficacy all things that are. Now we observe that all creatures, as they attain perfection, do not rest sterilely in themselves, but produce; even soulless things do this to the extent of their ability, as fire produces warmth and snow produces cold. How, then, shall the Sovereign Good abide in itself as if held by envy or impotence? There is a necessity that something should proceed from it by virtue of its sovereignty, and again something from this second, and something from this, infinitely, since the source is infinite.

The abstraction of reason is thus transformed into a potential energy. This is entirely self-sufficient, yet from its very infinity there will be an overflow, or procession, into actual energy.

[20]From this point through the three succeeding paragraphs I follow the account of the metaphysical descent in Henri Guyot's *L'Infinité divine,* where full references are given.

The question still confronts the monist: how does an absolutely unqualified One emit from itself a qualified and multiform world of being without itself undergoing any change or qualification? Of course the simple honest reply is, It doesn't,—at least so far as we have any experience of physical or psychical events there is no such thing as an effect or emanation which leaves its cause or source unaffected. But it is the function of metaphysics to transcend physical or psychical experience, while pretending to argue from such an experience, and so we have the Neoplatonists offering a meaningless answer to an impossible question raised by a gratuitous hypothesis. There are, says Plotinus, two kinds of energy. One is *of* the essence of a thing and is actually the thing itself; the other is *from* the essence of a thing and is the cause of another thing, which in turn will possess its own potentiality. Thus, in the case of fire, we distinguish between the heat which is the fire itself and the heat which flows from the fire without diminishing the fire. (Bad physics, for which however Plotinus should not be held responsible.) And so, in like manner, the First Principle remains unaffected, while from the energy which abides with it as its essential potentiality, and is It, there flows an actualized energy which takes a second place as Being and Nous.

Now this Nous, as proceeding immediately from the One, is itself in a fashion one; but, as mind, it instinctively tries to comprehend that from which it sprang. Or, we might say, in its primitive state it was not mind but vision which does not see; and so, in its striving to realize itself as vision, it becomes a seeing mind, no longer a true One, but as it were a one divided into the seer and the seen. What it beholds in itself, or tries to behold, is its sublime source, but by its inability to grasp absolute unity it breaks the seen up into multiplicity, and thereby as a divided One becomes the One-Many. It is the Logos and energy of the First Principle, a great God, but a second god, below the highest.

As the energy of the First Principle, Nous is a potentiality which cannot remain sterile, but in its turn, without diminishing itself, overflows to produce a lower energy, like itself though still further from the primal One. This hypostasis of mind is Soul. And as mind looks up to the One and becomes the One-Many, so Soul looks back to mind, and, being unable to grasp the noetic Many in a single comprehensive view, suffers a dispersion of energy in such manner as

to become the One-and-the-Many. It sees part
by part, in succession, and thus becomes the origin of time, in distinction from eternity which is
the property of noetic vision. In its weakened
power also it is unable to see the Many within
itself as Nous had done, and thus by going
out of itself for its vision becomes the origin of
space.[21] And, further, whereas the First Principle had produced mind and mind had produced
soul in a state of quiescence and without internal
change, the Soul, no longer an overflowing potentiality, can create only by an inner alteration and motion, producing thus a world of sense
as a moving image of itself in time and outside
of itself in space. Soul is the third God, complet-
ing the celestial trinity; divine itself, as the hypostasis of Nous, what proceeds from it is no
longer divine, but the beginning of mortality.
The golden chain is snapped, and metaphysics
has entered upon its agony.

VII

Plotinus is in fact well aware of the break in

[21]Ingenious but futile reasoning. Seeing in succession Soul produces time, and seeing outside of itself it produces space. But to
say that it sees in succession and outside of itself is to assume
time and space as already existent, not to explain their cause.
The whole metaphysical procedure in fact is a senseless attempt
to explain genetically what is already present.

his argument. His ethical and emotional philosophy had started from a strong sense of the dualism of consciousness, from a clear perception of two elements in the soul, the divine and the mortal. His metaphysics, down to the point here reached, by confining attention to one of the two threads of experience, the divine, had retained a certain consistency and even a kind of specious clarity. But now a different sort of problem lies before him: he has reached again the starting point of dualism, and how shall he maintain his deterministic monism.

Time, space, motion, and it may be added form, are results of the activity of Soul, which is the third and last member of the divine triad; they are, so to speak, the psychical elements of the phenomenal world. By the same necessity of evolution matter also should be an outflow from the Soul, or from these psychical activities; and this indeed is true of matter regarded as an object of the senses, regarded, that is to say, using the Greek terminology, as earth, air, fire, water, and as the formed and coloured bodies (*sômata*) of our handling. But behind, or beneath, these manifestations lies the obscure substratum of matter itself, the hylê, which eludes our senses, and whose existence, as Plato said, we conjecture by "a certain sort of bastard reasoning without true perception." As inexplicable, Plato in the *Timaeus* was content to leave it there unexplained, calling it the "errant cause," "mother and receptacle of this visible and otherwise perceptible world of creation," a "separate kind, invisible and formless, all-receiving, and in some most extraordinary manner partaking of the Ideal and intelligible, itself utterly incomprehensible." Such is the philosophical humility and privilege of one who recognizes the limitations of reason. But an avowed rationalist, like Plotinus, has no such ease. Having set out to derive all things from the absolute One by an unbroken process of emanation, or evolution, he must in some way fit this hylê into his chain, while at the same time he must explain why the chain should terminate at this point, and how this termination brings into the open a dualism which, despite his protests, must have been latent in his system from the beginning.

This feat of mental legerdemain Plotinus accomplishes by his definition of reality. The progress from the First Principle is not by addition to it from some source of reality—for nothing can be added to that which is already perfect—but from not-being. Mind and being, though an VI, v, 12 overflow from the First Principle, have in a way less of reality, or of absolute being, than their source which is beyond being; Soul has less of reality than mind and being; and so the whole process implies at once a constant dispersion and a gradual deprivation (*sterêsis*) of reality. At the last—for reason demands a last as well as a first—will come that which has no positive qualities to be dispersed, from which nothing more can be subtracted, which, in a word, is there, but is there as not-being, a nothingness which rises like a blank wall where reality ends. This is the hylê of Neoplatonism. It is not properly speaking a part or product of the universal evolution, but the indescribable principle of multiplicity and deprivation that lies below being as the ineffable One was above being. The sum of actual existence looks suspiciously as if it resulted from the conjunction of a descending and an ascending cause, though there has been a desperate effort to express the act in terms of a single direction.

Plotinus in fact has exhausted the vocabulary of rhetoric and the devices of logic to explain the origin of the phenomenal world out of the chaotic negation of the hylê. In general the cause of creation would appear to be an instinc-

tive repugnance of Soul for the indefinite and
unreal. Soul has a dread of sinking down into
the void; and so, when in its outgoing activities
it strikes upon the dark uttermost clouds of not-
being, it endeavours to impose on the formless
and unqualified those forms and qualities which
it possesses in itself as an inheritance from Nous.
Such is the origin of the material bodies in this
manifold world of genesis. But, though these
seem to be material, they are not really so in the
sense that hylê enters into their composition as
an actual substance. For this hylê, as the reverse
of the immutable and unqualified One, is in-
capable of transformation or modification; it
should, rather, be likened to a smooth, impenetrable surface which reflects the forms cast upon
it without retaining any vestige of that which
comes and goes:—

"Its every utterance, therefore, is a lie; it pretends to be great and it is little, to be more and it
is less; and the Existence with which it masks
itself is no Existence, but a passing trick making trickery of all that seems to be present in
it, phantasms within a phantasm. It is like a
mirror showing things as in itself when they
are really elsewhere, filled in appearance but
actually empty, containing nothing, pretending
everything. Into it and out of it move mimicries

of the Authentic Existents, images playing upon an image devoid of Form, visible against it
by its very formlessness. They seem to modify
it but in reality effect nothing, for they are ghost-
ly and feeble, have no thrust and meet none in
Matter (hylê) either; they pass through it leaving no cleavage, as through water; or they might
be compared to shapes projected so as to make
some appearance upon what we can know only
as the Void."[22]

III. vi, 6

Viewed thus from its lower source the phenomenal world fades into an insubstantial pag-
eant, an uneasy dream of the Soul, since all of
the Soul that is in body sleeps; yet in another
aspect, seen as an evocation of the noetic forms in
the Soul, though it be but as shadows of images,
these same phenomena are altogether wonderful
and beautiful and radiant with reflected light,
a glorious garment of the Deity, a field wherein
the Soul may exercise her loving care with no
derogation of her pure majesty.

VIII

If we find ourselves baffled by the ambiguous
character of the phenomenal world, the difficulties grow mountain high when we undertake to

[22]III, vi, 7, Mackenna's translation.

grasp the Neoplatonic theory of evil. There are
in fact two methods of approaching the problem
involved in this theory, between which Plotinus
wavers with no warning and apparently no sense
of their disparity. One of these is genuinely psychological, and, as was set forth in our discussion of the Plotinian philosophy, merely traces
the source of evil to the known principle of indolence and vanity in the human heart. It were
well if Plotinus had been content to pause here.
But the question *unde malum* as a thing in nature was still urgent upon his reason, and so we
find him entangling his psychology in metaphysical conceptions of the ultimate *why* and *how*.
Inevitably his arguments fall into devious and
dark ways.

In general, the great cause is an affection of
unlucky matter and of that which has been made
like to matter; in that view Plotinus is pretty
constant whenever he touches on the subject of
evil as a cosmic fact. But as he chances to be
swayed by imagination or by reason, the calami-
tous effects of matter are regarded differently,
just as matter itself was explained differently.
At one time it is almost Plato speaking. That,
he says, which underlies all patterns and forms I, viii, 3ff.
and measures and limits, and has no trace of

good by any title of its own, but, at best, takes order and grace from some principle outside of itself, a mere image in respect of things that truly *are,*—this substratum reason by search discovers to be the primal evil, evil absolute. For matter becomes mistress of whatever is manifested through it, corrupting and destroying the incomer, and substituting its own opposite character and kind. Body is evil so far as it partakes of this substratum. Soul is evil in so far as it becomes individual by entering into body and by that act is made subject to excess and disorder and false judgments. And thus, as going upward from virtue we come to the Beautiful and the Good, so, by going downward from vice, we reach essential evil. And the individual soul, when it abandons itself unreservedly to the extreme of viciousness, is no longer a vicious soul merely—for mere vice is still human, still carries some trace of good—but has taken to itself another nature, the Evil, and so far as soul can be, it is dead. And the death of the soul is twofold: while sunk in the body to lie down in matter and drench itself therewith; and when it has left the body to lie for a season in that nether world— which is our "going down to Hades and slumbering there."

All this is positive enough to satisfy the imagination of the most thoroughgoing dualist; but then comes the metaphysical qualm and reason has her revanche. If all things are evolved out of the One-Good, there can be no positive wrong in the world, but only in some unimaginable way an illusion of wrong. As matter lacks every positive quality and must be described in terms of pure negation, so the evil which seems to rise up from this abyss of not-being is nothing real, but a kind of not-good which becomes good when viewed positively, an insubstantial phantom that appears, and then vanishes away at the touch of reason, like a mist melting beneath the rays of the sun.[23]

The nearest approach in Plotinus to a reconciliation of these positive and negative views, his most characteristic attitude, is that which explains evil as remoteness from the source in a scheme of infinite expansion. Evil thus becomes a failure of good owing to the fact that one thing will be less good than another in accordance with their increasing distance from the focus of being, while their existence as individuals depends   III, ii, 5

[23]Augustine's theory of evil as not-being, or deprivation, was taken from Plotinus, and from him has become a part of our theology. But the Christian theory is modified by the non-Plotinian conception of free will, which introduces into Christianity a profound and gratuitous inconsistency.

on this separation. And so, granted that the I, viii, 7 Good shall not be left in sterile loneliness, there is a necessity in the outgoing from it, or the continuous down-going or away-going, that there should be a Last beyond which nothing more can be produced. This Last will have no residue of good in it, will be the necessity of evil. Call it the final failure, or deprivation; call it the fallen II, iii, 17 sediment of the Higher Order, bitter and em-II, iii, 18 bittering; say that evils are necessary here because of the diminishing energy in expansion,— the metaphysical sting is in this recurring word Necessity, *Anankê,* which for Plato was the characteristic term of dualism, as designating something *contrary to* the Good, but by Plotinus is translated into a term of monism, as designating something *inherent in* the Good. Oh, it is not the case of Tweedledum and Tweedledee—far from that. These speculative differences, though they seem to be spun out of thin air, have a way of reacting on our attitude towards the very solid facts of life; and so we find in Plotinus a whole group of theories of evil that lie midway between his metaphysics and his philosophy, and are fraught with consequences practical enough.

One of his courses leads him to the ancient

paradox of the whole and the part, which virtually denies the existence of any evil at all. This world of sense, he says, is no longer a unity like III, ii, 17 the world of mind, but a multiplicity, the members of which are moved by a desire for unification; but desire by its very nature is opposed to desire, so that life is filled with contention and contradiction. Thence flows evil, thence the spectacle of a world abounding in wrong. Nevertheless, it is the function of philosophy to see that, however vicious some of the parts may be, yet taken together the evils nullify one another so as to combine into a perfect and flawless whole. If evil is a factor in the design, then it is not censurable, not really evil. Or, life may be likened to a play, in which the poet gives to each actor a part as protagonist, or second, or third. Villains and virtuous clash together to make up the plot; and for every man there is a place,—a place that fits the good man, a place that fits the bad, and each man assumes naturally and reasonably the rôle for which he is suited. The vicious rôle is just as necessary as the virtuous for the completion of the drama. In like manner we should see that the evil in the single soul serves a good purpose in the universal system, and that what in the individual offends nature, profits nature in the total event. Even the executioner's ugly office does not mar the well-governed State, since such an officer fills a civic necessity; and the corresponding moral type may be equally serviceable. As things are, all is well.

That last metaphor ought to have been a warning to an honest thinker; for it should be clear enough that, however necessary the executioner may be for governing an actual State, there is something essentially wrong in a community which needs such an officer. Even Plotinus, hardened optimist though he be when he gets the metaphysical bit between his teeth, suffers a qualm of conscience, and asks himself whether a scheme that comes to such conclusions does not exonerate the basest wrong-doers of their guilt. IV, iii, 16 But no, he replies, the injustice of man to man is an evil in the doer for which he will be held responsible; although in the order of the whole his act is not injustice, since it was necessity, and to his victim it may be a good.

With this statement Plotinus passes to another aspect of his argument, which professes to take the sting out of evil by treating it as the III, ii, 5 proper gymnasium for virtue. Not only would II, iii, 18 this All be incomplete without evil, but vice in itself has many useful sides: it brings about much

that is beautiful, in the artist's work for example, and it stirs men to thoughtful living and to
the exercise of temperance, not allowing them
to drowse in security. In this vein, Plotinus will
not shrink from the harshest Calvinistic logic:
all things, he declares, are the work of the rul-   III, ii, 11
ing Logos, even so-called evils.

Now I confess I never meet with this specious
fallacy, whether in Neoplatonist or Stoic or in
the corrupt application of the Christian *ad ma-
iorem Dei gloriam,* without a feeling of revolt
and indignation. Doubtless good may be wrung
from resistance to temptation, and purity in a
measure may be wrested from contamination,
but to turn this fact into an argument for the
necessity of temptation in the world or into a
palliation of evil as not in its essence and consequences evil, is nothing less than the last degra-
dation of rational unreason. Plotinus also, it is
gratifying to know, felt something of this in his
clearer moments. It is true, he admits in a notable passage, that the courage of man is de-   VI, iii, 5
pendent on the existence of war, as all our practical virtues are called out by this or that accident of life; but if Virtue herself had a choice in
the matter, whether there should be wars in order that she might exercise courage, and injus-

tice in order that she might restore the right, and poverty as a call to generosity, or whether the earth should have peace from all these things, certainly, if the choice were hers, she would prefer that all things should go well, though it left her with nothing more to do. Would not a true physician, like Hippocrates, desire that no one should have need of his art?

IX

I have dwelt at what may seem disproportionate length on the problem of evil, because it is really the point from which Plotinus takes his start and that to which he comes back at the last. The curious fact is that in the course of this circular process the very solid reality from which his philosophy sought a way of escape, at the touch of rationalism melts into an aerial nothing. His metaphysics makes a jest of his philosophy, or his philosophy makes nonsense of his metaphysics—as you choose. And it is because of the union of these two disparate and finally irreconcilable elements in Neoplatonism that any just summing up of its value is so difficult.

Undoubtedly the *Enneads* contain the record of genuine and profound experience which has

entered into the religious inheritance of the race.
Now religion of a vital sort is not a common possession; it is a flower whose root is always alive
in our barren human nature, but which blossoms
only here and there; it should be regarded, I sometimes think, as the last fine luxury of the soul,
so costly that, if it were got only by buying, few
would pay the price. What little grace of faith
we enjoy comes to most of us, when it comes, by
the gift of those pure minds endowed with spiritual genius, as our poetical sense is fed by the
genius of the great poets; and the religious imagination is the supreme faculty, rarer far among
men than the poetical imagination.[24] Multitudes

[24]Religious imagination I call this faculty of spiritual genius,
and the phrase is correct, for it is the power of vizualizing what
in its nature is incorporeal and invisible. St. Paul meant this
when he spoke (II Cor. iv, 18) of "the things which are not seen."
But Plato, of course, was the first and not the least great of
those who possessed the gift. It was he who made current the notion of the inner eye of the soul, and his allegories in the *Phaedrus* and *Symposium* are the finest examples in literature of the
spiritual imagination. But we must not disguise from ourselves
the fact that there is a certain danger in the use of this gift. For
after all we do not really see the unbodied world, and sometimes,
when the poetic fervour has cooled, the reaction leads us to question the very existence of a world whose reality seems to depend
on an imaginative illusion. The danger becomes acute in the
Neoplatonic exaggeration of the function of vision. Heinemann
well says (*Plotin* 210): "In der Zusammenhang der Grundbe-
griffe im Begriff der Schau, die auch als γνῶσις bezeichnet wird,
kann man eine Nachwirkung der Auseinandersetzung mit den
Gnostikern erkennen. Dennoch bleibt die Erhebung der Schau
zum Wesen aller Dinge die originelle These Plotins; andere sagen:
das Wesen der Welt ist Wille, andere: Unbewusstes, andere:
Willen zur Macht, andere: Wasser, andere: Luft, Plotin aber:
Schau." To make knowledge identical with the imaginative faculty of vision is to bring religion perilously close to poetry.

can speak glibly of that other world hidden behind the veil of sensuous phenomena, but to how
small a number does it seem to be a vivid reality.
As it was said in the ancient mysteries: many
carry the wand, the visionaries are few. And certainly Plotinus had that realization of things
spiritual which we call seeing. There are passages scattered through his work, in the fifth
Ennead particularly, that leave no doubt of the
fact,—passages which evoke the splendour of
this visible world with its variegated charm, and
then suffer it to fade away (as one picture of a
magic lantern is dimmed and overlaid and withdrawn by the imposition of another picture upon the screen), while in its place rises the glory
of the archetypal world, where we contemplate
things eternal in the kingdom of the god Kro-
nos, whose name is compounded of *koros* (fullness) and *nous* (everlasting mind). No writing
about these passages or scanty quotation can
convey their force; to be felt they must be read
in their completeness and by one capable of
sympathy. Such a reader will know that the inspiration of Plato was not lost, but passed from
generation to generation, as the lighted torch
was handed from rider to rider in the mysterious night race described in *The Republic*. If

Plotinus has not the perfect art of words and the creative genius of the author of the *Phaedrus* and the *Symposium,* the substance of the allegory is nevertheless there, and at times a precision and directness of expression which prove that he was no bare copyist but a master of things spiritual in his own right. So much must be granted—and it is very much—to the teacher of Neoplatonism, and so far his philosophy is genuinely Platonic. Had he only stopped here, or been content in his voyage over the wide seas of the spirit to enrich the contents of Platonism with the spoils of true discovery, instead of succumbing to the Siren voice of the metaphysical reason and its promise of the "ampler mind"!

> "For the shrill Sirens, couched among the flowers,
> Sing melodies that lure from the great deep
> The heedless mariner to their fatal bowers,
> Where round about them, piled in many a heap,
> Lie the bleached bones of mouldering men that sleep
> For ever, and the dead skins waste away.
> Thou through the waves thy course right onward
>   keep,
> And stop with wax thy comrades' ears, that they
> Hear not the sweet death-songs which through the wide
>   air stray."[25]

[25]*Odyssey* xii, 39 ff., Worseley's translation.—Cicero (*De Fin.* v, 18) read in the verses the same allegory of the lust of knowledge.

What harm, it will be asked, can come from dallying with the enchantress? Granted, as one grants of Plotinus, that the genuine spiritual experience is there, why should reason be checked in the full expansion of its powers, and prevented from erecting its hypothetical scheme of the sum of things? Why not accept metaphysics as a good gymnasium for the brain, if nothing more? What harm? Well, to begin with, I think that the faculty of reason itself suffers from this licence. Our main reliance in the decisions of life must always be on the distinctions and assimilations of reason, nor should it be supposed for a moment that the dualist who rejects a metaphysical rationalism is therefore blind to the superlative need of reasonableness. But in order to keep our guide in the jungle of appearances trustworthy, it is of prime importance that we should retain our sensitiveness to the difference between the act of reason dealing with the data presented to it whether in the sphere of the senses or the spirit, and the act of reason usurping the right to subvert the truths of experience to its own insatiable craving for finalities. And just this sensitiveness to truth is imperiled by the Neoplatonic rationalism. I think there is a real danger in reading incautiously the eighth book of the sixth *Ennead,* in which Plotinus argues back and forth the question of free will and determinism in the Absolute One. He who is carried away by this sort of logic, and allows himself to forget that the whole thing is a huge logomachy corresponding to nothing in the heavens or under the heavens or in the heart of man, is likely to suffer a deep vitiation of the mind, or, awaking from his illusion, may be converted, as Plato says, into a misologue, a hater of reason altogether.[26] For Socrates the beginning of philosophy as the wisdom of life was to know what we know and what we do not know, and just this distinction is lost by the metaphysician who deals with words and logical formulae which have no positive content.

But beyond this corruption of the reasoning faculty itself—*corruptio optimi pessima*—the indulgence in metaphysics may have a retroactive effect on the philosophy of which it is supposed to be a legitimate outgrowth. This result can be seen clearly enough in the two great departures of the Plotinian philosophy from the Platonic—the new conception of Ideas and the mysticism, which are so closely connected that it is difficult to say which of the two, if either, is cause and which effect.

[26]*Phaedo* 89 D.

When Porphyry joined the school of Plotinus at Rome, he brought with him from Athens the Longinian doctrine that Ideas exist outside of mind as separate entities of some sort, and that our knowledge of them is by a process of mental intuition corresponding to the physical perception of material phenomena. And this, with the kindred theory that the Ideas on which the Demiurge patterned the world have an objective and eternal reality, is certainly, in my opinion, the genuine Platonic tradition. One of the early acts of Porphyry in Rome was to read a paper supporting the Longinian view; but he was argued down by a fellow student, and at last recanted in favour of the contrary view inculcated by Plotinus.

Now for his theory that Ideas are *in* the mind, and only there, being no more than the noetic activity of the soul itself, Plotinus had abundant authority. In the first place he could go back to the pre-Socratic philosophy and quote the saying of Parmenides that "thinking and being are one and the same," and " 'I sought out myself' as one of the things that are."[27] For Plato himself he could refer to Aristotle's statement (certainly misleading if taken alone) that the

[27]See V, iv, 5, and compare Plato's rejection of the Parmenidean sentence in the *Sophist*.

place of Ideas according to the Platonic psychology was in the soul;[28] and Aristotle's doctrine of contemplation would support the same
view. The *logoi spermatikoi* of the Stoics were
essentially the Ideas of Plato reduced by the
compulsion of monism to the forces of genera-
tive reason acting *within* the material world of
phenomena. For a later age Plotinus had the
name of Philo, who taught explicitly that the
Platonic Ideas on which the Creator modelled
the world were simply the design in His own
mind, like the plan in an architect's brain when
he starts to erect a building.

But what chiefly led Plotinus to adopt this
theory of Ideas was, I think, a desire to escape
the arguments of the agnostic, with their tendency to materialism and moral indifference.
Sextus Empiricus, the historian of scepticism,
had insisted on the fact that our only knowledge
is of our immediate affections, while of the actual objective world behind our sensations we
can know nothing. Plotinus sees that the same
argument is valid for Ideas, and that here too,
so long as a distinction is maintained between
the soul and what affects it, there can be no absolute knowledge; we may know how we are af-

[28]*De An.* III, iv, 5.

fected, but there we stop. Reason is balked in its desire to define those spiritual forces which operate upon us out of the Ideal world and impose upon us the law of our moral being. This barrier of ignorance Plotinus would overleap by simply breaking down the distinction, and identifying the mind with Ideas. And at the same time he hoped to give a new and more precise meaning to the Delphic command of which Socrates and Plato had made so much: Know thyself. For, he says, if Ideas are not outside of the mind but in the mind, are in sooth nothing but mind in the act of reflecting upon itself, then to know one's self is to know Ideas and to know Ideas is to know one's self.

v, iii, 5, 6

v, v, 1, 2

v, viii, 11

All this is highly ingenious, and to many will appear a legitimate interpretation, or it may be development, of Platonism, as the only method by which the doctrine of Ideas can maintain itself against a critical analysis. But is it? On the contrary is it not the sort of subtle perversion that undermines while it professes to confirm? In the first place the defence is not necessary. It does not follow that Ideas must become nonexistent for us if we leave them as objects which in their inmost being we can never, as our faculties are now constituted, know. It does not

follow any more than that the material world
ceases to exist in itself if our knowledge of it is
confined to our sensations. Our immediate affections in the spiritual order may give us just
as positive a conviction that we are in contact
with an Ideal world as is our conviction of the
material world; it may be even far more real, as
touching the deeper strata of our being and as
governing our psychical life.

And, pragmatically, the change from the Platonic to the Neoplatonic conception of Ideas
points straight to that perversion of Ideas into
ideals which is the note everywhere of a pseudo-
Platonism. Now this distinction between Ideas
and ideals, though often ignored (partly perhaps because we have only one abstract deriva-
tive, "idealism," for both of them), has far-reach-
ing consequences. The sham Platonism amounts
simply to this, that there is no difference between truth and falsehood determined by the
correspondence of our ideals with immutable
spiritual facts. Genuine Platonism holds, on the
contrary, that there is a truth dependent on our
right apprehension of the power and operation
of the eternal and impersonal Ideas; it holds
that our happiness depends on the discovery of,
and obedience to, such truth. One must add, in

fairness, that the change from the idealism of
Ideas to that of ideals is softened in Plotinus by
his strong persuasion of a moral law pervading
all stages of evolution, and by his rather illogical tenet that in the order of evolution the *noêta,*
as the thoughts of Nous, precede *noêsis,* as the
thinking activity of Nous. But then, theoretically, the dominion of law can be maintained in
the monistic scheme of a Plotinus only by extending the sway of necessity to the deadly tyranny of a spiritual determinism. And, practically, a sham Platonism runs with headlong speed
into a kind of spiritual licence which teaches
that, if ideals are a part of the mind, then they
are ours; if we create them by our own good will
and pleasure, and are answerable to no person
or law for their objective truth, then in a word
we are free to believe and desire and hope as we
please. Man becomes the measure in the full
Protagorean sense of the phrase.

Mysticism is a word of various import, and
should not be allowed to pass unchallenged. It
may be used to signify any form of the supernatural, including a genuine Platonic Idealism;
it may denote an emotional pantheism such as
Wordsworth expresses in his *Tintern Abbey,*
or any vague anti-rationalism. But, more strict-

ly, it is a metaphysical and religious system cen-
tring upon that ecstatic union, that absorption
in God or the Absolute, in which all sense of
distinctions, all positive sensation or thought
or emotion of any kind, even consciousness, is
swallowed up in a vast nothingness. It is, to
borrow the rolling language of Sir Thomas
Browne, "Christian annihilation, extasis, exolu-
tion, liquefaction, transformation, the kisse of
the Spouse, gustation of God, and ingression
into the divine shadow."[29] The pseudo-Diony-
sius, who introduced the ecstatic philosophy of
Plotinus into Christianity and was thus the be-
getter of a long line of mystics through the Middle Ages and down to the present day, was as
precise in his description as words can be:

"Unto this Darkness which is beyond Light
we pray that we may come, and may attain unto
vision through the loss of sight and knowledge,
and that in ceasing thus to see or to know we
may learn to know that which is beyond all perception and understanding (for this emptying
of our faculties is true sight and knowledge),
and that we may offer Him that transcends all
things the praises of a transcendent hymnody,
which we shall do by denying or removing all
things that are. . . .

[29]*Hydrotaphia,* conclusion.

"It is not soul, or mind, or endowed with the faculty of imagination, conjecture, reason, or understanding; . . . It is not number, or order, or greatness, or littleness, or equality, or inequality; . . . It is not immovable nor in motion, or at rest, and has no power, and is not power or light, and does not live, and is not life; nor is It personal essence, or eternity, or time; . . . nor is It one, nor is It unity, nor is It Godhead or Goodness; nor is It a Spirit, as we understand the term, since It is not Sonship or Fatherhood; nor is It any other thing such as we or any other being can have knowledge of; nor does It belong to the category of non-existence or to that of existence; . . . It transcends all affirmation by being the perfect and unique Cause of all things, and transcends all negation by the pre-eminence of Its simple and absolute nature—free from every limitation and beyond them all."[30]

This, with the exception of a Christian term or two which are inessential, is a fair statement of the Plotinian mysticism carried to its ultimate expression. Evidently we have here a product of the same spirit of introversion and unification as that which deprived the Platonic Ideas of their substantive reality and merged them with the Nous. And just as evidently it bears the marks of the Aristotelian Absolute, grafted on

[30]*The Mystical Theology* ii and iv, translated by C. E. Rolt.

the religious sentiment of the age and transformed into a complete cause of being as well as
of motion. It immediately raises three questions:
(1) the fact of the experience, (2) the interpretation of the fact, and (3) the consequences of
the interpretation.

As for the fact, I do not see how it can be denied. The literature of the world, Oriental and
Occidental, is too replete with accounts of the
mystical experience to leave any room for intel-
ligent doubt. And these accounts are singularly
uniform in their method of describing a state
which they all declare to be, positively speaking,
indescribable, unrecordable, unrememberable.
Something has happened to these mystics, something which is unfelt, or dimly felt, by the normal man, but which cannot for that be laughed
or argued away. There is a real experience here
to be explained.

Doubt, or difference of opinion, becomes legitimate, however, when we listen to the interpre-
tations given by those who have had the experience. It is true that by turning inwards the mind
can brood upon physical sensations in such a
way as to forget the body and the world of material forces; but it does not follow hence that
the body and the material world are really elim-

inated as causes contributing to our physical sensations. It is true that by the same brooding introspection the mind can think of itself as the source and only place of the world of Ideas; but it does not follow that Ideas have really lost their independent existence as powers which affect our inner life. And so also it is true that by a kind of self-hypnotization the soul can withdraw itself from all distinctions of thinker and thought, engulfing itself in the vacuity of utter abdication; but again it does not follow that our words have any authority when we interpret this spiritual catalepsy as evidence of a final and absolute Unity at the heart of the world. One may suspect that a terrible confusion of emotional values has played into a like intellectual confusion to create a strange and fascinating philosophy.

As for the emotional values, one cannot read the lives of the great and the little mystics without being impressed by the constantly recurring association of the ecstatic experience with ill health, mental derangement, sodden stupidity, morbid excitability, moral degeneracy, downright criminality, erotic mania. "The one thing known about the religious [*i.e.,* mystical] experience is that its occurrence is invariably due to a combination of lowered vitality plus emotional excitement." Too often the results point to a "dissociation of ethical standards from religious standards" as the "fundamental characteristic of mysticism." I quote these words, with some hesitation, from a writer who, in her fanatical hatred of everything approaching the supernatural and in her no less fanatical devotion to what she calls science, would throw overboard much that in my judgment characterizes the higher reach of true religion.[31] I know the power and moral stimulation that have gone out to mankind from the lives of some of the greater mystics; and, indeed, my distrust of this whole side of religion has come to me only after long and intimate intercourse with mystical literature and somewhat against my instinctive sympathies. But the record is too clear and too disastrous; mysticism of the Plotinian type is almost certain evidence of a physical or mental or moral taint somewhere in the devotee. No doubt the psychology is complicated; the phenomenon may go with magnificent powers, with refined

[31]Anna Robeson Burr, *Religious Confessions and Confessants.* Miss Burr takes for the motto of her book these lines from *The Duchess of Malfi,* which her record justifies only too well:
"O this gloomy world!
In what a shadow or deep pit of darkness
Doth womanish and fearful mankind live!"

devotion, and the noblest traits of character; but in itself it is from the weakness, not the strength, of religious experience. To regard the momentary coma of the intellect as the crowning act of submission to the will of God and as the consummation of faith is a radical, often a dangerous, confusion of emotional values. One can see how, in the finer souls, the error takes place. The ecstatic absorption, so called, may be a blank, without meaning or content, induced by physical causes of a doubtful character; but afterwards, when the mind has awakened to the distractions and dismay of actual life, that moment of quiescence will be glorified by the magic of memory into a realization of the perfect peace of God which the pious soul always craves and never consciously knows. So much we can understand; but we need not suffer our judgment to be warped by such an illusion, or forget the dangers that beset it. As a matter of fact the Christian Church has shown a wholesome reluctance to sanction extravagances that, in weaker men, too easily run into spiritual debauchery; "for every mystic she has canonized, she has silenced ten."

The emotional claims of mysticism, I suspect, would be less tolerated, were they not doubled

by an intellectual confusion which, in the darkness of extinguished consciousness, one might
say, suddenly juggles our supreme ignorance
into absolute knowledge. The Platonic philosophy admitted that the Father and Creator was
hard to know and impossible to express. And so
Christian theology, of a thoroughly orthodox
type, has had much to say about our incompe-
tence to grasp the fullness of God's being, and
has been wont to insist on the fact that our finite
reason in striving to reach His ineffable glory
can only grope awkwardly in terms of negation.[32] "Only this I can say, what He is not," St.
Augustine declares. "And now, if you cannot
comprehend what God is, at least comprehend
what He is not; it is much for you if you do not
think of God otherwise than He is."[33]That is
the wise humility of reverence, the recognition
of the truth that before the inmost reality of
things the intellect of man must shrink to a pro-

[32]See *Platonism* 146.
[33]*De Trinitate* viii, 2.—In his *Theological Orations* II, 4, Gregory
Nazianzen rebukes Plato for saying (*Timaeus* 28 c) that God is
hard to know and impossible to express to all men. According to
the Christian theologian Plato's words were meant to convey a
subtle intimation that he really knew the divine nature which in
fact is beyond all human comprehension. Passages of this sort
might be multiplied indefinitely. It will not be out of place here
to add that my chosen phrase the "inner check" is used in this
philosophical and religious sense, not as denying the positive
reality of what is for us ultimately the divine faculty but as dis-
claiming immediate knowledge of its nature and *modus operandi*.

fession of its incapacity. And it does not follow
at all that such ignorance cuts man off from the
consolations of worship or even from a certain
fellowship with the divine personality. St. Basil
in one of his letters touches the matter with his
usual acumen:

" 'Do you worship what you know, or that of
which you are ignorant?' If we reply that we
worship what we know, then we are met at once
with the question: 'What is the essence of this
which you worship?' And if we admit our ignorance of His essence, we are overwhelmed with
the retort: 'Therefore you worship what you
know not.' But we say that 'to know' has more
than one meaning. For the majesty of God we
say that we know, and His power, and wisdom,
and goodness, and His providential care for us,
and the righteousness of His judgments; not
His essence. So that the question is unfair. Since
he who confesses ignorance of God's essence does
not thereby admit that we have no acquaintance
with God through those operations which we
have mentioned."[34]

The argument of the Fathers is clear and honest. Of God's works in the frame of nature and
in the human heart any man may have sufficient
understanding to guide him in the path of religion and to the peace of communion prepared

[34]*Epist.* ccxxxiv Migne.—For a like idea in Irenaeus and Tertullian see Kidd, *A History of the Church* I, 323.

for all trusting souls; of God's love and com-
passion we have sufficient revelation in the in-
carnate Son; but of God Himself and the ultimate mystery of the Divine only a fool will say
that he has understanding, as only a fool will say
that there is no God.

Philosophy and religion agree then in this,
that they both leave man in a combined state of
ignorance and knowledge, scepticism and faith;
they agree in telling us that we are morally responsible and intellectually impotent. But it is
against just such a limitation of its authority
that the *intellectus sibi permissus* rebels, and it
is just here that a metaphysical monism sets up
its claim. How, the doubter will ask, can we
comprehend the hypothetic One to which all at-
tributes are denied? How can we think of that
which is beyond thinking and thought? It might
seem as if metaphysics had deprived us even of
the practical half-knowledge vouchsafed by religious philosophy. But no: reason is resolute
and cunning; it is ready at hand to hypostatize
the very incomprehensibility of God's being into
a comprehensible Not-Being, saying to itself:
"Because I know Him not, therefore I know
His essence as pure negation." Taken alone such
a vaunt rather savours of verbal quibbling; there

is not much satisfaction for the hungry heart or
the ambitious brain in abstractions of this sort.
But joined to mysticism it acquires, and lends,
a factitious reality. By a coalescence of the illusion of the emotions with the legerdemain of
logic the fabulous Not-Being will impose itself
on the believer as an equivalent for the fullness
of infinite being, and the absolute One will seem
to be the negation of multiplicity only because
it embraces all things. Ignorance has swooned
into perfect knowledge.

The consequences of this metaphysical abuse
of an experience questionable in itself are written at large through the *Enneads* and the literature derived from them. As a protest against
the material monism of Epicurus and Zeno the
spirituality of Plotinus has a lasting religious
value; but as a spiritual monism it cannot avoid
the charge of running out into a mockery of
tantalizing paradoxes. Evil in this actual life
has been virtually juggled out of existence. In
the noetic heaven, conceived as universal Nous
lost in contemplation of its own thoughts, there
is no place for memory of our lessons in the phenomenal world, no continuity of moral responsibility, no spiritual adventure in a new world
of veritable Ideas, no place for the soul as an

enduring and individual entity, no immortality
that corresponds to the craving of human nature. In the final stage of absorption there is
nothing, no approach to a divine Ruler consciously engaged in the tasks of providence, no
communion with a personality who can feel as
man feels,—there is only the oblivion of a perfection that annihilates what is perfected. In a
universe so constituted worship becomes a vapid
form, faith loses its substance, hope is emptied
of comfort.[35]

The rationalism of Plotinus, like that of Epicurus and Zeno, was a self-willed effort to transcend the limitations which the dualist accepts
humbly as a necessity of our mortal state; the
inevitable result of grasping at the forbidden
Tree of Knowledge is to dissolve philosophy and
religion into the limbo of metaphysics. And the
end of metaphysics is a Pyrrhonic agnosticism
or a lapse into gross superstition.

[35]Plutarch, *De Defectu Orac.* 37: Εἰ δ' ἀλλαχόθι που κἀνταῦθα τῆς
᾽Ακαδημείας ὑπομιμνήσκοντες ἑαυτοὺς τὸ ἄγαν τῆς πίστεως ἀφαιρῶμεν, καὶ
τὴν ἀσφάλειαν ὥσπερ ἐν χωρίῳ σφαλερῷ, τῷ περὶ τῆς ἀπειρίας λόγῳ, μόνον
διασῴζωμεν.

CHAPTER VI

DIOGENES OF SINOPE

BEFORE taking up the final breakdown of the Hellenistic heresies in scepticism it will be in place to tell the story of the Cynic who, from a licensed beggar and buffoon, was transformed by the alchemy of tradition into the legendary saint of philosophy. In him the beginning and the end are curiously brought together.

Of the events of Diogenes' life, as generally of the early philosophers, little is related, and even what information we have is confused and more or less questionable. He was born in Sinope of Pontus, but left home as an exile. The cause of his banishment is said to have been a charge of counterfeiting brought against himself or his father; but this may well be a false inference from his famous maxim, "Remint the coinage,"[1] by which, playing on the double sense of *nomima* and *nomisma,* he meant to enforce the cynic

---

[1] Παραχάραξον τὸ νόμισμα. The phrase is variously translated: "remint the coinage," "falsify the currency," "restamp the mintage," etc.

transvaluation of all moral values. When reproached with the fact that the people of his
town had condemned him to exile, his reply was,
"And I condemned them to remain in Sinope."
At any rate to Athens he came, and there for a
while attached himself to Antisthenes, forced
himself on the unwilling teacher, it is said, by
vowing that no stick was hard enough to drive
him away. In time he became the typical Cynic,
accepting the epithet blandly with the remark
that if he was a "dog" it was not because he bit
his enemies, but because he snarled at his friends
for their salvation. Apparently he travelled about
a good deal, and more especially haunted the
Panhellenic games and other celebrations, where
among the crowds of idlers he could exercise his
gift of scoffing wit. He had his following, and
even seems at times to have given regular courses
of instruction, though how and where and in
what it is hard to say.[2] At some date in his career he was captured by pirates, and when put
up for sale in the slave-market greeted prospec-
tive purchasers with his customary insolence:
"Come, buy a master!" For a number of years
he served as pedagogue to the children of Xeni-
ades in Corinth, seeming to enjoy great liberty,

[2]For Diogenes as a serious teacher of philosophy see H. von Arnim, *Dio von Prusa* 37 ff.

whether as slave or freedman. He died in **323**
B.C. in extreme old age, on the same day, tradition said, with Alexander.

That is a scant biography, and in fact it serves,
as in the case of Aristippus, merely as frame-
work for a collection of the pithy sayings actually uttered by Diogenes or attributed to him.
From the mass of these memorabilia recorded
by his namesake of Laerte I select a few of the
more characteristic:—

"Once when Plato had invited him and certain
friends to dinner, Diogenes trampled on his rugs
with the remark, 'I am trampling on Plato's
vanity.' To which Plato, 'With what vanity of
your own, Diogenes!' "

"He went about with a lighted lamp one day,
saying, 'I am looking for a man.' "

"Once he was begging of a statue, and, being
asked why he did so, replied, 'I am learning to
meet with refusal.' "

"To the query when was the time to marry he
answered, 'For young men not yet, for old men
no longer.' "[3]

"He was entering a theatre when the crowd
was leaving, and being asked why, he said, 'This
has been my practice all my life.' "

To these anecdotes may be added a few from

[3]Diog. Laert. has τοὺς δὲ πρεσβυτέρους μηδεπώποτε. Surely the word
should be μηκέτι.

the numerous references scattered through Plutarch's *Essays:*—

"He said that the safest course for a man was to possess good friends and hot-tempered enemies; for the former will instruct him and the latter will lay bare his faults."

"To the question how one should get the better of an enemy he answered, 'By making one's self a true gentleman.' "

"When some one was praising Plato, he asked: 'Why should that fellow be proud, who has been playing the philosopher all these years and never caused a pang to any one?' "

"Catching a boy making a pig of himself, he gave a slap to the boy's guardian, rightly putting the blame not on him who had learned no better but on him who had taught no better."[4]

" 'These men are laughing at you, Diogenes.' 'But I am not laughed at.' "[5]

(On the possible blessings of exile): "Leisure, walks, reading, undisturbed slumber;[6] the boast of Diogenes, 'Aristotle breakfasts when it pleases Philip, Diogenes when it pleases Diogenes.' "

These braggart and for the most part petu-

[4]Cf. Sophocles, *Philoctetes* 387 f:

Οἱ δ' ἀκοσμοῦντες βροτῶν
διδασκάλων λόγοισι γίγνονται κακοί.

[5]The Cynic version of the Aristippean *Habeo, non habeor.*

[6]*Moralia* 604 D: Σχολὴ περίπατος ἀνάγνωσις ὕπνος ἀθορύβητος—could the scholar's life be described more beautifully?

lant sentences may look poorly for the baggage
of one who was to be the canonized saint of philosophy, yet if we examine them we can see how
they bear directly on the goal towards which all
the Socratic sects were striving. Security, in one
form or another, had been the aim of Aristippus
and of Antisthenes, as indeed it was of all their
followers; and above any one of them Diogenes
could boast this advantage from his philosophy,
"that he had prepared himself for every hazard
of fate." For what adversity could happen to a
man who was, in the words of the tragedian,

"Cityless, hearthless, reft of fatherland,
  A wanderer begging food from hand to hand"?

Socrates had attained security by character and
by the power of endurance; Diogenes would do
more, he would not wait upon the assaults of
Fortune but would go out voluntarily to meet
her. So, at the sight of a mouse running about
at night with no need of a sleeping place or fear
of the dark, he sets himself to harden life by
giving up everything save a few necessary uten-
sils. Later, when he sees a boy drinking out of
his hands, he even throws away the cup he had
retained. And when the little house he has ordered is not ready for him, he makes his abode

in one of the great water-jars lying by a temple.
So he would flout the hedonist, and prove that
"the contempt of pleasure is the truest pleasure
after all."

Liberty was the other lesson that the Socratics had learned from their master—unless it
should be called only a phase of security—and
liberty also was carried by Diogenes to the last
point of licence (*parrhêsia*). The tongues of ordinary men might be hushed by reverence or
fear, but not the genuine Cynic's. When Alexander stands beside him while he is sunning himself in one of the gymnasium courts of Corinth,
and asks if he would have any favour, his reply
is, "Yes, remove your shadow from me." Ordinary men might submit to the conventional de-
cencies of life out of respect for public opinion
if for no other reason, but not Diogenes: with
incredible effrontery he chose the open highways
to exhibit the most disgusting acts. Security and
liberty, he thought, were the fruit of obeying
nature and spurning law and custom; and in
this way he did, to the amazement of Philistine
and philosopher, effect the transvaluation of all
values of which the Sophists had talked, and
over which in these latter days certain so-called
naturalists still rave.

And the world was amazed, and did not forget. In the fragmentary state of our information we cannot trace all the steps by which Diogenes grew into a legendary figure, but the main course of the progress is pretty clear. At an early date collections of memorabilia were made, into which no doubt genuine and spurious anecdotes were thrown together with little discrimination. Any current witticism or bold story with the true cynical ring would naturally gravitate to the great exemplar of Cynicism. It was on these memorabilia chiefly that Diogenes Laertius drew for his so-called biography. Meanwhile the popular professors of philosophy were busy expanding and embroidering and altering. To Bion of Borysthenes, pupil of Crates who himself was a pupil of Diogenes, is ascribed the invention of the brief exhortatory address, the influence of which is still seen in the *Discourses* of Epictetus and in the earlier appeals of Christian preachers to the populace. So far as we can judge from the tradition there was little teaching of a positive sort in Bion, but mainly criticism of conventional life and morals in a cynical vein. To lend vivacity to his diatribes he employed freely the Socratic dialogue, in the form of terse question and answer, examples of which may be found in the works of Plato. But in Bion it is clear that Diogenes begins to displace Socrates as the spokesman of wisdom.

More is known of Teles, a wandering preacher and pedagogue of the third century B.C., who imitated and quoted Bion, and of whose diatribes considerable fragments have been preserved in abridgement. They are dry enough reading, at least as they have come down to us, but they have some value as indications of the way in which the legend of Diogenes was taking shape. And in the second discourse (Hense) the position of the Cynic philosophy between the optimistic endurance of Socrates and the dogmatic optimism of the Porch is shown in a manner not without historical interest. Teles is quoting Bion:

"As the biting of wild beasts depends on the way you take them—for instance, grasp a snake by the middle and you will be bitten, grasp him by the neck and you are safe—so our suffering from circumstances depends on the opinion we take of them. If your opinion of them is like that of Socrates, you will not suffer; otherwise you will be made to suffer, not by the circumstances themselves, but by your own character and by your false judgment. Hence we should not endeavour to alter circumstances, but to adapt ourselves to things as they are. . . . And

so, as I say, I do not see how there is anything
hard or painful in things themselves, such as old
age or poverty or exile."

Socrates would overcome the evils of existence by strength of character and by trust in the
ultimate justice of the gods; the Cynic makes
the power of endurance an active principle of
life, and attains security from fear of suffering
by his contempt of hardship as a force inferior
to his own energy, and so in a way regards evil
as a matter of opinion or self-estimation; the
Stoic will go a step further and will assert that
there actually is no evil in the world except as
our opinion, or judgment, imagines it to be. The
commonplace illustrations of endurance drawn
by Teles from the life of Diogenes I have omitted
in the quotation, but even without them the passage must commend itself as a curious and in-
structive blend of these three stages of philosophy.

The next step apparently was taken when
some unknown rhetorician published a number
of letters supposed to have been written by
Crates to his wife Hipparchia and to various
friends. The compositions are very brief for the
most part, consisting each of a few sentences on
some saying of Diogenes or on some common-

place of the Cynic school. In one Crates instructs
his disciples to beg the necessaries of life only
from those who are themselves initiated in philosophy, for by so doing they will be accepting
what is their own. Another note admonishes a
friend that the country does not always breed
innocence nor the city vice, and that if he desires
his children to be good he should not send them
into the country but place them under the care
of a philosopher; "for," Crates adds, "virtue
comes by training, and does not insinuate itself
into the soul automatically as vice does." Com-
menting to another friend on the security and
freedom and salubrity of the simple life, he con-
cludes: "The philosophy that effects these things
is the best of all; and if you do not find it elsewhere, you will certainly find it with Diogenes,
who discovered the short path to happiness."
And again the writer says: "Long is the path to
happiness by words and argument, but the study
by daily practice is short,"—which is good doctrine, whether preached by Diogenes or by whom-
soever. The most elaborate of the letters tells the
story of Diogenes' adventure with the pirates
as reported to Crates by one of the fellow victims who was sold into slavery and redeemed.
It is really an amusing little picture, ending

with the naïve statement that the pirates were
so impressed by Diogenes' words when offered
for sale that they took him down from the block
and carried him off to their haunts, promising
him liberty if he would impart to them his wisdom. "Wherefore," the reporter ends, "on my
return home I did not send a ransom for him,
nor did I ask you to send it; but do you rejoice
with me that he is living a captive among the pirates, and that such a thing has happened as few
men will credit."[7]

The spurious correspondence of Crates would
appear to be an early creation, and may go back
to the age of Teles. A similar collection of letters, attributed to Diogenes himself, and addressed to various friends ranging from Alexander to the supposed writer's mother, must, I
think, be of later date. There are fifty-one of
these epistles, neatly turned and cleverly phrased,
which form on the whole one of the most enter-
taining products from the rhetorical workshop.
And, again, the method of composition is simple
enough; in most cases the author merely takes
one of the sayings or doings ascribed to Diog-

[7] The story of the capture and sale of Diogenes probably has a
kernel of historic truth. It seems to have taken literary form
under the hands of the satirist Menippus. For the part played by
Menippus generally in creating the legend, see Rudolf Helm,
Lucian und Menipp 231 ff.

enes, and then about this builds up an imaginary
scene from his life, with details added to taste
and with more or less of moralizing. Thus, in
one letter, we have the story of the slave (not a
child, as in the source-book of Diogenes Laertius) drinking from his hands. Another repeats
the anecdote of the water jar, with the addition
that Diogenes got his hint from the sight of a
snail in its shell. Alexander turns up, of course;
he duly casts a shadow on the Cynic (who now
represents himself as pasting the leaves of a
book and needing light for the task), and he observes, as a true monarch should, that if he were
not Alexander he would be Diogenes. In one
note Crates is advised to beg of statues, and in
another he is admonished not to beg of men unless he can give a *quid pro quo* in moral help. An
anecdote in the Life tells how Diogenes read
over the door of a newly married man this inscription: "Heracles Callinicus, son of Zeus,
dwells here; let no evil enter," and how he mis-
chievously added the words: "An alliance after
the battle." This anecdote the letter-writer expands into the pretty tale of a visit to Cyrene,
where Diogenes sees the inscription over door
after door, and bids the citizens put "Poverty"
in the place of "Heracles" as a better safeguard

against calamity and temptation, or, if poverty
is too austere for their taste, then the word "Justice." So visibly before our eyes, the sturdy beggar and licensed scoffer is changing to a model
of righteousness; even his shocking indecency
is translated into a plea for the sanctity of nature which would satisfy the most emancipated
naturalist of the twentieth century. One of the
longer communications, to an anonymous friend
whom Diogenes has met at the Olympian Games,
closes in this highly edifying tone:

"But I weighed the gifts of those who offered
me bread, and from those who had profited I accepted, while the others I refused, thinking it
not a fair thing to accept from those who had received nothing. And I did not dine with every
body, but only with those who needed my service as a healer. . . . On one occasion I went to
the house of a very rich young man, and was received on a couch in a room hung all over with
pictures and decked out with gold—so fine indeed
that there was nowhere for a man to spit. Accordingly, when I choked with phlegm and,
glancing about, could discover no more suitable
place, I just spat on the youth himself. He began to scold at this; but I stopped him with the
words: 'You'—and I named him—'why do you
blame me for what has happened, instead of
yourself? Here you have adorned the walls and
floor of your room, and have left yourself un-

adorned as the only fit place to be so used.' 'Your language,' he replied, 'seems to intimate that I am an uneducated boor; but you shall not have a chance to say this to me again, for I am going to stick close to your side henceforth.' And in fact, on the very next day, he disposed of all his property to his family, put on the Cynic's knapsack, folded his cloak, and followed me. These things were done by me in Olympia after your departure."

These are the things, indeed, done by the Diogenes of the epistles, but one may doubt whether the words and deeds of the actual man were quite so pious in their intention. If the closing incident at Olympia reads like a caricature of a scene in the Gospels, where, however, the rich young man did not follow, but went away, leaving the Master sad, there is another letter which describes the conversion of Diogenes himself in a manner suitable almost, barring the whimsical conclusion, for the investiture of a Galahad in the insignia of Christian knighthood. The newly appointed Cynic is supposed to be writing back to the home he has recently left:

"I am at Athens, dear father, and, having heard that the companion of Socrates was teaching happiness, I betook myself to him. He chanced at the time to be lecturing about the paths leading thither. They are two, he was saying, and not many, the one short, the other long; and it lies with each man to choose for himself by which of them he will go. I listened and said nothing; but on the following day I returned to his house, and besought him to expound to us the nature of these two paths. He was quite ready, and, leaving his seat, took us into the city, and through the city straight to the Acropolis. And when we had come to its foot, he showed us that there were two paths up to the height, one short and steep and difficult, the other long and gentle and easy. And, 'these,' he said, 'are the ways leading to the Acropolis, and the ways to happiness are like them. Each of you may choose which he will, and I will be your guide.' At this the others shrank back in alarm from the difficulty and steepness of the shorter path, and begged him to conduct them by the longer and gentler; only I, feeling my superiority to hardship, preferred the steep and difficult road, for the desire of happiness was urgent upon me though it should carry me through fire and swords. And then, when I had chosen this path, he divested me of my robe and tunic, and threw about me a folded cloak, and hung a knapsack upon my shoulder, first putting in it bread and a bit of coarse cake and a cup and plate, and attaching to it outside an oil-flask and a strigil. He gave me also a staff; and so he fitted me out.

"And I asked him why the cloak he had thrown

over me was doubled. 'In order that I may train you for both states,' he replied, 'for the heat of summer and the cold of winter.' 'But why,' I asked, 'would not a single cloak suffice for that?' 'No,' answered he; 'that would be a comfort in summer, but in winter too great an infliction for human endurance.'[8] 'And the knapsack, why have you hung that upon me?' 'That you may carry your home about with you,' said he, 'wherever you go.' 'And the cup and plate, why did you put them in it?' 'Because,' said he, 'you must drink, and you must have something to go with your bread, nasturtium seed or the like.' 'And the oil-flask and strigil, why did you attach these?' 'One,' said he, 'is for your labours, the other for cleanliness.' 'And why the staff?' I asked. 'For security,' said he. 'Against what?' 'Against that for which the gods used it, against the poets.' "

The date of these letters cannot be determined exactly, but from their character it is pretty clear that they are earlier than Dio Chrysostom and Epictetus, by whose time the buffoon of Athens and Corinth has been completely transformed into a personification of sacred wisdom.

Dio was an eminent rhetorician of a distinguished family of Prusa in Bithynia, who, for court reasons, was banished from Italy and his

[8]Crates in one of his letters says that Diogenes never wore the Cynic's cloak.

native province in the year A.D. 82. During his
period of wandering exile he underwent a conversion from rhetoric to philosophy. Later he
came into court favour again, and was particularly intimate with Trajan. Apparently one of
the first fruits of his conversion was a group of
essays wherein the ardent acolyte in philosophy
preached Diogenes to a surfeited world as a
model of the simple life. And it is curious to see
how he constructs these essays. The method is
precisely the same as in the case of the letters,
except that, in place of little scenes from Diogenes' life drawn for moral edification, we now
have full-blown sermons, some of which might
have graced a Christian pulpit. So the fourth
Oration (Von Arnim) grows and expands out
of the reputed meeting with Alexander. The circumstances are described more minutely than
in the letter and have all the air of an historical
novel. The King is in Corinth on political business, and, telling his retinue that he desires to be
alone, goes off to visit the famous Cynic—not
to his door, for door or house the sage has none,
but accounts the whole city his home, and at
that particular time is residing at ease in the
court of a gymnasium. There Alexander finds
him squat upon the ground; and we are told

how, on being greeted, the Cynic looked up at the intruder with the savage glare of a lion, and bade him stand aside a little. Alexander, like the good prince in a fairy tale, admires the man's audacity; for that is the character of the brave everywhere, to love freedom and truth and to hate falsehood and flattery. Whereupon king and philosopher enter into a conversation, which trails out in a long lecture from the one on the virtues and duties of a ruler, with a few humble questions interposed by the other. And, as if that were not sufficient, another essay gives an extended comparison between the life of a philosopher and that of the Great King, all placed in the mouth of Diogenes, and all, needless to say, going to prove that in virtue and security and true happiness the beggar in his tub is infinitely superior to the Persian monarch in his palace.[9] It is a pity rather to find the burly ruffian thus smoothed out into a prig; but these common-places seem to have been listened to seriously at the time, and they have gone on echoing through literature down to a comparatively recent date. Bolingbroke's treatise on the *Idea of a Patriot King* is one of their latest man-

[9] A beautiful illustration of the way in which a true and practical thesis of Plato's (cf. *Gorgias* 470 E) is transformed by rhetoric into a flaunting paradox.

ifestations, and that idea, working in the mind
of George the Third, helped to make a good deal
of sad history.

Again Dio takes up the brief statement of
Diogenes' presence at the Games and develops
it into an edifying discourse in which the Cynic
appears at once as text and expounder. Now we
see him in the throng streaming from Corinth
to the Isthmian Games. Some one asks him if
he too is going to be a spectator, and he replies,
"No, but a contestant." And then, when his in-
terlocutor laughs and begs to know who his an-
tagonists may be, he launches into a terrific diatribe on his own mighty combats with pain and
pleasure as compared with the poor sport of
wrestlers and boxers. The moral of the sermon
is that the true athlete will go out to meet labour
and pain and grapple with them and throw them,
but the strongest man is he who flees the furthest
from pleasure, for pleasure is an antagonist never
to be conquered at close quarters. That is the
kernel of the matter; but Diogenes' exposition
must have held his travelling companion all the
way out to the sacred grove of Poseidon, where
no doubt the patient hearer made an escape.

Elsewhere we learn that Diogenes was the
original primitivist. Zeus punished Prometheus,

he thought, not in envy or hatred of mankind, but because the gift of fire was the source of luxury and all the woes of civilization. And when some one remarked that men are tender and naked and need artificial warmth as other beasts do not, Diogenes pointed scornfully to the frogs, who have less hair on them than men, yet can live comfortably in the coldest water.[10] As for the exhibitionism (if I may use the hideous word) by which Diogenes sought to shock men out of their complacent acceptance of conventions, there is no shirking the worst of it by Dio, on the ground that deeds speak louder than words, as no doubt they do; but the stories would corrode the paper of a modern book.

Dio is not altogether at his best in these resuscitations of the old Cynic. The invention is too palpable; and one is tempted to discredit his praises of poverty and hardship as meaning no more than the common trick of the rhetoricians who sought applause by their contorted encomiums of flies or smoke or baldness or gout or fever or vomiting or anything else calculated to astound an audience satiated with eloquence. Yet one cannot study the life of Dio or go

[10]Compare the Socratic retort to Protagoras (*Theaetetus* 161 c), that he might as well make a tadpole, instead of man, the measure of all things.

through all his Orations without feeling that
there was more in the man than this and that he
really had a message to deliver. The contrast between philosopher and tyrant may ring hollow
when Diogenes is represented as haranguing
Alexander in the gymnasium of Corinth, but the
common-places on the duties and toils of king-
ship take a different colour when actually pronounced by the same Dio before Trajan and his
court. "Do not fear that I shall flatter you," said
the preacher, facing the ruler of the world; "it
is long since I gave proofs of my independence.
Formerly [under Domitian], when everybody
felt obliged to prevaricate, I alone was not afraid
to utter the truth at the risk of my life. And now,
when there is permission to speak freely, I am
not likely to be so inconsistent as to surrender the granted liberty. And why should I lie?
To gain money, applause, glory? But money I
have never been willing to take, though often it
has been offered to me; and what fortune I possessed of my own, I gave away and dissipated
for others, as I should do today had I anything
to give." The saintly robes of the old Cynic may
have been the work of legendary weavers, but
his example was strong enough four centuries
after his death to inspire a few men who were

striving for simplicity and sincerity and abstinence in a society at once brutal in its excesses
and terrified by its doubts. And at times a higher
note breaks through the moralizing of a somewhat sentimental primitivism. The tenth Oration represents Diogenes as holding forth on the
true nature of man's intercourse with God, rebuking the common practice of praying for
worldly gifts and prosperity, and ridiculing the
folly of wresting the oracular commands into
permission to follow our own desires.

With Dio, notwithstanding the sincerity of
his conversion, one feels that he never quite put
off the old rhetorical man, and that always he
was as much interested in displaying literary
talent as in enforcing a moral truth. But with
Epictetus we enter into a purer region, where
no suspicion of vanity mars the effect. And this
change is felt immediately in his use of Diogenes. The old themes recur which the rhetoricians had worn threadbare, the same lessons are
drawn, but with a vigour and earnestness of
tone, with a breath of new inspiration, one might
say, that lift them into the plane of true philosophy. One of the traditional stories told how,
after the battle of Chaeronea, Diogenes was
taken prisoner and carried to Philip, and how,

being asked who he was, he replied: "A spy upon your insatiability." The witticism is remem-
bered by Epictetus; but now the world itself becomes the battle-field, and life a warfare, wherein the Cynic's mission is to release himself from
all other obligations in order that he may be devoted solely to the service of God. So it is he goes
to and fro among men, without being involved
in personal relations, which if he violates he will
lose his character as a good man, and which if he
maintains he will destroy the Spy and Messen-
ger and Herald of the gods that is in him. Hence
Diogenes lived without city or hearth or property or slave, sleeping on the ground, with only
earth and sky and one poor cloak for his furni-
ture, yet lacking nothing, blaming no man, fearing no man, the master of himself and of Fortune.[11] We, exclaims Epictetus, looking at the
Cynics of his day, "dogs of the table, guardians
of the gate," who copy those of old in nothing
except perhaps in dirty habits, do not compre-

[11]Compare the epigram of the Hindu Bhartrihari:
One boasted: "Lo, the earth my bed,
This arm a pillow for my head,
The moon my lantern, and the sky
Stretched o'er me like a purple canopy.

"No slave-girls have I, but all night
The four winds fan my slumbers light."—
And I astonished: Like a lord
This beggar sleeps; what more could wealth afford?

hend the measure of the greatness of Diogenes.
Otherwise we should not be astonished at his abstention from marriage and the getting of children. The true Cynic is parent of all men, has
all men for his sons, all women for his daughters.
Nor does he rebuke the erring in a spirit of conceit; he corrects them as a father, a brother, as
a servant of Zeus who is Father of all. Do you
think that Diogenes loved no one, he who was so
gentle and philanthropic that he cheerfully took
upon himself those great labours and burdens for
the common good of mankind? As befits a servant
of Zeus, he had always the care of the world at
heart, yet in submission to the will of Providence.
As Heracles accepted the commands of Eurys-
thenes, so did he not count himself wretched under the hand of discipline, or shrink from pain,
or cry aloud in indignation. When the pangs of
fever took hold of him, he called to the passers-
by: "Base creatures, will you not stay? You are
going the long way to Olympia to watch the ath-
letes matched in battle, yet you have no curiosity to see this contest between fever and a man."
And he won the victory, as Heracles won it, presenting himself to mankind with the glow of
health on his face, as an illustration of the plain
and simple life in the open air, a model of ready

wit and native grace, whose very squalor was cleanly and attractive. He was the true physician. "Men," he says, "you are looking for happiness and peace not where it is but where it is not. Behold I have been sent to you by God as an example. Try me, and if you see that I am at peace in mind, hear my remedies and learn of me how I found healing." Such was the philosopher thought by Zeus worthy of the crown and sceptre; such is the Kingdom of the Cynic, in comparison wherewith the power and riches and glory of the kingdoms of the earth are vanity.[12]

Evidently the Stoic sage, or wise man, so much debated in the schools, has taken on flesh and blood and proved himself a possibility in the person of Diogenes, while the philosophic ideal has been modified by assimilation to the historic hero of the tub. But the reader, I think, cannot fail also to be struck by a certain similarity between the Diogenes of Epictetus and the Christ of the Gospels, as one whose life was a lesson for all mankind; even the "kingdom of the Cynic" has a curious suggestion of the kingdom of heaven. But the parallel is incomplete, and in the mind of Epictetus it was entirely unconscious. The last step remained to be taken by Julian the

[12]Put together from *Discourses* III, xxii; III, xxiv; IV, viii. The language is largely that of P. E. Matheson.

Apostate, who gathered together whatever plausible hints he could find in Greek philosophy and mythology, blended them with Persian and other Oriental beliefs that had been overrunning the Empire, and out of the compound brewed a strange new religion which, as he hoped, would give to men all that was luring them to Christianity, while at the same time it would save the world from the threatened break with the nobler traditions of antiquity.

For centuries the need of a mediating divinity had been growing upon mankind. The old naïve faith, which had held the gods so close to human society, was shattered by philosophic speculation and general scepticism. Immorality had spread over the world like a sickly taint; it may be that men were no more subject to the flesh than they had been in earlier ages, but they were more aware of uncleanness and less able to keep apart their lustfulness and the normal activities of life. Local conventions had been swept away with local autonomy, and the Empire, which had swallowed up city and State in its all-leveling unification, had failed to check the moral disintegration, was in fact itself showing signs of inner decay and dissolution. From this distracted world the gods seemed remote, and faith was growing cold, or manifested itself in waves of cringing or hysterical superstition. One need only read the prose hymns of Aristides, of the second century of our era, to Zeus and Poseidon, and then, after these, his addresses to Serapis and Asclepius, to feel the difference between the chilly conventional reminiscences of a dead worship and the palpitating warmth of the new daemonic naturalism. Hence the growing demand, if the fair Pantheon of Hellas was to be preserved at all, for a mediating divinity between a troubled world and the far-off peace of the greater gods. Little help could be expected from pure reason. Indeed, the Neoplatonism which offered itself to Julian, with its effort to lift the object of worship into the rarified air of metaphysics where no human soul could breathe, had suffered the inevitable reverse by falling into mystery-mongering of the crudest sort. Meanwhile the Logos of the Christians, at once the ineffable glory of God and His wisdom present in the world, was supplying what paganism failed to give. Under the strain of such a need and with conscious reference to the success of this hated rival, the Emperor turned for succour to the Sun-God Helios, who belonged both to the lower realm of phenomena, whither his light came down with healing purity upon the living creatures of the earth, and to the upper realm of the divine, where he shone with spiritual radiance upon the gods, thus uniting the two worlds in one vast organism. Plato, in the sixth book of *The Republic,* had long ago shown how the sun, as a visible symbol of the Good, offered a meeting place for the Idealism of philosophy and the stately cult of Apollo, the sender of light and the patron of art; and with this faith of ancient Hellas could now be united the more emotional and mystical worship of Mithra, the young conquering deity out of the East. Hence Julian's *Hymn to Helios,* surely of all attempts to evoke religious fervour by a brave and deliberate effort of the imagination the most extraordinary, of all attempts to stay the deep tides of change the most pathetic.

Having thus, as he thought, found a substitute for the Christian Logos, the Emperor— and this at least is to the credit of his mind and heart—saw that little was accomplished until he had inspired the guardians of the renovated cult with the zeal and virtues of the Christian ministry. Hence his *Letter to a Priest,* which has the unction of a bishop's charge to his clergy[13] and the moral fervour of a Puritan exhortation. The impious Christians, he declares, have gained the ascendency and drawn men into atheism by their philanthropic care for the poor and neglected; and this virtue of benevolence must be adopted by the priests of the gods. Charity to all men, good and evil alike, they must practise, and in their conduct they must show such a spirit of purity and piety and holiness as befits those who have been set apart to be ministers to the gods, and clothed in the high honour of office in order to inspire reverence in the people. They are to be constant in prayer and service, not given to profane jests, avoiding the contamination of the theatres, reading only such literature as will strengthen them in wisdom and devotion. History does not always present the Christian priests of that age, and especially the ruling bishops, in a very favourable light; they appear often as proud and grasping and contentious and uncharitable, models of anything save the evangelical virtues of humility and brotherly

[13]It may be fanciful, but the style of Julian reminds me of the non-juring Hickes's *Treatises on the Christian Priesthood*. At least Hickes himself was not afraid of the parallel. "Julian," he says (Works I, 85), "was a serious pagan, . . . and I have cited these things out of his works concerning the common notion of priests and priesthood," etc. Julian, it should be added, was not always so flattering to the Christian priests, as, for instance, in his 52nd Letter.

love. And history no doubt has good warrant for its harsh judgment. Yet this letter of Julian cannot be left out of the account, and its testimony, wrung from a hostile witness, affords the strongest and most unexpected evidence that the great body of the clergy, the simple men whom historians forget, were walking in the quiet ways of duty and grace.

But something more was needed for the Emperor's revival than a mediating god in the heavens and a disciplined priesthood. Christianity proclaimed a Saviour who was God yet lived as man among men, and who, by his victory over the world, was an example and present help for all who were struggling to liberate themselves from the bondage of the flesh. The old pagan mythology offered fragmentary hints of such a mediator upon earth; there was Dionysus, the son of Zeus, who "came from India and revealed himself as a very god made man"; there was Heracles, who endured more than human labours to break the slavery of mankind and in the end was translated to Olympus in the flames of sacrificial fire, and there was Asclepius, the divine physician, "whom Helios, in providential care for the health and safety of men, begot as the saviour of the world." These myths Julian

adapted to his creed; but most of all his imagination was kindled by the story of Diogenes, as
a helper more comprehensible than the half-
gods and heroes of the poets and as not less divine though fully human. Like Socrates, the
Cynic in his rough exterior resembled the Sileni
that sat in the shops of the statuaries, while within they contained the beautiful images of the
gods. But the wisdom of Diogenes was deeper
than that of Socrates and more immediately inspired. "The founder of this philosophy," Julian writes in his address *To the Uneducated
Cynics,* "is he who, I believe, is the cause of all
the blessings that the Greeks enjoy, the universal leader, law-giver, and King of Hellas, I
mean the God of Delphi. And since it was not
permitted that he should be in ignorance of
aught, the peculiar fitness of Diogenes did not
escape his notice. And he made him incline to
that philosophy, not by urging his commands
in words alone, as he does for other men, but in
very deed he instructed him symbolically as to
what he willed, in two words, when he said, 'Falsify the common currency.' For 'Know thyself,'
he addressed not only to Diogenes, but to other
men also and still does: for it stands there en-
graved in front of his shrine." And then in a

succession of striking paragraphs Julian expounds this philosophy of which Diogenes is the spokesman and personification, and by which he was raised up to be the saviour of mankind.

Now the goal of the Cynic doctrine, as of all genuine philosophy, is happiness, and happiness consists in living in accordance with one's nature. So to live is to recognize the godlike part of one's being, the soul, or reason, as the true man; and this is to know one's self. Such is the first command of Apollo, which all visitors may hear and read. And the second command, which only Diogenes comprehended in its full scope, was like unto it, "Remint the coinage." The coinage is simply the mass of current customs and conventions; and these the Cynic must disregard, stamping a private currency for himself, so to speak, with the image of his own inner nature. What has he to do with the opinions of the deluded mob? Men are trading for honours and riches and the comforts of life, which they regard as precious and worthy of labour and sacrifice. Not so Diogenes, who owned nothing, toiled for nothing, desired nothing, envied no man, caring only "to loaf and invite his soul":

> "Cityless, hearthless, reft of fatherland,
> A wanderer begging food from hand to hand."

But to exhibit the complete mastery of the soul and to express in visible deeds the false standards of society the Diogenes of the Roman Emperor went beyond mere renunciation to a contemptuous "abuse of the flesh." The body was a slave, and should be treated as such:

"Then let him who wishes to be a Cynic, earnest and sincere, first take himself in hand like Diogenes and Crates, and expel from his own soul and from every part of it all passions and desires, and entrust all his affairs to reason and intelligence and steer his course by them. For this in my opinion was the sum and substance of the philosophy of Diogenes. And if Diogenes did sometimes visit a courtesan—though even this happened only once perhaps or not even once—let him who would be a Cynic first satisfy us that he is, like Diogenes, a man of solid worth, and then if he see fit to do that sort of thing openly and in the sight of all men, we shall not reproach him with it or accuse him. . . . He must show the same independence, self-sufficiency, justice, moderation, piety, gratitude, and the same extreme carefulness not to act at random or without a purpose or irrationally. For these too are characteristic of the philosophy of Diogenes. Then let him trample on vaingloriousness, let him ridicule those who though they conceal in darkness the necessary functions of our nature—for instance the secretion of what is superfluous—yet in the centre of the market-place and of our cities carry on practices that are most brutal and by no means akin to our nature, for instance robbery of money, false accusations, unjust indictments, and the pursuit of other rascally business of the same sort. On the other hand when Diogenes made unseemly noises or obeyed the call of nature or did anything else of that sort in the market-place, as they say he did, he did so because he was trying to trample on the conceit of the men I have just mentioned, and to teach them that their practices were far more sordid and insupportable than his own. For what he did was in accordance with the nature of all of us, but theirs accorded with no man's real nature, one may say, but were all due to moral depravity."[14]

In this way the Cynic interpreted the public command of Apollo to "know thyself," and modelled his life on the private command to "falsify the currency." So he rendered himself the happiest of all men, happier than Alexander or the Great King; and so, as Julian believed, he might be upheld as the supreme exemplar of a philosophy capable of liberating the soul from the dominion of hypocrisy and of withdrawing mankind from the delusions of a false Saviour.

Our first reflection may be that a philosophy

[14]From Mrs. Wilmer Cave Wright's translation in the Loeb Library.

which could find no cleaner exemplar than Diogenes was bankrupt and ready to be swept away. And then the question may arise: Why was this coarse ruffian rather than Socrates chosen by men like Epictetus and Julian for canonization? Philo Judeaus, in his *Quod Omnis Probus,* makes much of the story of Diogenes' capture and sale, and ranks the hero of that adventure among his specimens of Stoic, Jewish, and Hindu sages. Even so thorough-going a Platonist as Plutarch succumbed almost to the tradition, and clear-headed divines like Basil and Gregory Nazianzen were not exempt from the spell.[15] The climax came when, under Theodosius, a professed Cynic of the Diogenic stamp was almost made bishop of Constantinople. Diogenes was canonized I think, because in him more ostentatiously than in any other philosopher, even more completely than in Plato's master, was seen the exemplification of that longing for security and liberty which had attached so many diverse minds to the teaching of Socrates. There is a passage in the oration of the good Platonist, Maximus of Tyre, on the *Superiority of the Cynic Life* that brings this out quite clearly. Which, Maximus asks, of the men commonly praised by the

[15]Basil, *Quomodo Possint ex Gentilibus Libris* 583 в Migne; Gregory, *Ep.* xcviii.

unthinking multitude is really free: the demagogue, the orator, the tyrant, the general, the sea-captain? Each of these is in fact the slave of other men or of his own passions or of fortune. But the philosopher? Yes, but what kind of philosopher, he asks; and then replies to his own query:

"I am ready indeed to praise Socrates; but then his words occur to me: 'I obey the law and go voluntarily to gaol, and take the poison voluntarily.'—O Socrates, do you not see what you are saying? Do you then yield voluntarily, or are you an involuntary victim of fortune?— 'Obeying the law.'—What law? For if you mean the law of Zeus, I commend the law; but if you mean Solon's law, in what was Solon better than Socrates? Let Plato answer to me for philosophy, whether it saved him from perturbation when Dio fled, when Dionysius threatened, when he was compelled to sail back and forth over the Sicilian and Ionian seas. . . . Wherefore I say that from this tyranny of circumstance the only liberation is in that life which raised Diogenes above Lycurgus and Solon and Artaxerxes and Alexander, and made him freer than Socrates himself."

So it was that by his renunciation of all things, even of philosophy, Diogenes attained to perfect liberty and safety. Socrates still clung to the

conventional law of the city; he was not bold
enough to falsify the currency. Plato might establish a dominion over the minds and hearts of
men by the power of his intellect and the majesty of his imagination, but for what he achieved
there was the need of culture and long quiet
years and many gifts of chance. What would the
name of Plato be now had he not escaped from
the court of Dionysius? What would have been
his peace of soul had he remained a slave in the
island of Aegina? In the days of Julian a Plato
might have held the place in philosophy which
the great bishops and enemies of the Emperor,
such as Athanasius and Gregory, occupied in the
Church. True servants of God they might know
themselves to be, and without them Christianity
might have suffered corruption and perished;
but something still, in their own conscience, was
wanting, something still required, as men then
thought, for their complete liberty in the service
of God and for their emancipation from the
world. And so Gregory, the eloquent theologian
who saved the doctrine of the Trinity, was never
weary of extolling the retired and silent and
untroubled lives of the eremites; and Athanasius, the master statesman of the Church, who
stood unflinchingly *contra mundum,* wrote his

biography of that fanatical anchorite, St. Anthony, as of one who had reached a perfection of Christian character denied to him by his duties in the world. Anthony and Diogenes were poles apart in their faith and in certain aspects of ascetic practice. Instead of the utter shamelessness of the Cynic, the Christian was so far subject to shame that he would never bathe or in any other way expose his naked body to his own eyes. Yet the two were one in their absolute *contemptus mundi* and in their consequent fearlessness and indifference to the conventions of society. I think the motive that impelled Athanasius to idealize Anthony was not unlike that which led Julian, the philosopher in the world, to turn from Socrates to Diogenes for his model of philosophy out of the world.[16]

And Diogenes alone, or let us say the legendary Diogenes, could stand with the martyrs of the Church, as he stood with the terrible ascetics; and in the readiness to meet martyrdom joyously men had come to see the final test of faith, whether in religion or philosophy. It might seem as if Socrates would have served such a purpose better than Diogenes, for he had in fact faced

[16]One seems to see a direct continuation of the Cynic tradition in such antics, often disgusting, of the "fools of Christ" as Miss Underhill records in her *Jacopone da Todi* 14, 62, 63, 64 *et passim.*

death for his convictions and conquered its fears.
But if Socrates had suffered the momentary or-
deal, it was yet, as Maximus asserted, in a spirit
of submission to the law; whereas the whole existence of Diogenes might be regarded as a voluntary and triumphant martyrdom in protest
against any compromise with social conventions.

And there was another cause for the choice.
The death of Socrates, as had been his life, was
too calm and reasoned to satisfy the religious
craving of that age. Julian might make a brave
pretence of appealing to the verdict of intelligence, but at heart he was a child of his own generation, and for centuries the world had been
growing further and further from the old hope
of finding salvation in the clear conception of
truth and of what we know and do not know.
The change shows itself in the eclectic merging
of the various, even contradictory, sects of philosophy, with a vein of Neopythagorean obscur-
antism predominating over all. It is notable in
the waves of emotional superstition that were
supplanting the humanized mythology of Olympus. Most conspicuously it is seen in the victory
of the Christian faith, foretold by St. Paul in the
declaration that God hath "made foolish the
wisdom of this world," and verified in the exult-

ant cry of Tertullian, *Quia ineptum est! quia impossibile est!*[17] Over and over again we find the Fathers, even those most favourably disposed to Plato and most ready to admit that God had not left Himself without a witness among the gentiles—again and again we find them reproaching philosophy with its inability to convert the stubborn hearts of men and to save the masses. And the Fathers were right. In whatever terms we may choose to state the fact, it is true, as Ambrose said, that "it hath not pleased God to give His people salvation in dialectic."[18] It is simply true that, in setting the emphasis so strongly upon knowledge and intelligence and in leaving so little room for the will and the instinctive emotions, classical philosophy, even the philosophy of Plato, had left the great heart of mankind untouched. Christianity, by transferring the source of good and evil to the will and by appealing more directly to the emotions and imagination, had in a measure succeeded where philosophy had failed—yet, even so, how small has been that measure of success!

Looking back over all that Christianity has done and has not done, we may ask ourselves

[17]*De Carne Christi* 5. The exclamation of Tertullian has been popularized, but scarcely travestied, in the maxim, *Credo quia absurdum.*
[18]*De Fide* i, 5: *Non in dialectica complacuit Deo salvum facere populum suum.*

whether God meant to save His people by the
emotions alone any more than by the understanding alone; we may broach the question
whether the tragedy of Christianity was not just
there, in its failure to achieve, or at least to impose on the world, a sound combination of dialectic and emotionalism. The effort was made,
no doubt, and made nobly, but it was never carried to a conclusion. Clement of Alexandria perceived the need fairly enough, and sought to
blend Platonism and Christianity, reason and
faith, knowledge and feeling; and in some respects his endeavour marks the most dramatic
moment in the whole period we are studying.
But Clement's in the end was a confused brain,
that left him fumbling in shadows. And though
after a fashion his work was carried on and clarified by Athanasius and the great Cappadocians,
the stream of theological thought was largely
deflected by his successor Origen from the direct
course of Platonism into the blind channels of a
Neoplatonic mysticism.[19] In the West also theology received a strong Neoplatonic bent from
St. Augustine; and then, soon after the close of

[19]It is not quite precise, of course, to call Origen a Neoplatonist
if we confine that term to the school of Plotinus. But Origen
was a fellow pupil of Ammonius Saccas and carried a good deal
of that philosophy into his Christian theology.

our period, there flowed over East and West alike
the desiccating winds of Aristotelian scholasticism. As a consequence our Latin Christianity
has been largely a mixture of unbridied emotion,
running up into pure mysticism, with scholastic
metaphysics—a mechanical, unstable mixture
and no true marriage of the intellect and the
will. The consummation of the movement in the
Occident is found in the theology of Thomas
Aquinas, from which the veiled rationalism of
Calvin and Luther was a revolt, inevitable no
doubt, but in the end more destructive of religion than the disease it sought to cure. I cannot
see any other escape: if the world is to be saved
by religion, if salvation is anything more than
an idle word, which, like Brutus, we have pursued in the vain belief that it was a reality, our
hope would seem to lie in a return to the path
indicated by Clement. There we must push on
where the Greek theologians groped for a while,
grew faint, and fell away.

But this is a digression. The main stream of
philosophy by the time of Julian was stagnating
in the bogs of emotionalism; even the mysticism
of Plotinus had lost its metaphysical backbone
and had loaded itself with the jumbled supersti-
tions of an Iamblichus and other baser necro-

mancers who possessed the ear of the court. In that atmosphere one can understand how a Diogenes should have been selected for the idealized personification of otherworldliness.

To be sure there were recalcitrant voices. At an earlier date, yet in the full tide of the legend, Lucian had satirized the philosopher of the tub as an audacious swaggerer, preaching his Cynicism thus to gods and men:

"The traits that you should possess in particular are these: you should be impudent and bold, and should abuse all and each, both kings and commoners, for thus they will admire you and think you manly. Let your language be barbarous, your voice discordant and just like the barking of a dog: let your expression be set, and your gait consistent with your expression. In a word, let everything about you be bestial and savage. Put off modesty, decency, and moderation, and wipe away blushes from your face completely. Frequent the most crowded places, and in those very places desire to be solitary and uncommunicative, greeting nor friend nor stranger; for to do so is abdication of the empire. Do boldly in full view of all what another would not do in secret; choose the most ridiculous ways of satisfying your lust; and at the last, if you like, eat a raw devilfish or squid, and die. That is the bliss we vouchsafe you."[20]

[20]*Philosophies for Sale,* translated by A. M. Harmon.

The satire is bitter enough, and closer to the original, one may well believe, than the tradition that was concealing the cloak of the sturdy old beggar under the drapery of a "fair soul." But Lucian was a mocker by profession who spared nobody, and it remained for a Christian preacher to say the last word on the subject. St. John Chrysostom certainly had Diogenes in mind, and so far was just, when he pronounced his criticism of the long search of our Hellenistic philosophers for the security and liberty of religion within the closed circle of naturalism: "Such was the philosophic life of the Greeks, but it was idle. They could make a show of austerity, but to no purpose, for they had no salutary end to which they looked; their eyes were set on vanity (*kenodoxia*) and on honour from men."[21]

[21]*In Eph.* 91 A.—Theodoret, *De Virtute Activa*, Col. 1132 Migne, has the same idea: Οὐ γὰρ ᾽Αντισθένει καὶ Διογένει καὶ Κράτητι παραπλησίως κενῆς δόξης, ἀλλ᾽ αὐτοῦ γε εἵνεκα τοῦ καλοῦ δρῶσιν ἃ δρῶσιν.

CHAPTER VII

SCEPTICISM

I

AFTER his haphazard manner Diogenes Laertius, in his life of Pyrrho, mentions various doubters who anticipated the founder of the school of Scepticism, such as Homer, and Euripides, and Zeno the Eleatic, and Democritus, and Plato, but does not name Socrates. Yet if the *Apology* reproduces, as it surely does, the genuine opinions of the master, one can scarcely avoid including the sceptics in the great and quarrelsome family of Socratics. Indeed, all that Pyrrho was to teach, with something more, is really implicit in the famous utterance on death: "Strange it would be if now, when the god, as I firmly believe and am convinced, bids me stand forth as one devoted to wisdom, a questioner of myself and all the world, I were to desert my post through fear of death or any other thing. . . . For the fear of death, my friends, is only an-

other form of appearing wise when we are foolish and of seeming to know what we know not.
No mortal knoweth of death whether it be not
the greatest of all good things to man, yet do
men fear it as knowing it to be the greatest of
evils. And is not this that most culpable ignorance which pretends to know what it knows
not?" The Epicurean sought for the admired
security and liberty of Socrates in the path of
pleasure; the Stoic looked for peace rather in the
contempt of pleasure and in the strength of endurance; Pyrrho, whether consciously or not,
laid hold of the Socratic doubt for the same end.
For leave out the spiritual affirmation of Socrates, his belief in the gods and in the eternal
reality of justice, as the Epicurean and, less
frankly, the Stoic also left it out; translate his
avowed ignorance in the face of alternative views
into suspension of judgment (*epochê*) ; for
"questioning" (*exetazein*) substitute "searching" (*skeptesthai*) ; for the resulting fearlessness use the term "tranquillity" (*ataraxia*) , and
the broad foundation of Pyrrhonism is laid, while
only the superstructure remains to be raised.[1]

That would seem to be clear enough, and, considering the influence of Socrates and the affini-

[1]See Appendix B.

ties between the school of Pyrrho and the later
Academy, I have no doubt the affiliation is historical as well as logical.[2] More immediately, however, Pyrrho would seem to have come under the
influence of the Democritean school, perhaps
through association with Anaxarchus, of that
sect, in whose company he followed Alexander
on the march into India. On his return from this
expedition Pyrrho settled at Elis, his native
town, where, with his sister, he lived in dignified
simplicity, dying in extreme old age about the
year 270.

How far Pyrrho assumed the rôle of teacher
it is not easy to say. Apparently he wrote nothing except perhaps a poem addressed to Alexander, and what wisdom he had to impart was
conveyed chiefly in pithy phrases and catch-
words, such as "No more" (*scil.* this than that),
"I decide nothing," "Balance" (*scil.* of evidence
and views), "Incomprehensibility," "Suspension" (of judgment), "Silence" (*aphasia,* "refusal to speak"), "Tranquillity." According to
his successor, Timon of Phlius, his philosophy
was a search for happiness, summed up in three

[2]According to Cicero the sceptics regarded themselves as followers of Socrates: *Fuerunt etiam alia genera philosophorum
qui se omnes fere Socraticos esse dicebant, . . . Pyrrhoneorum*
(*De Orat.* iii, 17).

questions: (1) What is the nature of things?
(2) What should be our attitude to them? (3)
What will be the result to us of such an attitude? To the first of these questions the Pyrrhonist will reply that we have no means of determining whether or not our sensations and
opinions correspond with the objects themselves, so that in their ultimate nature things are
for us indistinguishable and incommensurable,
and there is no court of appeal for settling our
differences about them. As Democritus said, it
is customary to call one sensation hot and another cold, but beyond that we know nothing,
and truth lies buried. Hence the answer to the
second question: we can put no faith in our opinions, and should hold our judgment in suspense,
saying simply in regard to each matter that it is
or is not, or both is and is not, or neither is nor is
not.[3] And, thirdly, the result of this refusal to
decide will be that unsolicitous state of mind
which may be called tranquillity, ataraxy, and
which, as Timon added, follows upon suspense
of judgment as its shadow.[4]

[3]These are precisely the replies Buddha used to make to those
who inquired about the entity underlying our sensations and to
metaphysical questions generally.

[4]The questions are quoted from Aristocles, a late Peripatetic,
by Eusebius (*Praep. Ev.* XIV, xviii, 2). The answers, as I give
them, are from Aristocles with some additions from Diogenes

How Pyrrho carried his conclusions into the test of life we may illustrate by his use of a pig, a philosopher, and a dog. For the first, being once at sea and caught in a storm, he rebuked the terror of the passengers by pointing to a little pig that kept on feeding through all the commotion, and declared that such ought to be the tranquillity of the wise man.[5] For the philosopher, we are told that once when he saw Anaxarchus fallen into a pond, he passed by without offering assistance—a display of philosophic calm of which the victim is said to have approved. But it was not always thus. When reproached for showing fear at the attack of a dog, he excused himself even more philosophically by observing that it is hard to put off the whole man.

Pyrrho at best, though he imposed his name on one of the greatest of all schools of thought, remains a shadowy figure, and it is impossible to separate with precision his own views from

Laertius.—Brochard (*Les sceptiques grecs* 71 ff.) makes ἀδιαφορία, resignation or complete renunciation, rather than ἐποχή, intellectual doubt, the keynote of Pyrrho's teaching, and believes that he was strongly influenced in this by observation of the Hindu gymnosophists.

[5] Yonge has a delicious version of this story in the Bohn translation of Diogenes Laertius: "He kept a calm countenance, and comforted their minds, exhibiting himself on deck eating a pig." I have fallen upon a good many strange blunders in the course of my reading, but never on a more diverting one than this.

those of his followers. But the tradition is probably in the main true, and if the three questions and their answers, as formulated by Timon, give the substance of his philosophy of life, I think we must admit that he laid down all that is essential to scepticism, and that later scholars, whether ancient or modern, have done no more than develop his axioms. The great philosophies, however rich their contents may be, rest finally on the simplest common-places of experience; and it is the honour of Pyrrho that he grasped the conscious sense of ignorance inherent in the minds of all men, penetrated to its source, and applied it relentlessly where other men faltered or drew back. Our criticism of the value and significance of scepticism we shall defer until we take up the systematic and historic work of Sextus Empiricus; but we shall not forget that the title of originator and master of the sect belongs to the obscure doubter of Elis.

From Pyrrho the defence of scepticism passed to the hands of Timon, not the misanthrope of that name, but one who might be called the *misophilosophe*. He was a wine-bibber; and he also wrote poetry, tragedies and comedies—which business, the historian naïvely observes, is scarcely fit for a philosopher, as if wine-bibbing were quite in the line of his profession. The dramas, fortunately for us perhaps, are all lost; but we have a few fragments from his three books of Silli, or Lampoons, which evidently were bitter and impudent enough to make a sensation. He seems to have possessed a full command of the terminology of abuse, compounded of far-fetched and often archaic words, such as had delighted the audience of Aristophanes, and these he poured out on the dogmatic philosophers, living and dead, with magnificent impartiality. In mock-Homeric language he describes the contentious Muse of philosophy as a pestilence walking among men:

"Waster of spirit and an empty sound!
Wherever discords of the brain abound,
There the dark sister of debate is found.

"Who sent this strife of tongues that twist and lie?
Silence is mobbed by mouthing ribaldry;
The talking-sickness comes, and many die."

A few chosen prophets of doubt are spared the lash, and notably, of course, Pyrrho, the eponymous hero of the school, who alone had learned the secret of a quiet and easy life, devoid of controversy and pretension, and heedless of the wiles of a deceitful wisdom. Only he, Timon says, as Lucretius afterwards was to say of Epicurus, had discovered how to enjoy upon earth the blissful calm of the gods.

II

But if Timon could sing the praises of peace, he certainly did not walk in the way thereof. It was in his days that Arcesilas changed the school of Plato into the so-called Middle Academy, which pretended to be more logically sceptical than those who had usurped the name of sceptics;[6] and it was particularly against Arcesilas, as his nearest rival in the field, that Timon's rage was directed, in accordance with the verse of Hesiod, often quoted by the sectarians from Plato down, to the effect that "potter is the natural enemy of potter, and poet of poet, and beggar of beggar." "What are you doing here where we freemen are?" was Timon's genial remark to Arcesilas, when they met one day in a public place; and at another time, to the query why he had come from Thebes, his answer was, "To be where I can laugh at you face to face." It was a

[6]Though Arcesilas and Carneades called themselves Academics, their purpose would seem to have been to reject what they regarded as the dogmatism of Plato for the more completely sceptical attitude of Socrates. That at least is the view of Cicero, *Acad. Post.* i, 16.

merry battle, no doubt, replete with joy for the
witty *flâneurs* of Athens, and so long as Timon
lived Zeus held the scales equal; but very soon
the bastard sons of Plato triumphed over the
children of Pyrrho, as later they brought confusion among the children of Zeno, and for a
hundred years and more the Academy was the
acknowledged home of scepticism. Until the rise
of Aenesidemus, if there were any avowed Pyrrhonists, they are the shadows of a name and
nothing more.

Of the actual teaching of Arcesilas we know
very little, and still less of his successor Lacydes, save the foolish but not insignificant story
which I have related in the chapter on the early
Stoics. The Middle Academy attained its full
growth under Carneades, who presided over the
school until his death in 129 B.C., and of whom,
thanks mainly to Cicero, we have more definite
information. Carneades was a subtle dialecti-
cian and pugnacious fighter; philosophy for him
consisted not so much in what could be deduced
from the doctrines of his nominal and remote
master, as in what could be said against his very
near enemies of the Porch. Now the Stoics,
craving some final stay for the mind and conscience, had developed a pure rationalism based

on the assumption that certain knowledge of the
truth can be obtained from the senses. Starting
then from the sensations which convey knowledge in the form of a mechanical impression on
the mind, they created a theory of the world as
a vast fatalistic machine. But at the same time,
with a fine inconsistency, their rationalism, forgetting its origin in the mechanical laws of gross
matter, produced its own theory of the world as
a process of evolution absolutely determined by
a divine indwelling reason. In either case the
logical end, whether mechanistic or pantheistic,
was to shut up the human spirit in a prison
house of Destiny, without door of exit or win-
dow of outlook. The only escape from this out-
rageous restraint was to attack the principles of
sensationalism and rationalism as adequate instruments of the truth, or as capable of giving
us any knowledge of things as they are in themselves; and this attack made the joy of Carneades' life. With the sensational hypothesis of the
Stoics, based on a self-evident distinction between true and false impressions, he made short
shrift; it was, indeed, as we have seen in an earlier chapter, vulnerable from every side. Manifestly the criterion by which we distinguish between truth and falsehood, if it exist at all, must

be sought outside of the sensations themselves. But no such criterion can be found in reason. This fact Carneades demonstrated by bringing out certain fallacies inherent in the syllogism, and, more generally, by showing that every rational proof depends on premises which themselves need to be proved, and so on *ad infinitum*.

The result was a complete scepticism; neither sensation nor reason can carry us beyond the circle of appearances. And this destructive analysis of the instruments of knowledge Carneades confirmed by exhibiting the contradictions involved in the conclusions actually reached by the dogmatists. God an infinite abstraction and also a reasonable, personal being; right and justice a remorseless law of fatality and also a matter of human responsibility; a sequence of events eternally predestined and also a liberty of the individual will,—all the terrible and insoluble antinomies that later were to enter into the Stoic theology of St. Augustine, were dragged out by Carneades and used as battering rams to beat down the stronghold of the Porch.

Meanwhile, brought to bay in turn with the assertion that his scepticism left no motive for action and made life impossible, Carneades de-

fended himself with the theory of probability.
It is demonstrable, he says, that reason affords
no criterion of absolute truth, but we can attain
to varying degrees of probability in our own
conviction of truth, and this conviction, if exam-
ined and tested, may provide a security sufficient at least for practical ends, if not for the
complete satisfaction of the inquisitive intellect.

The persuasive, the probable, as a pragmatic
sanction for action, whether introduced by Arcesilas and only developed by Carneades, or actually invented by Carneades, is the great addition to philosophy of the Middle Academy. But
just how far the canon was carried by Carneades as a nominal follower of Plato is a delicate
question to which no positive answer can be
given. For it will be seen that there is a legitimate extension of the principle—legitimate,
that is, for the Academician—and an illegitimate extension. Legitimately, it might be applied to an extension of our convictions in the
Ideal realm, to justify there a practical compliance with the great dogmas of theology and
mythology; but that was a door which, apparently, Carneades did not open, or opened so nar-
rowly, as to obtain only a glimpse of the path
leading to religious liberty. Illegitimately, the
canon might be employed not as a fortification

within, but as an escape from, scepticism. According to a rather doubtful statement of Sextus the scepticism of Arcesilas was only a blind by which he tested the suitability of his pupils to receive the esoteric doctrine of Ideas; so that the Stoic Aristo could satirize him as having "Plato before, Pyrrho behind, and Diodorus for middle."[7] If this means that Arcesilas used the canon of probability to establish the doctrine of Ideas, it can only be said that the procedure, so far as it prevailed, removed the Middle Academy from the sceptical fold, without bringing it any whit closer to a genuine Platonism. It was not, as we shall see later, by way of the probable that the Platonist reaches his fundamental philosophy of Ideas. And, whatever may be said of Arcesilas, there is no evidence that Carneades took this line. On the whole, then, the safest conclusion will be that Carneades himself was in essential matters a firm sceptic of the Pyrrhonic type, and limited the scope of probability to justifying his participation in the practical business of life, without using it as a criterion of objective truth.[8]

[7]*Hypotyposes* I, 234. Diodorus was a follower of the Megarian school.
[8]Augustine *Con. Acad.* iii, 18: *Quamquam et Metrodorus* [a pupil of Carneades] *id antea* [*i.e.,* before Antiochus] *facere tentaverat, qui primus dicitur esse confessus, non decreto placuisse Academicis, nihil posse comprehendi, sed necessario contra Stoicos huiusmodi eos arma sumsisse.*

III

After the death of Carneades something happened like the peace of exhaustion that falls upon two armies which fight all day in doubtful
battle and at night slink away, each claiming
the victory. The Academics surrendered the
field, but consoled themselves by declaring that
they had never really cared to occupy it; scepticism fell into abeyance, until, some time about
the beginning of our era, a certain Aenesidemus
undertook to revive and strengthen the old arguments of doubt as they were originally pro-
posed by Pyrrho. The works of Aenesidemus,
the first systematic writer of the school of Scepticism properly so called, are lost, but so far as
we can infer from the records his great achievement was the formulation of the arguments of
doubt in ten tropes (*tropos*, "method" or "procedure") leading to suspension of judgment,
and in another set of eight tropes against the
principle of causality. For the tropes of suspension it will be sufficient to say that they were
subsumed by Sextus under three heads. The first
four have to do with the differences in the active
agent in any judgment; as that, for instance,
no two men are alike in their constitution and

faculties, and consequently there is no standard by which we can bring their judgments into agreement. The seventh and tenth have to do with the object judged; as that, for instance, the same object under different conditions presents different qualities (colours, etc.), and consequently we have no means of telling which of these qualities is indicative of ultimate reality. The fifth, sixth, eighth, and ninth combine the difficulties presented by the judge and the object judged. Further, Sextus shows that these three groups may all be subsumed under the eighth trope, which reduces all our judgments to relativity (*to pros ti*).[9] Another division would group the first nine tropes together as showing the impossibility of a "comprehensive impression," while the tenth exhibits the contradiction of opinions that necessarily results from this impossibility. The argument in the eight tropes destructive of the principle of causality we may pass over for the moment.

The next sceptic to be noted is Agrippa, of whom we know virtually nothing save that he reduced the ten tropes of suspension to five, while at the same time extending their scope to include the processes of reason. The first of

[9]The ten tropes are given in a different order by other authorities.

Agrippa's five is based upon contradiction, and
embraces all the ten of Aenesidemus except his
eighth. The second is the famous *regressus ad
infinitum,* based on the fact that every proof requires its hypothesis to be proved, and so on
without end. The third corresponds with the
eighth of Aenesidemus, and argues the relativity of all judgments. The fourth is virtually a
repetition, or confirmation, of the second, and
denies the right to assume any unproved hypothesis as the ground of argument. The fifth,
as complementary to the second and fourth, expounds the "vicious circle" which arises when the
hypothesis used to prove a thesis requires itself
to be proved by the assumption of that thesis.

Later some unknown systematizer com-
pressed the five tropes of Agrippa into two by
combining the first and third together in one and
the second, fourth, and fifth together in a second and complementary trope. The final form
of the tropes, then, may be stated thus: anything
known must be either (1) self-evident, or (2)
proved from something else; but (1) nothing is
self-evident, as is shown by the disagreement of
philosophers over all questions of sensation and
conception, and (2) nothing can be proved from
something else, since any such attempt involves

either the *regressus ad infinitum* or the vicious circle. In the end the analysis of the sceptical arguments started by Aenesidemus thus resolves itself into a simplified and clarified statement of the position taken by Pyrrho at the beginning: we cannot be sure of our comprehension of things (*katalêpsis*), since men differ in their opinions about them and there is no tribunal to which we can appeal for decision (*isostheneia*) ; hence we have no source of knowledge.

IV

With the anonymous formulator of the two tropes the development of scepticism reaches its climax. For our information in regard to the whole school, apart from Cicero, who writes as an Academic and confusedly at that, we are mainly dependent on Sextus Empiricus, the most important of whose works fortunately are preserved. Of the man himself we know virtually nothing. The time of his life is doubtful, falling somewhere within the limits of A.D. 150 and 230. The place where he taught, whether Athens or Rome or Alexandria, is disputable; and, curiously enough, though his cognomen would indicate that he was one of the Empirics of medicine, his own words imply rather that he belonged to the hostile camp of the Methodics.[10] His extant works are the *Hypotyposes,* or *Outlines of Scepticism,* in three books, and the *Adversus Mathematicos,* in eleven books, in which the condensed arguments of the *Hypotyposes* are extended and applied to the various schools of philosophy and science. In neither of these treatises does the author make any pretension to add anything of his own to the method developed by his predecessors; but he has gathered together and arranged in masterly fashion the whole sceptical thought of the centuries. Despite an occasional lapse into quibbling and an occasional confusion of ideas, he has presented once for all and in its final form the matter of what is certainly one of the most persistent and most important attitudes of the human mind towards the world in which we live. On the whole I am almost inclined to reckon the works of Sextus, after the Dialogues of Plato and the New Testament, the most significant document in our possession for the Greek Tradition as we are dealing with it in these volumes.

Before discussing the value and limitations of scepticism as the subject is presented by Sex-

[10]*Hypotyposes* I, 240.

tus, it may be well to summarize the difference between the Pyrrhonic school to which he professed allegiance and the schools to which he was more or less antagonistic. The conflict, as we have seen, verges upon two terms, *katalêpsis* and *isostheneia,* which express the gist of the sceptical contention as finally summed up in the two tropes.

Katalêpsis means seizing, comprehension, apprehension, hence knowledge which we know to be knowledge. So far the meaning is clear enough. But there is an ambiguity in the word, which seems not to have been firmly grasped by the disputants, and which has introduced a good deal of confusion into their discussion of its validity. On the one hand *katalêpsis* is concerned merely with the perception of objects as they present themselves to our senses. For instance, a stick, half in the water and half out, appears to be bent. Or, again, a coil of rope seen in the dark appears to be a snake.[11] The first question would be whether we have any means of rectify-

11These two illustrations, the bent stick and the coiled rope, were among the favourite tests by which the Hindus demonstrated the illusory nature, or *mâyâ,* of the phenomenal world. The first of them was in common use among the Greeks at an early period (cf. Plato, *Republic* 602 c); but the second illustration, the coiled rope, is so peculiarly indigenous to India as to lend support to Brochard's theory of Hindu influence upon Pyrrho.

ing such impressions of sight by the test of other faculties so as to reach an assured judgment of this stick or this rope as an object of the phenomenal world. On the other hand, the question of *katalêpsis* goes much deeper, and is concerned not with rectifying our judgment of appearances, but with our apprehension of what lies behind appearances. We may come to a conclusion as to the proper epithet to be applied to the stick or the coil of rope as phenomena, but have we any means of comprehending what this stick or this rope is in itself apart from what it appears to be? Can we in any way apprehend what, if anything, is the cause of our sensation of a certain form and colour and hardness? Can we, so to speak, go behind the returns?

Isostheneia means equal weight of evidence, or balance of divergent views, and is involved in the same ambiguity as *katalêpsis*. In its lower sense it denotes a disagreement over phenomena as phenomena, when, for instance, one man believes on the evidence that a stick in the water is really bent, and another asserts on other evidence that it is straight. In most cases of this order, agreement of a practical sort at least may soon be reached; though there are obscure phenomena less easy to decide. But in its higher range the

word signifies the discord of views in regard to
ethical opinions, such as justice, piety, decency,
and, beyond these, in regard to the ultimate nature of things, where the battle between dogmatists and sceptics has been, and still is, hotly
waged.

Now, if we take the attitude towards these
two terms as a key to classify the various sceptical and non-sceptical schools, it will be seen
that there are four combinations possible:

(1) Acceptance of *katalêpsis* and denial of
isostheneia,
(2) Acceptance of *katalêpsis* and acceptance
of *isostheneia.*
(3) Denial of *katalêpsis* and acceptance of
isostheneia,
(4) Denial of *katalêpsis* and denial of *isostheneia.*

Of these four combinations the first manifestly
is dogmatic; the other three, whether by the acceptance of *isostheneia* or by the denial of *katalêpsis,* are in different ways and degrees sceptical.

(1) In the actual war of the schools at the
time we are considering the Stoics were the fighting champions of dogmatism, although Epicurean and Neoplatonist are in other directions
equally divergent from scepticism. The chil-

dren of Zeno held that an impression might or might not correspond to objective reality, and hence might be true or false, but that in the *phantasia kataleptike* we have an impression which carries its own guarantee of veracious correspondence. Furthermore, they held that in the "sign" (*sêmeion*) of cause and effect we have evidence by which reason can attain to a comprehension of the universal laws of nature. They would admit, of course, that men do actually disagree in their views (witness the mad dogs of the Academy), but they argued that only the views of the wise need be considered, and that among the wise there is complete agreement—as to the truth of Stoicism. Thus the Stoics accept *katalêpsis* and, in the strict sense of the word, reject *isostheneia*.

(2) The Sophists of the Protagorean stripe, going back to Heraclitus for their principles, took as their motto the famous dictum, Man is the measure of all things, meaning by man his immediate sensations. Now on this basis there is manifestly no agreement among men, or in the same man with himself from day to day. Thus, honey is sweet to one man, but to another man with the jaundice or to the same man if he falls into that state honey is bitter, and each is right

in the statement of his sensation. So far, in making the shifting sensations of men the source of
isostheneia, the Protagoreans are in accord with
the Pyrrhonists. But the Protagoreans go a step
further, and add that man is the measure of all
things *whether they are or are not;* that is to say,
if honey gives to one man the sensation of sweetness, then the honey is in itself sweet so far as it
is anything, and if it gives to another man the
sensation of bitterness, then it is in itself bitter,
and by the same token it is at once both sweet
and bitter. In this way the Protagoreans combine the acceptance of *isostheneia* with the acceptance (inferentially at least) of *katalêpsis.*
Whatever a man feels, or thinks he feels, that is
true, not only in respect of his sensation and belief, but in so far as there is nothing in the nature of the external object to falsify that belief.
There is no distinction between true and false
determined by correspondence, but all opinions
are equally true.[12] The title of such a philosophy
may be set down as a kind of negative dogmatism or affirmative scepticism, as you choose; the
objective world becomes a mere chaos of contradictory qualities, and the subjective world cor-

[12]Sextus, *Adv. Math.* VII, 60: According to Protagoras πάσας τὰς
φαντασίας καὶ τὰς δόξας ἀληθεῖς ὑπάρχειν.

respondingly a mental chaos. The outcome, if carried logically into the moral realm, is that rule of brute force which we find actually advocated by Thrasymachus and other unflinching sophists in the Dialogues of Plato. Since there is no inherent distinction between true and false, right and wrong, but that is true and right which each man takes to be so, the struggle of life will be to make my true and right prevail over other men's true and right.

(3) However it may have been with Aenesidemus and his relation to Heraclitus,[13] the complete Pyrrhonist inclined rather to the side of Democritus, in so far as, like Democritus, he denied *katalêpsis* and accepted *isostheneia*. Man is the measure, but he is the measure of his immediate sensations only. Of things themselves the Pyrrhonist does not say, for instance, that they are sweet or bitter, or both sweet and bitter, nor of acts that they are right or wrong, or both right and wrong, but uses the words sweet and bitter, right and wrong, as purely conventional terms. Our judgments may or may not correspond with the nature of things; they may be true, but, as is shown by the complete absence of agreement among men, we have no criterion

[13]See Appendix C.

to determine whether or when they are true. Hence there is no truth for us in the sense of certain knowledge. There is even no way of knowing whether we are approaching to, or diverging from, the objective truth, or whether there is any stable law to which we can approach. In all these matters the Pyrrhonist insisted on suspension of judgment.

(4) Finally, there are the sceptics of the Middle Academy, who deny both *katalêpsis* and, in a manner, *isostheneia*. In demonstrating the inability of physical sensation and reason to discover the ultimate nature of things, they rejected *katalêpsis* just as the Pyrrhonist did. In regard to *isostheneia* their relation to the followers of Pyrrho is more complicated. Having shown the irreconcilable diversity of human opinions, the Pyrrhonist saw that, as a simple matter of fact, a certain mode of thinking and acting did prevail in the society which immediately surrounded him, and this convention of the time and place he simply accepted as a rule of life with no question asked as to ultimate truth or agreement. The Academic argued that the agreement in certain matters took a wider circle than the Pyrrhonist acknowledged and that this larger accord might be used as guide to a sort

of pragmatic truth. Even here was indeed no ground for absolute certitude that we were choosing the wiser course so long as any disagreement could be pointed to or could be supposed to exist, but some ground for probability there might be, varying in cogency as the agreement among men prevailed more or less widely. Practically, the substitution of conviction based on probability for mere conformity based on suspension of judgment gave a larger basis to the sceptical manner of life, strengthening the right of an individual citizen's judgment against the opinion of the narrow circle about him, yet limiting the presumptuous claims of individualism by the broader, if never unanimous, consensus of mankind. Theoretically, the canon of probability is in line with the scepticism of the Platonic, or Socratic, stamp, which differed essentially from that of Pyrrho. The position of the Middle Academy, in fact, wavers between the fixed poles of Pyrrhonism and Platonism, and is less stable than either.

V

We can now consider a little more fully the philosophy of Pyrrho in its final development as presented by Sextus. Then the last stage of our discussion will be to show how the Pyrrhonist and the Platonist, though votaries of the same method, reached very different conclusions; and by following their paths we shall, I trust, obtain a clearer insight into the scope and value of scepticism generally. As a preliminary I will ask the reader to examine with some care the subjoined diagram, and to have it ready for reference at the successive steps of the argument.

IMMEDIATE AFFECTIONS		PHILOSOPHY	METAPHYSICS
	Physical affections	Science	*Monism of chance or determinism*
		Ataraxy	*Absolute hedonism or optimism*
	SPIRITUAL AFFECTIONS	IDEALISM	*Transcendental monism*
		EUDAEMONISM	*Antinomianism or asceticism*[14]

If we get behind the scenes, so to speak, if we reach the forces that animated the various sects and set them at one another's throats, we shall find that the aim of the sceptics in a special man-

[14]Words in l.c. Roman (*e.g.*, Science) indicate what both Pyrrhonist and Platonist accept.

Words in Italics (*e.g., Monism, Transcendental*) indicate what both reject.

Words in sm. caps. (*e.g.,* SPIRITUAL) indicate what the Pyrrhonist rejects but the Platonist accepts.

ner—an honourable aim in the best of them—
was to live in a world of facts. Pyrrhonism developed in an age when the thinking men of
Greece were divided into hostile camps, each of
which claimed the sole possession of the truth,
and was ready to contend for the field against
all comers—Eleatic against Heraclitean, Peripatetic against Academic, Cynic against Cyrenaic, Stoic against Epicurean; not to mention
Megarian and Democritean and Sophist and I
know not what other roving guerilla bands.
Where lay the truth for which they were fighting? Who should decide among these implacable combatants? And might it be that there was
no such truth at all, and could this fair valley
land of their desire be only a mirage of the brain,
which would vanish away at approach, and leave
the victor, if victor there should be, still pursu-
ing phantoms in a waste of sand? Such a state
was not peculiar to that era of Greek philosophy; it has occurred many times, and will occur
again whenever men are swayed by the *libido
sciendi*. It was only yesterday that one of our
poets wrote:

> "And we are here as on a darkling plain
> Swept with confused alarms of struggle and flight,
> Where ignorant armies clash by night."

Now all this embittered confusion the sceptic brushed away with the single magic word *isostheneia*. Where there is no agreement and no umpire, there can be no certitude of truth, no knowledge; where theory only provokes counter theory, and discussion proceeds to endless division of beliefs, he simply withdrew from the field and took refuge in suspension of judgment: Away with the vain chase altogether, let me plant my feet here at home on indisputable ground. The facts beyond dispute he expressed by the phrase "immediate affections" (*oikeia pathê*). Certain perceptions, he said, I have about which no man can argue, from the knowledge of which no logic can evict me. This chair I see, this table I do here and now perceive: I say nothing about the chair itself, or the table itself; apart from my sensation I make no assertion about anything whatsoever, leaving you to wrangle over your theories of ultimate reality like dogs over a bone; but the image in my mind, which I call a chair or a table, that I have and know. And so with my present sensations of pleasure and pain; my hopes and fears; my memory of past sensations, whatever memory may be; my passing reflections, however they may come to me,—all these are immediate, they are my own, they are not inference but fact.

So far the attitude of the sceptic is perfectly simple and comprehensible. But the sceptic, like every other man, must live; and the question arises on what basis he shall conduct his life, and how he shall escape falling into the same sort of theorizing as that which he has condemned in the dogmatists. Here enters the distinction I have indicated in the diagram by the rather arbitrary use of the words philosophy and metaphysics. The terminology, I confess frankly, is not that of the ancient Pyrrhonist, who denied categorically that he had any *philosophia* and admitted only an *agôgê,* or manner of life; philosophy and metaphysics in his language were all one, and equally objectionable. But our tongue has no equivalent for the Greek *agôgê,* and in accordance with the usage in the previous volumes of this series I shall here confine the term philosophy to the narrower scope of reason permitted in the sceptical and in all the other schools, and apply the term metaphysics to that further use of the reason, different indeed from philosophy in kind as well as in degree, where sceptic and dogmatic drew apart.

This distinction granted, it remains to show

what philosophy the Pyrrhonist followed, and
how he justified his adherence to any philosophy.
In the first place Sextus emphatically asserted
his right as a sceptic to work in the field of science, properly defined and limited. "The phenomena of nature," according to the well-known
division of Mill, "exist in two distinct relations
to one another; that of simultaneity, and that of
succession."[15] Hence the two categories of the
"uniformities of coexistence" and the "uniformities of causation," by which scientific procedure
falls into the two types of (1) classificatory or
descriptive, and (2) genetic or mechanical. And
in both of these types, with due restrictions, the
sceptic might feel himself perfectly at home,
since both simultaneity and succession he accepts as immediate affections. He perceives as
simple facts of sensation that certain phenomena
appear together and certain others apart from
one another, and hence can be classified by description; he perceives also that certain phenomena appear regularly in succession, and hence
can be classified in the manner of the genetic or
mechanical sciences. So in the science of which
Sextus himself was a student, he found no in-
compatibility in joining the profession of com-

[15]*System of Logic* III, v, 1.

plete scepticism with the practice of the Me-
thodic branch of medicine. So, too, in the books
written by him against the encyclical studies
(grammar, rhetoric, geometry, arithmetic, astronomy, music), the arguments in each case are
directed not against, *e.g.,* grammar as an empi-
rical study of the observable facts of speech, but
against theories of language based on rational
analogies and the supposed nature of things.

Why is it then, one asks, that the sceptics have
been accused of "denying the possibility of all
science"?[16] The error, apparently, must be attributed to the differences of terminology which
are the source of endless other misunderstand-
ings in modern commentators; and to this source
of error should be added, as particularly virulent in our treatment of the sceptics, the deeply
ingrained conceit of ourselves as wiser than our
progenitors. Now it is a remarkable fact that
the Greeks, though they gave the impulse to
scientific procedure in the western world and
were indeed eminently scientific in their method
of thought, yet had no specific term for science
as a field lying between the utilitarian arts

16M. M. Patrick, *Sextus Empiricus and Greek Scepticism* 96.—
The German critics are sounder. See Goedeckemeyer 261, 283;
Richter 97ff. It is fair to add that Antiochus was brought to
reject scepticism on the ground that it made science as well as
every other human activity impossible.

(*technai*) at the one extreme, and at the other extreme physics (*ta physika*), which in the Hellenistic use of the word includes also metaphysics and theology. The case, let us admit, presents its difficulties; for while Sextus is really inveighing against those who deal with art and metaphysics as if they were science, the historical critic, owing to the lack of a specific word for science, is in danger of overlooking the fact that true science is not embraced in the destructive arguments. There is, however, this compensation in the linguistic ambiguity, that it points to a like and almost universal ambiguity in thinking. For it happens today, as it happened in the far past, that the scientist, so soon as he lays down his scalpel and his scales, and begins to generalize and define, is tempted to break through the hampering circle of permitted classification and to indulge in abstractions as unreal as those of the professed metaphysician or theologian, whom he so often despises. And it was against this metaphysical extension of science that the sceptic directed his batteries.

Now the ultimate data of science (or physics in our use of the word, not the ancient) are mass (*sôma* the Greeks called it) and motion and energy; and the first fatal step in rationalism is

taken when the scientist, not content to employ
these immediate and inexplicable facts of sensation, tries, as it were, to go behind the returns,
and seeks by some legerdemain of definition to
comprehend what these phenomena are in themselves. The Stoics started the merry game when,
for the sake of a supposedly clarifying simplifi-
cation, they undertook to define energy (*tonos*)
in terms of mass and motion, and then, pushed
by their foes of the Academy, were compelled
to define mass and motion in terms of energy,
and so, in their eagerness to embrace a cloud,
found themselves like Ixion nailed to an ever-
revolving wheel.[17]

If the deluded scientist attempts to escape
from this vicious circle by defining his physical
data in terms of mathematics (number, addition
and subtraction, whole and part), the sceptic is
at his heels with arguments to show that we have
no clearer comprehension of what number itself
is than of what mass itself is, nor of the process
of addition and subtraction, nor of the relation
of whole and part. These elements of mathematics are the immediate data of the mind, behind which we cannot go, as mass and motion
and energy are the immediate data of the senses,

[17]See Appendix A.

and the endeavour to explain the latter by the former is merely a vain effort to define *obscurum per obscurius*. And the metaphysical scientist is no better off if he undertakes to get behind the data of the senses and the mind by defining them in the terms of space and time. This indeed is to fall into a depth of confusion which might be described as *obscurius per obscurissimum*. To begin with the sceptic had no difficulty in demonstrating that any attempt to make either space itself or time itself comprehensible to the understanding is of all metaphysical follies the most foolhardy. And there is this last inextricable entanglement, that any psychological definition of either space or time, of the sort desired by the deluded scientist, involves the use of both space and time together, and this coordinate use of space and time means that space will be expressed in terms of time and time in terms of space, although each of these is so contrary in its nature to the other that any such reciprocity of terms results in the virtual abolition of both as immediately given to us in experience.[18]

This is a thorny brake through which I have dragged the reader, and unprofitable as well, I fear, unless he has had the good will to follow up

[18]*Adv. Math.* II, 6 ff., 169 ff., III, 19 ff., 85 ff., I, 161 ff., 311 ff.; *Hyp.* III, 131, 142.

the references. But, however thorny and repellent the discussion may be, it is a fact that no scientist of antiquity, who sought to go behind appearances, could escape the dilemmas into which
his sceptical antagonist threw him; and the
makers of hypotheses today in regard to mass
and energy would fare no better, had not the
critical sense been pretty well frightened out of
the field by the superstition that whatever is said
by a man of science must be science.

The next step towards the bog of metaphysics is taken when we proceed to deal with the relation of succession and the genetic branch of
science in the terms of sensation. Now in one
sense the sceptic no more denies causality than
does the dogmatist. "The law of causation," says
Mill, "the recognition of which is the main pil-
lar of inductive science, is but the familiar truth,
that invariability of succession is found by observation to obtain between every fact in nature
and some other fact which has preceded it; independently of all considerations respecting
the ultimate mode of production of phenomena,
and of every other question regarding the nature of 'things themselves.' " To this statement
the sceptic would in the main assent, though
he would refuse the word "law" quite the full

meaning it has in Mill, and would regard causation rather as a subordinate division of the general principle of classification than as a principle antecedent to classification. But, however that may be, the sceptic does not deny the sequence of cause and effect as a matter of observation. That is to say, he admits freely as one of his immediate affections the memory of a certain invariability of succession. He knows that as a fact of memory, whatever memory may be, he has seen colts always born from horses and children from men, and he knows by the same token that he has acted on the supposition that this invariability in the past would continue in the future and has not been deceived in so acting. So far he is ready to admit that the existence of causation as a term for observed sequences is convincing by its own evidence.

The sceptic withholds his assent only when the rationalizing scientist proceeds to analyse the operation of causality, or to define its nature, or to draw inferences from it as from a rationally comprehensible and ultimate law. Here Sextus brings forward the contradictions into which the rationalist falls the moment he begins to define a cause in terms suitable to what is corporeal or what is incorporeal, or as operating in

space or in time, or as dissociated from or associated with its effect, or as simple or as multiple.[19] In the end his destructive argument
amounts to this: the phenomenon of physical
causation, like the previously discussed phenomena of mass and motion and energy, is conditioned on the two simultaneous factors of time
and space; but each of these factors presents
conditions peculiar to itself and exclusive of,
even contradictory to, the conditions presented
by the other factor, so that when we attempt to
define a cause in the terms of these inevitably
concomitant factors we become entangled in a
network of incoherencies. Again, we are blocked
by a wall of ignorance. If, to escape these entanglements, the dogmatist will limit his efforts at
definition to the simple statement that cause is
a matter of relativity, Sextus will assent; but he
will add that relativity is purely a conception
of the mind, as he elsewhere sufficiently demonstrated, and that it gives us no knowledge of an
objective operation.[20] To say that causality is a
causal relation leaves the term causal still to be
defined.

The conclusion then of the whole argument,

[19]*Adv. Math.* IX, 203, 210, 227, 232, 237, 252, 246.
[20]*Adv. Math.* IX, 207; VIII, 453 ff.

developed from the eight tropes of Aenesidemus, will be that causality, as a phenomenon of
experience, seems to exist, but that, if the existence of an operation is made to depend on our
ability to give a coherent definition or rational
explanation of its nature, then causality seems
not to exist; and between these two positions the
sceptic will hold his judgment in suspense.

It might seem as if this debate with the scientific dogmatists were little better than quarrel-
ing over words; for, after all, if you grant the
facts, or apparent facts, of mass, motion, and
energy, number, time, and space, causality, as
elements of our immediate experience, what difference does it make whether you deny our ability to go behind the returns and to define the nature of these elements? Well, it does make a serious difference. For the assumption that we can
arrive at any rationally definable knowledge of
these things is, as it were, the half-way house between legitimate science and pure metaphysics,
and having gone so far, the mind is urged on
almost irresistibly to the last plunge into the
abyss, of which plunge the results are palpable
enough. So long as physical causation is accepted as nothing more than the memory of certain
sensations which have appeared in succession,

the mind is checked in its impulse to draw rigid
and absolute conclusions from these phenomena;
but once grant that physical causation is an immutable and universal law of mass and energy,
a law of whose nature and operation we have
sure knowledge, grant this and what can save us
from leaping to the metaphysical conception of
the world as a vast all-embracing mechanism of
matter, wheels within wheels for ever grinding
on in ruthless indifference to whatever may be
caught in their cogs? The Epicurean may define his world as composed of atoms dancing
frantically through the void, the Stoic may define the same world as a continuous substance
for ever palpitating with a kind of internal contraction and expansion; the Epicurean may deny the presence of any design in his rain of
atoms, the Stoic may deny the presence of anything but design in the everlasting recurrence
of change—all is one. In either case the liberty
and security of the spirit, which these philosophies started out to discover on the pathway of
physical law, end in the mockery of an inhuman fatality. It was against such a result that
the sceptic was fighting. For this purpose he
harped with exasperating tenacity on the contradictions within each of the metaphysical sys-

tems, and on the contradictions of system with system; and so, by virtue of the universal *isostheneia* of reason and opinion, confirmed the position of Socrates, that in regard to the ultimate nature of things our only knowledge is that we know nothing.[21] "There was in Sais," says Plutarch in his essay on Isis and Osiris, "a statue of Athena, whom they call Isis, with this inscription: 'I am all that has been, and is, and

[21]A neat illustration of the false extension of thought from scepticism and legitimate science to metaphysical pseudo-science may be found in the works of Huxley. His scepticism, or agnosticism, has as its positive side this "clear result of the investigation started by Descartes, that there is one thing of which no doubt can be entertained, . . . and that is the momentary consciousness we call a present thought or feeling" (Works, Eversley edition, VI, 65). This is precisely the Pyrrhonic *oikeion pathos,* "immediate affection." Huxley's practical work as an observer of nature and experimenter, and his theory of science as concerned with the classification of our observations, are still purely Pyrrhonic. So too is his acceptance of Hume's analysis of causality: "The relation of cause and effect is a particular case of the process of [mental] association; that is to say, is a result of the process of which it is supposed to be the cause" (VI, 83). This, I take it, is the Pyrrhonic canon of *to pros ti.* So too Huxley remains a Pyrrhonist in his acceptance of Hume's distinction between science and metaphysics (VI, 69). But when he goes on to make cause and effect an absolute and universal law of nature, to doubt which would be self-destruction on the part of science (V, 70), when he declares that Darwinian evolution is "no speculation but a generalization of certain facts" (V, 42); and, further, that "the materials of consciousness are products of cerebral activity" (VI, 94), that we are pure "automata," that all causation is of a material, mechanical sort, and that "man, physical, intellectual, and moral, is as much a part of nature, as purely a product of the cosmic process, as the humblest weed" (IX, 11), then he slips from scepticism and genuine science, to rationalizing science and pure metaphysics. I have dealt with this subject at length in *Shelburne Essays* VIII.

shall be, and no mortal ever yet has withdrawn
my garment.' "

VI

Such was the philosophy of the Pyrrhonist in
the intellectual sphere, and such his rejection of
any theory of truth approaching metaphysics.
What will be the limits of his philosophy in the
practical and emotional sphere? How shall a
man bear himself in a life surrounded and shut
in by walls of ignorance? Should the sceptic,
having surrendered the hope of positive knowledge, carry his denial on to what may seem at
first its logical conclusion in nihilism and black
despair? Such, certainly, has been the outcome
of doubt in many minds. It was the undernote
of the epigrammatists of the Greek Anthology.
In modern times it has been voiced by James
Thomson with dismaying clarity:

> "For life is but a dream whose shapes return,
>   Some frequently, some seldom, some by night
> And some by day, some night and day: we learn,
>   The while all change and many vanish quite,
> In their recurrence with recurrent changes
> A certain seeming order; where this ranges
>   We count things real; such is memory's might."

That was precisely the stand taken by the an-

cient sceptic so far as science was admitted into
his philosophy; and, one may add, it was the attitude of Plato towards the moving shadows
cast on the wall before the prisoners of the cave.
But what of the moral effect of this illusion, as
Thomson depicts it on the face of the "Image"
that sits enthroned above his City of Dreadful
Night, the woman of Albrecht's Dürer's *"Mel-
encolia"*?

"But as if blacker night could dawn on night,
    With tenfold gloom on moonless night unstarred,
A sense more tragic than defeat and blight,
    More desperate than strife with hope debarred,
More fatal than the adamantine Never
Encompassing her passionate endeavour,
    Dawns glooming in her tenebrous regard:

"The sense that every struggle brings defeat
    Because Fate holds no prize to crown success;
That all the oracles are dumb or cheat
    Because they have no secret to express;
That none can pierce the vast black veil uncertain
Because there is no light beyond the curtain;
    That all is vanity and nothingness."

Such may be one of the fruits of disillusion,
but not of the kind indulged by Pyrrho and Sextus. They would say that this tragic bitterness
of defeat meant the rebellion of a mind con-

vinced that it had laid bare the foundation of the
world and saw all things rooted in ignominy:
"For out of unreason spring all things that are."
That, they would say, is not doubt at all, but a
kind of inverted and sullen dogmatism. The true
sceptic, they maintained, was of all men most
justified in claiming a certain ease and tranquillity of mind, owing to the very fact that he refused to pass any judgment at all on the ultimate nature of the world.

If we analyse this boasted ataraxy of Pyrrho it will appear to be made up of about equal
parts of the Socratic hedonism and apathy.
What pleasures life affords the sceptic will grasp
and enjoy, asking no question as to their hidden
source or end. If troubles and pain befall him,
as they come in varying guise to all men,—

> "For not of ancient oak nor yet of stone
> He springs, but doth a human kinship own,"—

these too he will accept, and render as light as
may be by endurance, not denying their reality
nor rebelling against them as an outrage put
upon him by some malevolent Power. Such is
the proper mood of one who limits his knowledge to the immediate affections.[22]

[22]*Adv. Math.* XI, 141 ff.

As for the attitude towards society and the kind of conduct best suited to secure this state of tranquillity—for like the partisans of the other sects the sceptics also aimed at a measure of security—Sextus states his position fairly: "We follow a certain sort of reasoning based upon appearances, which instructs us to live in accordance with the manners and laws and character of our people, and with our own immediate affections." If our fellow citizens worship the gods, we too will worship, not in scornful superiority, but with humble acquiescence in what men believe; if they cherish the family and make a virtue of the other amenities of the heart, we too will be domestic and kind. All this the sceptic will do on no fixed principle of morality, but rather in despair of discovering any better guide than the custom and beliefs in which he has been brought up.

In practice the code of the Pyrrhonist comes pretty close to that of the Cyrenaic; but it differs in so far as the Cyrenaic makes particular pleasures the set purpose of his life and the test of wisdom, whereas the Pyrrhonist simply welcomes what pleasures may come to him with, so far as possible, a genial indifference to fate.[23]

23 *Hypotyposes* I, 215.

Further, the two schools differ in their attitude
towards society, as conformity differs from adap-
tability. The Pyrrhonist conforms to the prevalent customs and sentiments in a spirit of genuine scepticism; the Cyrenaic finds his profit in
adapting himself to current opinions with a
more or less cynical contempt for what he believes to be false, fluctuating between the modesty of a Pyrrho and the insolence of a Thrasymachus.

Should the dogmatists turn upon the sceptic
and charge him with choosing and avoiding, in
general with not practising his boasted suspense
of judgment, the sceptic will reply that they do
not understand the distinction between a metaphysically determined goal, for which if he
waited he would never act at all, and a philosophical observation of phenomena, whereby he
has a perfect right to choose this and avoid that
among the actual experiences of life. As the
sceptic did not see himself debarred from the
practice of legitimate science, but refused to go
with the scientists into their abstract definitions,
and so on to their absolute theories of the world;
so, in the exigencies of daily business, he is not
shut out from adopting a rule of conduct sug-
gested by appearances, while rejecting every

absolute definition of Good, whether it lead to
the Epicurean's frantic flight from pain or to
the Stoic's pitiless affirmation of optimism. He
thinks he has found the pleasant home where
Tranquillity resides; but his mistress is not the
ataraxy of Epicurus or the apathy of Zeno (the
words he uses, but divests them of their metaphysical associations). On the contrary, he sees
that these fixed principles not only lead to logical absurdities but defeat themselves practically; since the moment a man sets up an absolute
ataraxy or an absolute apathy as the goal of a
rational hedonism or optimism, he adds an un-
necessary anxiety to life by aiming at what he
can never attain. Rather, the Pyrrhonist takes
to heart the story told of Apelles, who, painting
a horse and finding it difficult to reproduce the
foam, finally in a temper threw his sponge at the
picture, and lo! there was the effect he had been
striving for. So, Sextus said, the sceptic, looking about for a philosophy in which his mind
could repose, found himself balked at every step
by the disagreement of the sects; thus he was
forced to hold his judgment in suspense, when,
lo! by good chance the tranquillity he was seeking followed as the shadow a body.

VII

I cannot see that the logic of Sextus has left anything essential to be added by the sceptics of a later age. Doubtless Kant, to take the greatest of the moderns, has thrown the arguments of the ancient school into a new and imposing scheme, and has given them a different psychological slant; but so far as Kant's philosophy remains truly "critical," it seems to me to move within the circle prescribed by his predecessors in the Greek Tradition. Both Sextus and Kant show, and for reasons of the same character, that our perceptions are confined to appearances and tell us nothing of things as they are ultimately in themselves. Both show that we are obliged to use time and space in our perception of phenomena, but can neither define the nature of time and space nor employ them to define the nature of that which we perceive by their means. If anything Sextus is here more thorough than Kant, in his insistence on the difficulties which beset the mind, owing to the fact that any attempt to analyse our sensations in the terms of time and space obliges us to express the relations of time in the incompatible relations of space, and *vice versa*.

Again, Sextus deals critically with what Kant calls the Ideas of Reason—the soul, the Cosmos, God—and with the same destructive results. Of any guide or superior principle of the soul distinguishing man from the beasts we have, according to Sextus, no certain knowledge; indeed of the soul itself we can make no affirmation, since to some reason proves its existence and to others its non-existence, and, having no higher court of appeal, a wise man will hold his judgment in suspense. And so it is of the Cosmos as an orderly, rational whole; between those who reason that all is chance and those who reason that all is design, in our ignorance of the nature or existence of causality, what resting-place is there for the critical mind? And so, also, it is with the being or not-being of God. I cannot see how in any of these cases the famous antinomies of Kant have added anything of significance to the *isostheneia* of Sextus; indeed, for scope and thoroughness, though not in schematic clarity, I submit that the palm belongs rather to the ancient champion against the dogmatists.

The break between the ancient and the modern comes when we pass from Pure Reason, where Kant, remaining true to his "critical"

creed, is at one with Sextus, to the Practical
Reason, where he ceases to be critical. It is true
that Sextus also, after a fashion, used the Ideas
of Reason pragmatically as necessary assumptions. Thus he introduces his discussion of the being of the gods in the *Hypotyposes* with the statement that, so far as the practice of life goes, the
sceptic will accept the common belief and will
act as if the gods existed and exercised a providence over the world; but he will do this *adoxas-
tôs,* that is to say, without permitting his practical conformity to prejudice his judgment of
the fact. Least of all will he, in a panic of fear,
suddenly throw overboard his whole critical
method, and rationalize this practical conformity into a "categorical imperative" which commands him to give an unselecting assent to the
universe as a whole. He will remain a consistent sceptic, and will not, like the Kantian of today or like the last beaten leaders of the Academy, try to speak as a sceptic and a Stoic in one
and the same breath.

Nor can I see that the logic of Sextus has left
open any loophole of attack for the enraged
dogmatists. One objection, however, to his conclusions has been raised so often and stated so
complacently, that it cannot be passed over with-

out mention. It was thrown against the Pyrrhonists and Academics of antiquity time after
time; St. Augustine reechoed it in his *Contra
Academicos* as if it were unanswered and un-
answerable; it is repeated by some of the historians today with the same assurance of final-
ity. In a word the argument asserts that scepticism is self-destructive: that is to say, the very
use of reason to prove the invalidity of reason
assumes that the process of reasoning is valid,
and the conclusion that we know nothing is itself an assertion of knowledge. Or, as Mr. Maccoll expresses the criticism: "The sceptics do
not appear to have seen that their supposed disproof of reasonings, if valid, disproved their own
reasonings, if, indeed, we can allow those who did
not allow of proof to talk of disproof."[24] Now to
say that the sceptics were unaware of this sort
of objection is, as a matter of fact, an extraordinary misstatement. It was flung in their
teeth, so to speak, by every passer-by, and Sextus, not to mention his predecessors, has it constantly in mind. There would be more truth
in the statement that the sceptic's replies to it

[24]Norman Maccoll, *The Greek Sceptics* 100.—In the issue of *Mind*
for July, 1894, there is an excellent criticism by Alfred Sidgwick
of Professor Bradley's *Appearance and Reality,* dealing clearly
and vigorously with the attempt of modern idealism to resusci-
tate this ancient charge against the futility of scepticism.

25

were too frequent and were not always wise. More than once, after a destructive train of reasoning, Sextus pulls himself up at the end with a kind of apologetic defence, to the effect that he is neither proving nor disproving, but holds his judgment in suspense. Such an apology is not quite candid, and is certainly a strategical mistake. Indeed, both the attack and the defence are no better than a quibbling evasion. On the one hand, to prove by good logic that we have no criterion of knowledge, and then to add that this is not to assert the non-existence of a criterion but only to use, *ad captandum,* such methods as will convince the dogmatist—that, I say, is a feeble trick of evasion, unworthy of a child of Pyrrho.[25] The sceptic's position is stronger than that. To employ reason in such a way as to show that it is self-destructive as an instrument for defining the ultimate nature of things, is not to assume the validity of reason in any sense of the word under discussion; to conclude thereby that we know nothing beyond our immediate affections is utterly different from concluding that we do know something beyond these affections, and leaves the sceptic and the dogmatist at opposite poles of philosophy. To

[25]*Hypotyposes* II, 79.

retort that the affirmation of ignorance still implies the holding of dogma, is a quibble which, if it brings satisfaction to any hungry dogmatist, let him, o' God's name, make the best of it.[26]

VIII

At this point I would ask the reader to refer back to the diagram on page 330. It has been made clear, I trust, how a genuine scepticism is consistent in admitting a philosophy (as I limit the word) of science and conduct, while rejecting the metaphysical extension of this philosophy in any direction. But it will be seen by the diagram that I also classify among the sceptics those who accept a whole range of philosophy which the Pyrrhonist excludes, and which I designate as spiritual. Something has been said about the connexion of Pyrrhonism and the Middle Academy; the last topic, and the most important for our purpose, will be concerned with the true children of Plato.

In the introductory chapter of my *Platonism* the three main theses of the Socratic teaching were stated as scepticism, a spiritual affirmation, and the identity of virtue and knowledge,

[26]See Appendix D.

the third of these propositions being capable of a double interpretation, one of which easily glides into rationalism. Now the affiliation of the Hellenistic philosophies may be indicated by saying that the Epicurean and the Stoic followed the rationalizing tendency of the third thesis taken alone (not forgetting, however, the ambiguity of the Stoic position), that the Neoplatonist rationalized the spiritual affirmation, and that the Pyrrhonist clung to the scepticism and rejected the other two theses. In such a sense these schools may be grouped as imperfectly Socratic and as the heresies of philosophy, whereas Plato alone developed the full doctrine of the master by uniting the three theses into one harmonious system of thought.[27] How Plato accomplished his great task I have tried to set forth in the two previous volumes of this series; but of the part played by scepticism in his philosophy not much was there said, and indeed could not very well be said until after the works of Sextus had been considered.

That Socrates did actually in his own mind effect a union of scepticism and spiritual affirmation is shown by the quotation from the *Apology* given at the opening of this chapter.

[27]See Appendix B.

That there was also a strong vein of interroga-
tion and doubt running beside the Platonic
Idealism must be clear enough to any one who
has read the Dialogues. It was thus no accident
that the leaders of the Academy at an early date
beat the Pyrrhonists at their own game, and became for many years the representative spokes-
men of scepticism. The customary "it is likely"
(*eikos*) of Plato's speculations needed only a
shift of emphasis, an extension of scope, to pass
into the "it is probable" (*pithanon*) of the Middle Academy, and the thing was done. When
Pyrrhonism revived, the Dialogues were still a
reservoir of anti-dogmatic arguments on which
the sceptic could draw, as may be seen by the
large use of them in Sextus.[28] It is true, of
course, that the sceptical thesis of the Dialogues,
written before Pyrrho was born, is implicit rather than fully developed, so that our discussion
may seem more pertinent to a certain kind of
Platonist than to Plato himself; but, with this
granted, what is the relation of the Platonic
scepticism to the Pyrrhonic? how can it be maintained along with a spiritual affirmation? is it a
true scepticism at all? Three questions which are

[28]*E.g.*, the use made of *Meno* 80ᴅ and *Theaetetus* 147ʙ, 165ʙ
in *Adv. Math.* I, 33; *Theaetetus* 204 in I, 135; *Ion passim* in I,
300; *Sophist* 233ᴀ in I, 300; *Timaeus* 35ᴀ in I, 301.

really one: they touch the Christian faith as well as the Platonic philosophy; and they must be met and answered by any believer who, having freed himself from the fetters of rationalism, desires a larger world for his liberty than can be seen by the eyes of the flesh.

Now the very essence of scepticism is the admission that our knowledge is limited to those immediate affections about which there is no dispute and can be no doubt. So far the Pyrrhonist and the Platonist and the follower of any other philosophy must agree, if they lay claim to the sceptic's liberty of reasonableness. The issue will arise between the Pyrrhonist and the Platonist over the scope of these immediate affections. Both, as may be seen by looking back at our diagram, will admit the reality of what is there designated as the physical affections— pleasure and pain, and all those sensations and perceptions which are connected with the body and the world of material phenomena. But the Platonist asserts that he lives also in a whole range of affections, equally immediate and certain, which are not material in their origin, and which belong to a subjective and objective world of another order.

The character of these spiritual affections, as

they may be termed for lack of a better word, I
need not here dwell upon. They are comprised
under what, in the previous volume of this series,[29] I have denominated the philosophy of Plato as distinguished from the two other elements,
theology and mythology, which enter into his
religion; and I have there, to the best of my ability, analysed and described them. Briefly stated,
they come down to a recognition of something
called the soul as an independent entity apart
from the body, and of those immediate facts of
consciousness which belong to the soul as a moral, self-determining agent. Against these claims
the Pyrrhonist opposes a virtual negative; he
does not indeed directly and positively deny the
existence of the soul and its moral experience,
but, theoretically, he holds his judgment in suspense regarding them, and, practically, he ig-
nores them by basing his rule of life on the physical affections alone. Beyond these there is for
him nothing to consider save the shifting customs of society which have no obligation other
than what men choose for the time to attribute
to them. In this sense the Pyrrhonist is an agnostic, and the agnostic, whether ancient or modern, has always been a more or less disguised materialist.

[29]Particularly *The Religion of Plato,* chap. iii.

Who is right, the Pyrrhonist or the Platonist?
Judged by the canon of *isostheneia,* the Pyrrhonist would appear to be your only genuine sceptic, since it is an open fact, so at least he avers
with plausible assurance, that, whereas all men
agree upon the existence of physical affections,
there is no such agreement upon the existence
of the spiritual affections, and it is presumptuous to affirm knowledge where contradictory
opinions prevail. This was the question that
Plato faced in the *Gorgias,* when to Socrates'
unflinching announcement of the spiritual affections Polus replied that his language was
highly paradoxical and would be generally ridiculed by his countrymen. And Socrates admits
the paradox. It is a fact, he says, that you can
bring a host of witnesses who will swear that
they have no belief in these things which I affirm; but I, he adds, though I be alone in my
conviction, will not assent to their views, nor
can you force me to assent, for all the evidence
you bring to dislodge me from the truth. And
what is this clamour of the mob to us? Here we
are, you alone and I alone, debating together on
this great concern of the soul; and I think only
this will satisfy you, to convince me, as I am sure
that all I desire is the honest confession of what

you, and no other, have felt and do know. For the rest of the world, what is it to you and to me how they believe?

Such an argument from individual consciousness might seem to be a sufficient answer to the cavilling of the Pyrrhonist; for, after all, logical demonstration ceases, and personal appeal begins, when we come down to the rock bottom of first premises. Have I, or have I not, this particular affection? But even here an honest man may well be shaken in his conviction if he finds himself solitary or with a loud majority against him. He will ask himself whether he does really feel what his words imply, whether he may not have been deluded in holding this affection, however vivid, as in very truth of a spiritual order. And so Socrates does not rest with the personal argument, but proceeds to show that all men, by the intuitive meanings they put into language and by the involuntary voice of conscience, do in their hearts know these spiritual experiences which in their lighter moments they deny.[30]

If Socrates and Plato are right, the case would stand something like this. The spiritual affections are immediate and universal, just as

[30]This is the truth, I think, veiled in the famous saying of Heraclitus 113 Diels), ξυνόν ἐστι πᾶσι τὸ φρονέειν.

are the physical affections; all men alike live in these two distinct orders of experience. But, in comparison with the coarser sensations of the body and the train of emotions they awaken, the sense of things spiritual in the natural man is evanescent and elusive, coming and going with a kind of shy reticence.[31] And so it is that reason, which is always in a state of rebellion against any irreconcilable dualism, begins to argue within us that these finer sensations are not so much elusive as illusory, being in fact not of a separate order from things physical, as they claim to be, but material in their origin like all our other affections. And in this monistic argument reason is abetted by the strength of our natural desires, which are uneasy under any abridgement of their validity. Against this tendency of rationalism the Platonist will contend that he, and not the follower of Pyrrho, is the complete sceptic, since he accepts the whole range of our immediate affections, whereas the Pyrrhonist is but an imperfect sceptic, in so far as he suffers reason to tyrannize dogmatically over one-half his consciousness.

However that may be, and whether the Pla-

[31] Cardinal Newman has dwelt on this fact with the conviction of a priest and the eloquence of a poet. See, for example, the passage quoted in *The Religion of Plato*, Appendix C.

tonist is right or not in assuming a dualism of
affections, it is a fact that he is able to carry the
sceptical attitude into the spiritual realm, granted the existence of that realm, in a manner that
runs quite parallel with his and the Pyrrhonist's
attitude in the physical realm. Thus, if the reader will cast his eye down the column headed philosophy in the diagram, he will see that the doctrine of Ideas corresponds to science in the physical order. In the lower order of experience the
sceptic accepts the existence of a physical reality as a fact given him in his immediate affections; that is to say, the sense of something objective and impersonal, something outside of
himself which has the power of affecting him, is
just as real and immediate to him as the sense of
colour or the feeling of pleasure. The very word
"affection" implies that something not himself
affects him, and in his view the position of the
Berkeleyan idealist and, *a fortiori,* of the solip-
sist is not sceptical at all but dogmatic and metaphysical to the last degree.[32] And so in the high-

[32]Thus phenomena, the sense of something appearing to us, are
identical with immediate affections as τὰ κατὰ φαντασίαν παθητι-
κὴν ὑποπίπτοντα (*Hyp.* II, 10), ἀβουλήτως(*Adv. Math.* VIII, 316),
τὰ κατὰ φαντασίαν κατηναγκασμένα πάθη (*Hyp.* I, 13), τὰ ἐξ ἑαυτῶν εἰς
γνῶσιν ἡμῖν ἐρχόμενα (*Hyp.* II, 97), etc. The Pyrrhonist would account it a metaphysical absurdity to argue that pain is not an
affection produced by something outside of ourselves, or that
our sense of the body is not of something objective and impersonal.

er order the Platonist holds that it is not the
function of scepticism, but of a perverted rationalism, to deny the existence of a world of objective reality underlying and shaping his spiritual
affections. The forces of this immaterial world,
with which in some way he is in contact, are simply in his vocabulary the Ideas. The Platonist
perceives further in the realm of spiritual phenomena a relation of simultaneity and succession which gives him the two categories of the
"uniformities of coexistence" and the "uniformities of causation," precisely as he finds them in
the realm of physical phenomena. So far as his
experience goes he sees that certain laws prevail here as they do in mechanics, that certain
consequences invariably attend certain moral
acts or states; so that a fair and adequate definition of the doctrine of Ideas would be "the science of the spirit." He thinks that his experience here is even more exact and cogent than his
experience of physical law, for the reason that it
comes down to the centre of his being; and hence,
in comparison with the science of the spirit, he
is inclined to regard the so-called science of
physical phenomena as a mere body of relative-
ly unstable opinions. To permit the insistence
of physical phenomena to obscure the reality of

the soul and the Ideal world is to the Platonist
the last illusion of wilful ignorance, and he who
lives in such a state is as a man walking in his
sleep.[33]

Again following down the column under philosophy in the diagram we see that corresponding with the ataraxy of the Pyrrhonist stands
the Platonic eudaemonism. Here, in obedience
to the radical dualism of his experience, the Platonist divides his feelings into two distinct orders: pleasure and pain on the one hand, which
are the result respectively of this or that conduct
in the realm of physical phenomena, and which
he accepts with the Pyrrhonist; and on the other
hand happiness (*eudaimonia*) and misery, which
accompany our spiritual volitions, and which
the Pyrrhonist rejects, or at least refuses to
separate in kind from pleasure and pain. In
the higher order the Platonist finds his goal in
that immediate sense of happiness which comes
with a life governed in conformity with the philosophy of Ideas, as at once the effect and confirmation of spiritual knowledge. Eudaemonism to him is not necessarily antagonistic to
ataraxy, but supplements ataraxy as the final

[33]Iamblichus, *Protrepticus* pp. 68, 69, 79 Pistelli, has some excellent observations on this illusion (ἀπάτη), drawn from the
Phaedo and the Platonic Dialogues generally.

rule of conduct owing to its vastly greater significance and cogency in the fulness of life. By virtue of his complete scepticism he has attained to a peace in the soul incomparably more precious than the bare imperturbability of mind boasted, but in fact rarely, if ever, possessed, by the Pyrrhonic half-sceptic.

To this point the philosophy of scepticism goes, and here it stops. The sceptic of any sort must rest in the impossibility of defining in rational terms the nature of that objective reality which lies behind material phenomena and which he accepts as a given fact. So it is with Ideas. Of their nature in themselves, how they exist, where they dwell, if indeed the word "where" may be applied to them at all, and in what manner they operate,—of this, if he is wise, the Platonist will profess ignorance. Plato himself insisted on describing Ideas as separate (*chôrista*) from material phenomena, yet as in some way capable of affecting these phenomena by "participation" or "imitation"; and it may be that at times he was led on, by a very human impulse, to play with rational definitions of their nature which should explain this paradox of separation and participation; but such attempts were abortive to say the least, and in the main, and when true to himself, he left to the spiritual imagination a field wherein reason finds herself hopelessly baffled. But for the existence of Ideas, that was a matter the truth of which was not dependent on logical deduction or poetical imagination, but was given in the immediate consciousness of all men, however denied by some. Certainly in the end, if my interpretation of the *Parmenides* and the *Sophist* is correct,[34] he denied emphatically the right to translate the doctrine of Ideas into a transcendental monism corresponding in the spiritual realm to the metaphysics of Epicurus and Zeno in the physical realm. How far such a transcendental monism strays from the true philosophy of Plato I have tried to show in the chapter on Plotinus.

And the same limitation will be respected in the volitional and emotional sphere of philosophy. As the Pyrrhonist refrains from extending his ataraxy to the absolutes of hedonism or optimism, so the Platonist will refuse to carry his eudaemonism on into an absolute antinomianism or an absolute asceticism. Happiness, as he knows it, may be different in kind from pleasure, and may pertain to the soul alone as distinct from the body; he will not therefore allow

[34]See *Platonism* chap. viii.

his pursuit of happiness to merge into the anti-
nomian's indifference to life in the flesh as a
matter of no concern to the soul, nor into the
ascetic's condemnation of the flesh as something
utterly hostile to the soul and so to be ruthlessly
crushed down and silenced. Both antinomianism and asceticism he will regard as illegitimate
extensions of a dualistic philosophy into metaphysics; there are no rational absolutes for the
sceptic.[35]

So far I have endeavoured to show how the
philosophy of Plato embraces both scepticism
and the spiritual affirmation, and how by virtue
of this inclusiveness it proves itself more thoroughly positive than the materialistic exclusive-
ness of Pyrrho. For the relation of theology and
mythology to philosophy in such a scheme I must
refer the reader to the appropriate chapters in
my *Religion of Plato*. The problem of philosophy is to ascertain what spiritual knowledge is
consistent with a legitimate enlargement of Pyrrhonic scepticism; with theology and mythology, so far as we remain true to our Platonism,
we pass from the assurance of knowledge to that
land of varying probability which was discovered, but never occupied, by the great explorers

[35]See Appendix E.

of the Middle Academy. If there is any escape from the restrictions of probability in the religious sphere of theology and mythology, it cannot be achieved by the guidance of unassisted reason, but must wait on a revelation which comes with its own authority of immediate conviction. Such a revelation the Christian theologian found in the life and words of the historic Jesus, and this belief will be the theme of our next two volumes in the Greek Tradition.

THE END

APPENDIX A

Lactantius (Arnim, *Stoic. Vet. Frag.* II, 1041) has a clear statement of the confusion of monism and dualism in the Stoic system, resting finally on their assumption of active and passive as merely two aspects of an ultimate unity, which thus becomes God or matter, energy or mass, as the argument demands. It is fair to add that in this slippery use of active and passive, perhaps the fundamental fallacy of their whole metaphysics, the Stoics were victims of an inherent trait of the Greek language. At another time I have in mind to follow this peculiarity from the morphological ambiguities of the Greek verb and adjective, through its philosophical implications in the active and passive use of such words as κακόν and ἀγαθόν, to its final results in the theological dogmas of faith and grace and justification. There is, as I see it, a profound truth in these philosophical extensions of a linguistic ambiguity, as well as obvious dangers. The whole matter is a striking illustration of the close connexion between the Greek tongue and the Greek Tradition.

As for *tonos*, so far as I can guess at its meaning, it is a further attempt to reduce mass and energy to the same terms. It is the vibratory tension in the mass of any object, energizing from the centre to the periphery and from the periphery to the centre. By its inward thrust it gives unity and essence, cohesion we should say, to an individual body; by its outward thrust it gives magnitude and form and the secondary qualities. So far the definition leaves a radical distinction between matter and energy; to escape this mechanical dualism *tonos* is then regarded as itself simply a subtle kind of matter (ether, or warm air), which penetrates a solid body and acts upon its mass by contact and thrust. But this leaves the mechanical operation of contact and thrust still definable only in terms of energy. And so the argument proceeds in an endless circle from mass to energy and from energy to mass. It is not strange that the ancient critics of the Stoic physics were bewildered.

The use of *tonos* was extended by the Stoics from *hexis*, which is the constitution (including essence and quality) of inorganic bodies, to *physis*, which is the constitution of plants, to *psychê*, which is the constitution of animals, and finally to *nous* (reason), which is the constitution of man. More generally expressed, *tonos*, the sustaining and constitutive element regarded from *hexis* upwards to *nous*, becomes the *logos* of the universe when regarded from *nous* downwards to *hexis;* or, put the other way, the *logos* becomes the *tonos* of the universe when regarded from the starting point of our corporeal experience. *Logos* and *tonos* are, so to speak, the same principle taken now in a downward, now in an upward, direction.

Our knowledge of the Stoic conception of *tonos* is derived from a few fragments (Arnim II, 439-462), largely the work of hostile critics, and the whole subject is avowedly obscure. But one cannot read the arguments without surmising that the fundamental hypotheses of physics were grasped by Chrysippus with a clearer sense of the metaphysical problems involved than is commonly shown by modern scientists, although, of course, without our apparatus of experimental facts. The relation between *logos* and *tonos* is, I suspect, much the same thing as the modern relation between mathematical equations and physical operations, expressed by us in terms more useful practically, less suggestive metaphysically.

If any reader is curious to follow the Stoics further in their divagations regarding the materialism, or submaterialism, or whatever it may be called, of qualities and forces and relations, let him study the fragments dealing with the four categories of Chrysippus. He is likely to come out with a headache and nothing more. As Plutarch says (Arnim II, 380), ταῦτα πολλὴν ἔχει ταραχήν. Again one might draw a curious and illuminating parallel between the Stoic definitions of ποιά and συμβεβηκότα, as material yet differing from ordinary matter by not being subject to the known laws of mechanics, and some of the modern hypotheses of physics and chemistry. The Stoic hypotheses are on the whole more logical, but they lack the audacious fancifulness of our scientific creations.

APPENDIX B

I HAVE referred several times to the relation of Platonism and the various Hellenistic philosophies to the doctrines of Socrates. For the sake of obtaining a summary view of the matter we may set down these affiliations in a diagram, remembering, however, that such a schematization is of the roughest sort and does not pretend to completeness or exactness.

The intellectual method of Socrates may be described as combining scepticism and the equation virtue = knowledge. Owing to the ambiguous sense of the word knowledge, the equation, taken in one way, leads to a rationalism, or metaphysic, quite incompatible with scepticism, while taken in another way, it leads to reasonableness and a kind of intuition which consort easily with scepticism. This distinction I have treated at length in my *Platonism*. Passing on to the data of life, we may say that Socrates applied his method in such a manner as to obtain a calculating hedonism, an optimistic endurance of things as they are (*karteria*), and a spiritual affirmation. The practical outcome of this application is the two traits of character, liberty and security, which together form self-sufficiency (*autarkeia*).

Now the various schools dealt with in this volume are all imperfectly Socratic in the sense that they each laid hold of certain of the Socratic theses to the exclusion of others, while they all aimed at the one common end of *autarkeia*. Manifestly the Epicureans built their philosophy on the rationalism and hedonism of Socrates, the Stoics on his rationalism and optimistic endurance, while both excluded the scepticism and, in varying degrees, the spiritual affirmation. Plotinus takes the rationalism and the spiritual affirmation, while rejecting the hedonism and at least the optimism properly belonging to the attitude of endurance. The Pyrrhonists accepted only the scepticism combined with hedonism and endurance. The affiliation of the sects may then be schematized as follows:—

Epicureanism: rationalism with hedonism
Stoicism: rationalism with optimistic
         endurance
Neoplatonism: rationalism with spiritual   liberty   *autarkeia*
         affirmation   security
Pyrrhonism: scepticism with hedonism and
         endurance

Platonic dualism is the true Socratic philosophy (beside which the various sects run much as the heresies run parallel with Christian orthodoxy) by virtue of uniting the Socratic theses in one harmonious system, developing the ethical equation in the direction of reasonableness and the higher intuition, while repudiating a metaphysical rationalism. Together with these Socratic traits Plato contains also hints of a religious element which later will be developed and made dominant by Christianity. The radical change to Christianity will come with the substitution of revelaton for *autarkeia*.

APPENDIX C

Pyrrho connected his doubt with one aspect of the Democritean philosophy, whereas the Sophists were rather followers of Heraclitus, the difference being pointed out succinctly by Sextus, thus: "From the fact that honey appears bitter to some and sweet to others Democritus argued that honey itself was neither sweet nor bitter, but Heraclitus said that it was both" (*Hyp.* II, 63). That is to say, from the *isostheneia* of our sensations the Pyrrhonist, taking a hint from Democritus, concluded that we have no knowledge of the nature of things, whereas the Sophist from this same *isostheneia* argued the knowledge of a like *isostheneia* in things themselves. Yet, in the very chapter in which Sextus draws out his distinction between the Sceptics and the Heracliteans, he inserts the curious statement in regard to Aenesidemus, the reviver of true Pyrrhonism, that "he said the sceptical school was the way to the philosophy of Heraclitus." Here is a crux to which no satisfactory solution has ever been given, which indeed, with the data at our command, can only be answered conjecturally. One may guess that Aenesidemus, being impressed by the discord of our sensations and opinions, felt that in some way it must correspond with, or be a part of, some sort of instability in the world at large. Now, if we consider the fact that his ten tropes are all summed up under the one head of relativity, and the further fact that he seems to have referred the variation of our sensations and opinions to the flowing character of time as the corporeal essence, so to speak, of all things (*Hyp.* III, 138), we can understand how he was led, tentatively at least, into the camp of Heraclitus; for the universal flux of Heraclitus is just the union of relativity and time. But we may conjecture also that his theory remained within the bounds of a vague correspondence, and did not venture upon hardening this correspondence into such a criterion of *katalêpsis* as underlies the position of the Sophists. At any rate we may be sure that he would have rejected the sophistic dogmatism of a Thrasymachus, who believed that by sheer exercise of will-power a man could impose his own desire as a temporary canon of right and truth.

APPENDIX D

It is to me a surprising thing that Pyrrhonism in general and Sextus in particular have received such scant consideration in our day from English commentators. The only translation we have of Sextus is Miss Patrick's version of the first book of the *Hypotyposes* in her *Sextus Empiricus and Greek Scepticism,* and unfortunately her work shows a very imperfect acquaintance with technical Greek. As an illustration of the grudging spirit of the critics I may cite the comment on Sextus with which Mr. Alfred Benn closes an otherwise acute study of scepticism in his *Greek Philosophers* (2nd edition, p. 470) :

"It will be enough to notice the singular circumstance that so copious and careful an enumeration of the grounds which it was possible to urge against dogmatism—included, as we have seen, many still employed for the same or other purposes,—should have omitted the two most powerful solvents of all. These were left for the exquisite critical acumen of Hume to discover. They relate to the conception of causation, and to the conception of our own personality as an indivisible, continuously existing substance, being attempts to show that both involve assumptions of an illegitimate character. Sextus comes up to the very verge of Hume's objection to the former when he ob-

serves that causation implies relation, which can only
exist in thought; but he does not ask how we come to
think such a relation, still less does he connect it with
the perception of phenomenal antecedence (1); and
his attacks on the various mental faculties assumed by
psychologists pass over the fundamental postulate of
personal identity, thus leaving Descartes what seemed
a safe foundation whereon to rebuild the edifice of
metaphysical philosophy (2)."

Now (1) Sextus does clearly enough imply, if he
does not actually state, that our conception of causality is connected with the regularly perceived sequences
of phenomena (*Hyp.* III, 17, 18; *Adv. Math.* IX,
200-203).

(2) Descartes is fully forestalled. If his dictum
Cogito ergo sum has any value as the starting point
of a metaphysical philosophy, it must mean this: "I
think, therefore I have knowledge of myself as a thinker, and from that knowledge can deduce other knowledge." But Sextus (*Adv. Math.* VII, 310 *et al.*) dem-
onstrates to the hilt that the *dianoia*, or thinking faculty, has no means of knowing itself; and, if this is so,
the Cartesian *Cogito* is left as a mere immediate affection from which no such deductions as he desired can
be made. Moreover, Sextus argues more than once
(*e.g., Hyp.* II, 32; *Adv. Math.* VII, 55) that the soul
itself is unknowable, and that therefore its existence
is a matter of doubt. And soul, in his modest vocabulary, is nothing less than the fundamental postulate
of personal identity.

Mr. R. D. Hicks, in his *Stoic and Epicurean* (p.
312), is something more than grudging:

"The scepticism of antiquity," he says, "busied itself with the problem of knowledge. But when compared with cognate inquiries in modern philosophy, it
appears in its scope and range almost ludicrously ten-
tative, jejune, and superficial. That the object of cognition was external reality, nay more, that it was material reality, was not in that age seriously questioned.
No one ever challenged the existence of a real world of
things lying behind the phenomena of which we are
conscious."

Now that the arguments brought together by Sextus were neither jejune nor superficial, I trust has been
made evident. At least one may say that to character-
ize the philosophy of Carneades and Aenesidemus as
ludicrous is merely bad taste or ignorance. As for Mr.
Hicks' specific objections, they are simply amazing.
Does he mean to imply, in the face of page after page
and book after book of Sextus on the cognition of internal reality, that the only object of cognition at-
tacked by the sceptics was external and material reality? And then, in view of the Neoplatonic theories of
hylê and the *mê on*, how can he say that "no one ever
challenged the existence of a real world, etc."? As for
the sceptics, it was distinctly not their business to determine what the object of cognition is, but to demon-
strate that we have no knowledge of any object (beyond our immediate affections) whether external or
internal. To argue against the existence of an external reality, as Mr. Hicks implies that the sceptic
should have done, leads not to scepticism at all, but to
a dogmatism of the most metaphysical sort, such as we
see in Plotinus and Berkeley. To arguments of the

Berkeleyan sort Dr. Johnson's retort by kicking a
stone was good reason and good scepticism. Johnson
simply meant that we have an immediate and irrefut-
able affection of an objective material world, different
in character from personality. Pyrrho and Sextus
would have applauded his *beau geste*. But to state that
we have such an affection of an impersonal objective
world does not imply that we know what that world is
positively.

Mr. Maccoll, in his study of *The Greek Sceptics*, is
more generous than Mr. Hicks, but still has his reservation. "It [Pyrrhonism] disputed the possibility of
subjective, as much as of objective, truth," he says,
p. 19, "and so wide was its range, that, had it not been
regarded only as a speculative means to a practical
end, a philosophy that taught the great secret of how
to be happy, Pyrrhonism would have been very closely
akin to the doubt of modern times." That is scarcely a
fair criticism and does not correspond to the historic
fact. Doubt was forced on the Pyrrhonist by the *isostheneia* of the wrangling schools; he did not doubt in
order to obtain happiness, but learned by experience
that a certain tranquillity of mind followed a withdrawal from the contest, and he then justified his position by proving to his own satisfaction that all the
wrangling claims of rationalism were equally inadmis-
sible. Mr. Maccoll is nearer the fact, but still, I think,
in error, when he says, p. 100: "They only stopped
short when the absurdity of their position was shown
by their application of it to practical life: but their
arbitrary attempt to cut the knot by admitting a criterion in practice and excluding it in theory cannot be

accepted." Mr. Maccoll is here virtually repeating the
well-known criticism of Hume in his Essays (II, 131,
Green and Grose):

"A Stoic or Epicurean displays principles, which
may not only be durable, but which have an effect on
conduct and behaviour. But a Pyrrhonian cannot expect, that his philosophy will have any constant influence on the mind: or if it had, that its influence would
be beneficial to society. On the contrary, he must acknowledge, if he will acknowledge anything, that all
human life must perish, were his principles universally
and steadily to prevail. All discourse, all action, would
immediately cease; and men remain in a total lethar-
gy, till the necessities of nature unsatisfied, put an end
to their miserable existence. It is true, so fatal an event
is very little to be dreaded. Nature is always too strong
for principle. And though a Pyrrhonian may throw
himself or others into a momentary amazement and
confusion by his profound reasonings; the first and
most trivial event in life will put to flight all his doubts
and scruples, and leave him the same, in every point
of action and speculation, with the philosophers of
every other sect, or with those who never concern
themselves in any philosophical researches. When he
awakes from his dream, he will be the first to join in the
laugh against himself, and to confess, that all his objections are mere amusement, and can have no other
tendency than to show the whimsical condition of
mankind, who must act, and reason, and believe;
though they are not able, by their most diligent inquiry, to satisfy themselves concerning the founda-

tion of these operations, or to remove the objections,
which may be raised against them."

Hume's antinomy between theory and practice seems
to me to hold good against scepticism of the Protagorean and Heraclitean variety (see *ante* p. 325),
which would reduce nature to a positive chaos, and
against which Plato's philosophy is directed; it seems
to me to hold good also against the militant and dogmatic agnosticism of the nineteenth century. But I
cannot see that the true Pyrrhonism is under any such
liability. As a matter of fact the logical and perfectly
tenable position of the Pyrrhonian is very much like
that of the man in the street, as we should say today,
who accepts things as they are without concerning
himself in philosophical researches, unless he is worried by the missionary zeal of a reformer. That is precisely the Pyrrhonian *agôgê*.

A good account of Greek scepticism, though it forces
the evidence for a regular development, is Goedeckemeyer's *Geschichte des griechischen Skeptizismus*. The
most searching analysis and criticism of the subject
is in Richter's *Skeptizismus in der Philosophie*. But
learned and acute as are Richter's efforts to break
through the sceptical net, it would be possible, page
after page, to show how, misled by the methods of
modern metaphysics, he fails to meet the point at issue.
On the whole the best treatise on ancient scepticism is
Brochard's *Les sceptiques grecs*.

APPENDIX E

THE scepticism of Plato, as I have said, was not formulated by him systematically, but its character may be learnt from passages in the *Theaetetus, Republic, Timaeus, Sophist, Parmenides,* and *Phaedrus.* The outcome of the *Theaetetus* is to show that we have no absolute or direct knowledge, or at least that we do not know what knowledge is. We must be content with opinion. Right opinion is distinguished from wrong opinion only by the pragmatic test of experience. Right opinion is thus a kind of *ex post facto* knowledge of events; it is not knowledge of causes or of what nature in itself is. In his treatment of astronomy in *The Republic* and of the phenomenal world generally in the *Timaeus,* Plato shows that science is only an approximate, never an exact or final, statement of physical law, and furnishes no basis for metaphysical theory.

In the *Sophist* it is proved that Ideas do exist, at least as *dynameis* (forces whose effects we perceive), and that the realm of Ideas is a living world of power and law. But again of the ultimate nature of Ideas, as of matter, we have no knowledge, owing to the fact that any attempt to define them or to explain their relation to the phenomenal world involves the use of spatial terms, whereas Ideas are not in space. This difficulty is brought out in the discussion of the *Par-*

384

menides. Nevertheless, as is demonstrated in the *Theae-tetus,* we have this test of the conformity of our moral judgments with the operation of Ideas, that if a city, for example, decrees certain laws as just, the future consequences to the life of the city will expose the fact if the conception of justice was false. Our condition might be summed up in the sentence that we are morally responsible and intellectually impotent. And this state of moral responsibility and intellectual impotence, it may be observed, is the essence of tragedy as worked out on the Greek stage. (On this point I may refer to the profound study of Aeschylus and Sophocles in P. H. Frye's *Romance and Tragedy.*) The vision of Ideas and the theory of reminiscence, as described in *The Republic, Phaedrus,* and other dialogues, are a mythological expression of a philosophy which combines a spiritual affirmation with scepticism.